SPIRITUAL AUTOBIOGRAPHY
IN EARLY AMERICA

WISCONSIN STUDIES IN
AMERICAN AUTOBIOGRAPHY
William L. Andrews, General Editor

SPIRITUAL AUTOBIOGRAPHY IN EARLY AMERICA

DANIEL B. SHEA

THE UNIVERSITY OF WISCONSIN PRESS

Published 1988

The University of Wisconsin Press
114 North Murray Street
Madison, Wisconsin 53715

The University of Wisconsin Press, Ltd.
1 Gower Street
London, WC1E 6HA, England

First Wisconsin printing
Originally published in 1968 by Princeton University Press

Printed in the United States of America

Library of Congress Cataloging-in-Publication Data
Shea, Daniel B.
    Spiritual autobiography in early America.
    (Wisconsin studies in American autobiography)
    Includes bibliographies and index.
    1. United States—Church history—Colonial period,
ca. 1600–1775.   2. Autobiography.   3. Quakers—United
States—Biography.   4. Puritans—United States—
Biography.   5. Spirituality—United States—Biography.
I. Title.   II. Series.
BR520.S5   1988   277.3'07'0922   87-40375
ISBN 0-299-11650-6
ISBN 0-299-11654-9 (pbk.)

FOR MY FATHER

CONTENTS

Part One:

The Quaker Journal

Part Two:

Puritan Spiritual Narratives

T he work here republished remains, I believe, a useful introduction to a number of the more prominent examples of spiritual autobiography written by Puritans and Quakers before 1800, as well as to the affective dimension of religious experience in that period. But twenty years are a great many in the history of modern scholarship and criticism, and readers wise enough to begin a study of American autobiography at the beginning also need to be prudent enough to read this work in the light of recent studies on the same subject and discriminating enough to distinguish the approach of this work from current approaches, the better to situate themselves against the day when what is current will be what none of us has guessed.

A principal object of *Spiritual Autobiography in Early America* was simply to read seriously a body of writing that had been little read until that time. In so doing it seemed possible both to enlarge the literary record, or as we now say more politically, the canon, and at the same time to complicate and refine our sense of what a spiritual autobiography in the colonial period was like. A simultaneous awakening of interest in autobiography and in literary approaches to early American literature, of which this book was a product, has since 1968 had the effect of putting before the student of the period an increasing number of important texts. Of the works treated here, the autobiographies of John Woolman, Edward Taylor, Anne Bradstreet, Thomas Shepard, Cotton Mather, Nathan Cole, and Benjamin Franklin have now been given to the reader in authoritative editions.[1] Jonathan Edwards' *Personal Narrative* will appear in the Yale edition of his works as originally printed by Samuel Hopkins in 1765 (see pp. 189–90n below). And the *Account* of Elizabeth Ashbridge, indentured servant turned Quaker, will finally reach a wider audience through a new publication of colonial women's autobiographies from The University of Wisconsin Press.

Increased attention and closer scrutiny have also brought corrections of the record. The reader should be warned in particular that, as Patricia Caldwell has demonstrated, the *Experiences* of Elizabeth White, described in chapter 6, were published first in England in 1671; and Mrs. White, an English autobiographer after all, never came to America.[2] While the *Experiences* may be seen, by virtue of their 1741 Boston publication, as part of the promotional literature associated with the Great Awakening, their chief literary use, as in Caldwell's suggestive explorations, may be to serve as a reference point for distinctions between English and American versions of spiritual autobiography, or more speculatively, of national autobiographical expression in general. Phillips Moulton's edition of the *Journal* of John Woolman makes possible further and more authoritative study of the process of autobiographical self-effacement undertaken by Woolman through a series of manuscript revisions. It must still be argued that those revisions are an index to what is most characteristic of Woolman's autobiographical act, but the new student of Woolman should now rely on the Moulton edition, which, although it does not

[1] For editions of autobiographies referred to in this text that have appeared since 1968 see the "Primary Works" section of the "Bibliographical Supplement, 1988" beginning on p. 277.
[2] Patricia Caldwell, *The Puritan Conversion Narrative: The Beginnings of American Expression* (Cambridge: Cambridge University Press, 1983), pp. 1–41.

provide all manuscript variants, nevertheless corrects the errors of the Gummere edition on which section 5 of my Woolman chapter is based.[3]

The book's second object was, as I have said, a more literary reading of texts that, when they were read at all, tended to be seen as direct reflections of the writer's piety or as formulaic instances of the theology of conversion. These things there were, but it seemed too that there were literarily discernible arguments, shaped not out of the ordinary loci of rhetoric but out of the "life" as it had been remembered and imagined by the autobiographer at a crucial point in time. Exemplary autobiography seemed inevitably rhetorical even when, as in the accounts of Anne Bradstreet or Nathan Cole or Samuel Hopkins, the argument dictated by formula only appeared to encourage a counterargument or to provoke divergent patterns of language that suggested the writer's struggle to achieve a textual unity and finish that would serve in the stead of a more recalcitrant spiritual experience.

Some reviewers objected that this approach, in its elaborated detail, relied too heavily on the analytic techniques of the New (but even then somewhat middle-aged) Criticism. By an irony of critical history, the same objection might be made against it today, though for entirely different reasons. In 1968, the staple of much critical publication continued to be readings of ironies and paradoxes and tension-begetting patterns of imagery in the most eligible works of English and American literature, so that reviewers were objecting not to the method itself but to its application to such sub- or extra-literary materials as the autobiogra-

---

[3]*The Journal and Major Essays of John Woolman*, ed. Phillips P. Moulton (New York: Oxford University Press, 1971). See textual appendices A–F, pp. 273–99.

phy of John Dane, whose literary strategies, to be sure, did not recall those of John Donne.

II

Almost twenty years later, the situation has reversed itself. A student of spiritual autobiography in early America, writing now with a diminished sense of the autonomy of the author and of the author's art, and according no special privilege to the belletristic, would not hesitate to approach literarily unsophisticated texts whose discourse could compel interests—cultural, political, linguistic—other than that of authorial strategy. But if texts now have a larger permission to be unsophisticated, readers do not. The searching ray of critical self-consciousness, after extending itself far beyond the bounds of the autonomous New Critical text, turns back reflexively, at once illuminating and threatening the act of reading itself. Even, or especially, in the matter of spiritual autobiography, readers are apt to discover first that they have created the texts they read and then, in a Pyrrhonist variant of the divine *I am*, have created and undone themselves as well. In 1968, complication was less complicated than now.

Given such a development, and thinking of reading as an autobiographical gesture, it is not surprising that autobiography should have moved from the periphery to something like the center of literary studies, taking its phantasmal child, spiritual autobiography, with it. Twenty years ago, one felt almost apologetic about dealing with spiritual autobiography rather than with "real" autobiography of the sort most nearly represented here by Benjamin Franklin's narrative, the sort that appears to present an almost tangible moral and psychological identity in the autobiographical self, that rests structurally and thematically on patterns of chronology and development, and that creates a world of others thick with incident and social texture. In spiritual autobiography, by contrast, the self is no more, and no less, than the soul, whose intangible existence is an invention of faith, whose social existence is only the shadow of its better being, and whose representation, the autobiographer concedes, must finally be impossible since the soul's activity in time is ultimately divine activity out of time. Were it not, in fact, for the mediation of scripture, the text whose figures of deliverance permit spiritual experience to attain textual body among fallen men and women, spiritual autobiography would be spiritual indeed, unspoken, unspeakable. Far from being a poor relation, then, of those more robust, socially grounded autobiographies that seem so sure of their referent, the spiritual autobiographer is more truly all autobiographers *in extremis,* confessing the incapacity of language to register its putative referent, the soul or self, all the while relying on language to create the terms and conditions of that subjectivity in which "self" has its magic-lantern existence.[4]

One might paraphrase the late Paul de Man who, having characterized autobiography as a figure of reading that occurs to some degree in all texts, concludes that "just as we seem to assert that all texts are autobiographical we should say that by the same token, none of them is or can be."[5] In the same way we can say that all autobiography, at its spectral, nonreferential heart, is spiritual autobiography, though spiritual autobiography is an oxymoron. As so

[4]On the subject of "Self Invention in Autobiography," see Paul John Eakin's *Fictions in Autobiography* (Princeton: Princeton University Press, 1985), pp. 181–278.
[5]"Autobiography as De-facement," *MLN* 94 (Dec 1979): 922.

often, Cotton Mather may be relied upon to suggest the poles of possibility. The unnamed speaker in the autobiographical *Paterna* writes himself out, we are told, "without the least Fiction in the World," banishing to the outer world of "fiction" all that, from the soul's point of view, never was and never would be. Yet Mather, whose own name is a felt absence in the manuscript he addressed successively to a son (Increase) who would shame, then another (Samuel) who would more gloriously continue that name, could also assert in *Paterna* that there is "not One word, that shall discover unto any One man living who I am!"[6] An autobiography that is absolutely true but in which the identity of the autobiographer is felt to be inessential: it is difficult to imagine the contemporary theorist of autobiography who could state more succinctly than Mather the situation of the autobiographer who, making a kind of fiction, nevertheless feels a sense of the true to be an enabling pretext and who, while prodigiously inventing himself at every turn, asserts the final unavailability of his subject.

Lest this characterization of spiritual autobiography appear too singularly bodiless, it is well to be reminded by recent psychological-historical studies of the Puritans how thoroughly communal was the autobiographical act among them. And the thesis must apply as well to the Quakers, for whom the condition either of silence or of speech, referred to the authority of the Inner Light, was in an important sense authorized by the communal Meeting. It is not only that, as David Leverenz has pointed out, the conflicts of the Freudian family romance may be traced from the writings of the last English through the first several American gen-

---

[6]*Paterna: The Autobiography of Cotton Mather,* ed. Ronald A. Bosco (Delmar, N.Y.: Scholar's Facsimiles and Reprints, 1976), pp. 4–5.

erations of "tender mothers and grave governors."[7] Beyond the little commonwealth of the family lay too the concentric circles of gathered church and elect nation, all of these figurally related. It was only from the center of these circles that a Puritan autobiographical voice could arise, although with the Great Awakening an urgency of individual experience began to unsettle their concentricity.

The historian Edmund Morgan has been on record for some time as stressing the exceptional emphasis among the early Puritans on the necessity of a spoken or written confession of faith for admission into church membership.[8] In effect, the requirement of autobiography operated as a reification of the self, and the community was empowered, theologically, socially, and politically to decide which autobiographies were authentic, which selves were, by virtue of grace, "real." With the publication of 51 confessions recorded by Thomas Shepard between 1637 and 1645 in his church at Cambridge, several new studies have suggested ways in which the individual and the community were linked in New England's peculiar autobiographical institution.[9]

The most literary of these works, Patricia Caldwell's, makes clear the individual's tendency to locate itself among scriptural figures and to find support in its shared faith with the congregational audience even more than in the sometimes feeble words of the confession itself.[10] Charles

[7]The quotation is from the title of chapter 3, David Leverenz, *The Language of Puritan Feeling: An Exploration in Literature, Psychology, and Social History* (New Brunswick: Rutgers University Press, 1980).

[8]*Visible Saints: The History of a Puritan Idea* (New York: New York University Press, 1963).

[9]*Thomas Shepard's "Confessions,"* ed. George Selement and Bruce C. Woolley. Collections of the Colonial Society of Massachusetts, vol. 58 (Boston: The Society, 1981).

[10]*The Puritan Conversion Narrative*, pp. 107, 168–78.

Cohen, arguing that these early personal narratives "show multiple forces sculpting the experience of regeneration," goes on to demonstrate that congregational audiences, out of their need to identify signs of grace in themselves, both participated in the confessions and, as in the example of Roger Clap, could be affected, moved toward regeneration, by them.[11] A final tumbler falls in place, literary and historical approaches enabling each other, when John O. King III surveys the literature of the Puritan drama of the soul and makes the more extenuated argument that "Textual expressions . . . are in themselves capable of creating a person's character."[12] The Puritan anguish of soul becomes an American anguish of soul, argues the psychohistorian, because men and women in early New England fashioned their experience out of a language of melancholy that would continue to create character long after the institutional sanction for spiritual narratives had withered away.

The implication of these several theories taken together is that while the community may in some sense generate the autobiographical text, the continued transmission of that textual reality generates an identifiable psychic profile, the "iron of melancholy" King finds in the voices of Shepard's collection, in Nathan Cole, in Edwards and Hawthorne and William James. King's thesis is a local application of Paul de Man's suggestion that it may not be the referent who determines the figure, that is, not the autobiographer who determines the autobiography, but the other way round.

---

[11]*God's Caress: The Psychology of Puritan Religious Experience* (New York: Oxford University Press, 1986), pp. 21, 158–59.

[12]*The Iron of Melancholy: Structures of Spiritual Conversion in America From the Puritan Conscience to Victorian Neurosis* (Middletown, Conn.: Wesleyan University Press, 1983), p. 7. But see also Cohen's criticism of King's text-centered approach, *God's Caress*, p. 19n.

Even so, de Man goes on, the created fiction of a self "in its own turn acquires a degree of referential productivity."[13] The autobiographical self is no less "real" for all that when it can become the cornerstone of New England ecclesiology and, if we accept the theses of Caldwell and King, the author in some sense of later American texts. The referent of spiritual autobiography may not be there, may be only a trick of verbal mirrors; yet it does the same work as if it existed and in so doing appears to satisfy quite nicely both the demands of European theory and American pragmatism.

III

Autobiography is creation myth written in the first person. Hence it is not surprising that American literary history, which is often much absorbed with deriving the origins of *its* referent and with articulating America's special literary identity, should want to focus on autobiography and most especially on the earliest of our literary texts. The burden of that historical concern is more, perhaps, than many of these early texts can bear. Certain among them, however, like Jonathan Edwards' *Personal Narrative*, will always repay study, and appear to have a capacity for representing themselves to each new critical generation, as for example in recent studies by Wayne Lesser and R. C. De Prospo.[14]

While claiming few certitudes for the natural man in him, Edwards is an unhesitating historian when he locates

[13]"Autobiography as De-facement," p. 920.
[14]Wayne Lesser, "Jonathan Edwards: Textuality and the Language of Man," in *Critical Essays on Jonathan Edwards*, ed. William J. Scheick (Boston: G. K. Hall, 1980), pp. 287–304; R. C. De Prospo, *Theism in the Discourse of Jonathan Edwards* (Newark: University of Delaware Press, 1985), pp. 175–83.

the occasion from which he marked the beginning "of that sort of inward, sweet delight in God and divine things"[15] that constituted his spiritual and therefore his only real identity. Memory associates the moment of grace with the reading of a passage from 1 Timothy and thus links the self's derivation to the preexistent identity of the father, Timothy Edwards, supplying at the same time a barrier between the autobiographer's natural and gracious existence. But that clear memory of origin also creates a narrative threshold beyond which the questions of self-discovery and development become problematic. At the narrative's end, the didactic autobiographer will have sketched a pattern of growth in grace by which the awakened soul moves from a state of imminent combustibility, arising from a new sense either of divine things or of its own natural worthlessness, to a more settled state in which the religious affections have come to a balanced and harmonious economy, egregious ardor being replaced by the ultimate order of divine principle. Against that backdrop of theme, the problematic of Edwards' and of much autobiography is set in relief.

The last word of any autobiography is its closest approach to the living, biochemical, language-making phenomenon whose psychic origin the autobiography seeks to explain. The last word of the autobiography laps on that shore but can never engulf it. Let it be written again and again and never in the same words, the autobiographical text must eventually terminate and confess its finite status just where its effectively transcendent creator, the source of all its life and language, begins. The autobiographical

[15]The quotations from Edwards' *Personal Narrative* are taken from *Jonathan Edwards: A Profile*, ed. David Levin (New York: Hill and Wang, 1969), pp. 24–39, which reprints the narrative included by Hopkins as part of his 1765 biography, *The Life and Character of the Late Reverend Mr. Jonathan Edwards*.

creator, for his or her part, is by definition restless with transcendence alone and in order to avoid the merely hypothetical existence of an autobiographer outside any autobiographical text seeks entry into the invented "life" of the text where, as a first act, it must invent its origin in order to establish a point of entry, create the illusion of a seed from which the illusion of a "life" can grow. The text's version of "I began here, in this fashion," is perpetual genesis and endless rebirth for the autobiographer, whose need for descent into verbal life the personal scripture confesses.

As a result, the autobiographical text negotiates always between the energies of two imperatives. One is developmental, the pressing on of the autobiographical self to become (what it never shall be) the autobiographer. The other energy is the autobiographer's movement backward to his or her origin and life source, an energy expressed sometimes by the most exacting inquiry, sometimes simply as nostalgia, a huddling close to the originary fire. Both these energies are intense in Edwards' *Personal Narrative,* and the latter energy finds both rigorously analytic as well as nostalgic expression there.

There is on the one hand a language cognizant of the process of sanctification and teleologically oriented toward the saint's glorification in eternity, an end point infinitely beyond the narrative's limit. Speaking that language, the autobiographical character has "an eager thirsting after progress" in divine things, is put upon "pursuing and pressing after them," studies and contrives at the "ways and means" of holiness, and looks beyond the self to the advancement of Christ's kingdom and the fulfillment of the scriptural prophecies.

An even stronger flow of language, though, carries the "I" back to a hallowed and fully temporal "then" in which

xix

the first fresh vision of holiness conferred beatitude on the affections and a constant "inward ardor" sought vent in chant, soliloquy, and the speech of a singing voice. Indeed, one of the achievements of the *Personal Narrative* is to suggest that its rhythmic, hymning paradoxes are only a weakened echo of the original singings which are their supposed referent. While the autobiographical character may be said to long for an eternity in which the principle of holiness will "freely and fully vent and express itself," the autobiographer, in the long afterglow of grace's first infusion, struggles to create, in memory's image, the soul's first days and its first unfettered songs. In this way, the myth of the self's creation arrays its energies against the forward movement of the narrative and would, if it could, make of the autobiographer's "then" an eternal narrative now.

Edwards cannot effect closure on a process whose end point is eternity, but he will do well to effect an ascendancy of the language of a future eternity over the language of a past creation, elevating impersonal prophecy over a myth of personal origin. Since, however, the essence of autobiography is its umbilical tie to figures of self-creation, the implications of such a triumph are dire for the form in which it occurs. Of a possible catastrophe there have been occasional warnings. There has been a tendency in the narrative for the "I" to slip momentarily out of existence: "Used oftentimes to dwell long on one sentence to see the wonders contained in it"; as if the narrative's rush toward recovery of those wonders were squeezing out the first person as an expendable intermediary. The autobiographer has also registered alarm that the self and all its engendering and testifying language—the raw matter of the autobiographical act—are threatened from both above and below. Transcendently, it is the ineffable excellence of Christ that threatens to swallow up all thought and conception. Temporally, "since I lived in this town," the thought of the self's equally ineffable wickedness appears capable of "swallowing up all thought and imagination. . . ." In each case, either "a flood of tears" or "a kind of loud weeping" signifies the self's strandedness as it recognizes first that its language cannot create all that it proposes, that it can only invent and reinvent itself, and then sees even more painfully that only by undoing itself, extinguishing the "I" created by autobiography, can it survive the limits of autobiography and resist the nostalgia of origins.

The signal that immolation is about to occur comes in Edwards' last paragraph, with its quite casual mention of "another Saturday night" in 1739, another experience of divine things recovered out of the increasingly proximate past. Immediately, though, the self is cancelled, immurred in its tell-tale weeping behind fastened doors. We will hear no more directly of its speech. Its behind-doors tribute to religious duty appears quoted but is in fact mediated by an "as it were." In the narrative's final sentence the self is permitted to rejoice in God's governance of the world, then forced to withdraw. It is in the end as it was in the beginning, that "God reigned, and that His will was done." Nostalgia burned away, it is for all we know as if the autobiographer had never existed, though we know also that the text has urged us to read his autobiographical absence as absolute existence.

It may be that in these earliest American autobiographies something is tellingly said about the idea of origins, not so much that our literature has derived from them—though the reader is invited still to consider Thoreau and Whitman and Dickinson and Henry Adams in their possible procession from these Quakers and Puritans—rather that the myth of origins exerts a powerful spell, wonderfully mesmerizing the autobiographer into his or her first self-creative act, but then by continued replenishments from the well of nostalgia threatening to transform its charm into a curse. American literary history is national autobiography. We who write that literary history are therefore well-advised to search early American autobiography closely, for if there are autobiographical texts capable of escaping autobiography, there may some day be a kind of American literary history capable of disdaining the attempt to explain America.

PREFACE

It is perhaps understandable that of the 6,377 items listed in *A Bibliography of American Autobiographies* only a few have received close attention, and that those few are the narratives of men whose place in our literature depends only partially or not at all on their autobiographies: Jonathan Edwards, Benjamin Franklin, Mark Twain, Henry Adams, Henry James. Selection must begin somewhere, and it seems rash to forsake proven literacy as one confronts a list which begins with the title, *My Life as a Dissociated Personality*.[1] More than prudence is involved in this hesitancy to approach the autobiographies of the obscure. If men will surrender to the confessional instinct, we say, it is not our unavoidable duty to hear them out. The rewards of eavesdropping appear too slight and too unsavory.

Admitting these difficulties, one can still make a plausible case for more ambitious exploration of the full scope of American autobiography, beginning with the earliest contributions to the genre. The present study needs no other justification than the chronological priority of Quaker and Puritan autobiographies, but it has been stimulated by the conviction that we must examine prevailing generalizations about early American spiritual autobiography, which too often assume its contents to be foreknown and predictable. General descriptions may well remain useful; yet they may also seem empty or stale when applied to the persistent singularity of many individual narratives. Increased interest in the pervasiveness of autobiographical form in American literature makes such an examination doubly necessary,

[1] Louis Kaplan, *A Bibliography of American Autobiographies* (Madison, 1961).

since the most inclusive discussions of this mode of writing must touch on its earliest exemplars. I have written toward the end that in any such discussion the Quaker and Puritan autobiographers shall receive a full and just estimation.

In determining what works to discuss and how to approach them, I have been guided by the desire to be specific and to deal mostly with particulars. An historian of spiritual autobiography or of other forms of spiritual writing in this period might have wished to include denominational groups not represented here. It would be misleading to suggest that before 1800 only Quakers and Puritans composed narratives of their spiritual experience, and yet no other groups offer the possibility of compact treatment within that period. Methodist autobiographies, like Peter Cartwright's,[2] are not abundant until the middle of the nineteenth century. An historian might have cared to keep better statistical watch over the phenomenon of early spiritual autobiographies by turning to genealogical sources and the manuscript holdings of historical societies more often than I have done here, where statistical inclusiveness was not the aim. Yet the twenty narratives which I have selected for discussion, though comprising only a fraction of all spiritual writing in seventeenth- and eighteenth-century America, are fully representative of the range and variety of those which are first-person narratives.

Finally, because this is not a developmental history of spiritual autobiography, I have attended to chronology only in a general way. The section on Puritan autobiographies begins with early examples and concludes with Samuel

[2] *Autobiography of Peter Cartwright*, with an Introduction, Bibliography, and Index by Charles L. Wallis (Nashville, 1956). The *Bibliography of American Autobiographies* lists four autobiographies by Methodist clergymen before 1800, but seventy-five in the period 1800-1850, and twice as many again from 1850 to 1900.

Hopkins at the end of the eighteenth century. Most of the important American Quaker autobiographers lived in the eighteenth century; they have been considered first, not for any historical reason, but because their writing is usually less dense, less complex ideologically, than that of the Puritans. Discussing them first has made it possible to establish an approach to spiritual autobiography before attempting to apply it to more difficult texts.

In place of inclusive historical description, I have sought instead to locate the principle by which a given autobiographer selected from the details of his experience and according to which he shaped the narrative which was finally allowed to stand as the image of his soul. Social, intellectual, and religious historians have provided us with an extensive description of the principles which informed Quaker and Puritan experience, though differing frequently about their relative importance. I have intended no contribution to these debates, feeling myself disqualified, partly by ignorance, partly by the conviction that spiritual autobiographies, of whatever origin, do not reduce to the credal assertions of the writer, but are instead a form of argument in which the narrator's attempt to assemble and fashion evidence out of his experience may easily falter or yield an unexpected conclusion.

The explicit arguments of early spiritual narratives were highly conventional. A Puritan sought to assemble the evidence for divine favoritism toward him, and many Quaker journals recount the protracted search of the narrator for Truth, which he inevitably finds in the doctrines of the Society of Friends. But conventions are always more apparent from a distance, and by getting close to individual narratives I hope to show that the argument of early American autobiography is considerably more various than scholars have assumed, and fraught with more difficulties than its avowed didactic purpose would suggest. The two worst temptations of this approach are speculation on an autobiographer's unacknowledged motives and a tendency to deprecate successful, that is orthodox and exemplary, arguments in favor of intriguing failures. I have not rejected either temptation with complete success, but I can say that my respect for the successful arguments of John Woolman and Jonathan Edwards was increased, not diminished, by closer acquaintance. Knowing what the argument was supposed to be about is precisely what lends interest to unexpected developments.

To pursue these interests, I have had to exclude autobiographical writing that was periodic in composition. To the social and intellectual historian of the period, diaries and autobiographies are equally useful, but terms of literary analysis cannot be applied to this body of writing without a basic distinction. The entries of a diary may possess considerable homogeneity and may even accumulate into a number of discernible "themes." Nevertheless, autobiography represents a further stage in the refinement of immediate experience, a stage at which the writer himself has attempted to introduce pattern and moves consciously toward generalization about his life. The very circumstances of composition determine that the autobiographer shall consider the possibility of a relation between personal events widely separated in time, whereas the diary keeper is almost invariably a prisoner of the present.

Some straining of the distinction is unavoidable. Much autobiographical writing by Quakers was done in relatively brief periodic entries in their journals, a habit enforced by their frequent travels in the work of the ministry. The works isolated for study, however, are either whole narratives, or journals whose original entries were later revised and unified in retrospect. The autobiographies of two Puritans, Increase Mather and Samuel Hopkins, show interruption at various stages, but my remarks focus on the longest section of introspective writing in each narrative. Cotton Mather presents a special problem. His manuscript autobiography, "Paterna," begins with a section of original personal narrative, but it soon becomes an anthology of entries from his *Diary*. Yet the *Diary* itself is not an ordinary one, since Mather seems to have revised its entries in the manner of the Quaker journalist, leading his biographer to call it a compilation of "annual autobiographies."[3] So strenuous an autobiographical writer could not be left out.

Despite its potential vagueness, the term "spiritual" requires little explanation when applied to American autobiography of the seventeenth and eighteenth centuries. The spiritual autobiographer is primarily concerned with the question of grace: whether or not the individual has been accepted into divine life, an acceptance signified by psychological and moral changes which the autobiographer comes to discern in his past experience. The spiritual autobiography of early America ought not to be categorized exclusively, however, as a narrative of conversion. The question of grace may only serve to focus the themes of a narrative and provide it with a dynamic center. Quaker journalists dealt less with the subtleties of the conversion process than with the witnessing life wrought by conversion. Surprisingly few Puritan autobiographers devote large space to the description and analysis of their conversions; most of them extend the scope of their inquiry to include any experiences and events that might bear on their spiritual condition.

[3] Barrett Wendell, *Cotton Mather: Puritan Priest*, with a new Introduction by Alan Heimert (New York, 1963), p. 172.

Contrary to the usual assumption, these writers told more than one story in reply to the searching questions they had asked themselves. The earnest and vigorous colloquy of the arguments they made, to their posterity, to their country-men, to God, and to themselves, deserves a fuller reporting.

With two exceptions I have treated only published sources, which throughout have been identified in an in-itial footnote. For a further discussion of sources, see the Bibliographical Essay. Acquiring the necessary texts was made easier through the help of the reference staff of Olin Library, Washington University, and of Edward H. Milli-gan, Librarian of the Friends House, London. I wish to thank the Connecticut Historical Society for permission to quote from the Nathan Cole manuscript volume, which includes his "Spiritual Travels," and the University of Vir-ginia Library for permission to quote from Cotton Mather's "Paterna," still in manuscript in Virginia's Tracy W. Mc-Gregor Library. Duke University Press has kindly given me permission to use my article, "The Art and Instruction of Jonathan Edwards's *Personal Narrative*" from *American Literature*, xxxvii (March 1965), which with minor re-visions appears here as part of Chapter Six. Quotations from Edward Taylor's "Spiritual Relation" are with the permission of its editor, Donald Stanford, and *American Literature*.

Arriving at the space customarily set aside to express gratitude to those who have given one assistance, I discover how little these statements are a matter of form, how much a recording of simple fact. In various ways, this book has derived from my teachers: Herbert Slusser of the College of St. Thomas, who taught me to read and introduced me to autobiography; the late Yvor Winters of Stanford Uni-

PREFACE

versity, who taught and exemplified the literary consequences of ideas; and David Levin of Stanford, who has
long argued the importance of non-fictional narrative
in American literature, who guided this project at its outset
more than six years ago and has since given help and encouragement unfailingly. The work of Perry Miller on the
American Puritans has nourished and stimulated my thinking in all seasons. I have been fortunate in my colleagues
at Washington University, John Murrin, Guy Cardwell,
and Richard Ruland, each of whom responded generously
to my need for advice, correction, and encouragement. Final
preparation of the manuscript was made possible by two
grants from the Graduate School of Washington University,
and I am grateful to Jarvis Thurston, chairman of the De-
partment of English at Washington University, for finding
providential ways to arrange my time during the period of
the book's preparation. In untranslatable ways, I owe much
to my children, who reconciled themselves to my doing a
book without pictures, and to my wife, who sustained me
when it also lacked words.

PART ONE

THE QUAKER JOURNAL

CHAPTER ONE

VARIETIES OF QUAKER JOURNALS

A shelf of Quaker literature must always exhibit the *Journal* of George Fox in a position of pre-eminence. For the immediacy of its earnest and hectic prose and for its historical significance the personal record left by the founder of the Society of Friends has first claim on the attention of anyone who studies historical Quakerism. But the founder's journal should not be allowed to define the pattern and the tone of all Quaker autobiographical writing, English and American, in the seventeenth and eighteenth centuries. The historical context of Fox's writing is all turbulence: revolution, civil war, regicide, the proliferation of religious sects alternately denouncing one another and drafting pleas for toleration. A sense of the end of the ages pervades Fox's *Journal,* and the narrator's distinctive tone is urgent and apocalyptic:

". . . and [we] came to an inn where the townspeople were gathered together, being half drunk, a very rude place. And I was moved to admonish them and exhort them of the day of the Lord and to leave off their drunkenness and turn to the Lord and turned them to the light of Christ in their hearts which would let them see all their evil deeds, ways, and words. And the priest was amongst them and I admonished him and bid him see the fruits of his ministry. And so as I was turning them to the Lord Jesus Christ and his teaching, the priest and his clerk were in a rage and got up the tongs and fire shovel; and had not the Lord's power preserved us, we might have been murdered amongst them; yet nevertheless some received the Lord's Truth then and stand there to this day."[1]

As the dramatic action indicates, Fox preached in a time of general war. The raised voice of the prophet matches the pitch of antagonistic emotion aroused in the two representatives of established religion. Before long, though, the Society of Friends would enter into its own period of establishment. The persecutions of the Restoration delivered 1,400 Friends into prison at a peak time,[2] but adversity also had a consolidating effect. Quaker meetings, always a source of mutual encouragement, proliferated into the structural network by which the Society governed itself and insured regularity in its witness.[3] Then, under William and Mary, a Toleration Act was finally passed, and by the year of Fox's death, 1691, Quakers had begun to experience not only greater tolerance but, thanks to their proverbial thrift and honesty, a measure of respectability as well. As the eighteenth century began, Friends were gently reproving those who continued to prophesy in the old apocalyptic fashion.[4]

Most autobiographical writing by American Quakers dates from the period following these changes. English Friends had, of course, recorded their missionary efforts in the colonies, but journals by native Quakers are an eighteenth-century phenomenon. Until the various Quaker populations

[1] *The Journal of George Fox*, ed. John L. Nickalls (Cambridge, 1952), pp. 278-279.
[2] Charles M. Andrews, *The Colonial Period of American History* (New Haven, 1937), III, 276n.
[3] William C. Braithwaite, *The Second Period of Quakerism*, second edition prepared by Henry J. Cadbury (Cambridge, 1961), p. 228.
[4] Hugh Barbour, *The Quakers in Puritan England* (Yale, 1964), p. 234.

in Rhode Island, the Jerseys, and the Carolinas had matured, and before the settlement of Pennsylvania, there was no stable group of sufficient size which could produce a body of spiritual autobiography. American Quaker literature thus lacks the numerous testimonies of suffering and imprisonment and the gallery of embattled Quaker autobiographers produced in seventeenth-century England, though Boston's Puritan magistracy, at the height of its power, attempted to supply the deficiency when they repulsed or executed evangelizing Quakers. In general, the eased conditions which had muted the aggressive tone of English Quakers prevailed also in America, especially in Pennsylvania, where more than half the colonies' 40,000 Quakers lived, where freedom of belief and practice were guaranteed by William Penn's Quakerism, and where the hands of Friends wielded political control.

Recording his spiritual experiences and gospel labors against this more tranquil background, a Quaker autobiographer would not be reduced to writing a mere tale of survival nor forced to exhaust his eloquence against the representatives and followers of dead religion. For the edification of other Friends and in conformity with the aims of the Society, he might hope rather to isolate the essential phases of Quaker thought and experience from his life—the influence of pious parents, decisive or extraordinary spiritual experiences, adoption of Quaker beliefs, and the evangelizing activities, frequently involving extensive travel, which followed from his new convictions.[5]

The same group-mindedness which set the Quaker to his task of compiling a journal and which defined his objectives

[5] Luella Wright, describing the development of the Quaker journal out of diverse forms of experiential writing, gives these as the standard contents of the genre, *The Literary Life of the Early Friends, 1650-1725* (New York, 1932), pp. 193-197.

in doing so also tied him to new conditions confronting the Society of Friends in America. Quaker experience in the economic and political life of the colonies demonstrated that power and affluence might be as great trials as the persecutions suffered by the previous generation. Quakers had always been known, often disparagingly, as frugal businessmen. Obligated to perform worthwhile labor in the world as both a material and spiritual duty, and adhering closely to the strictest notions of honest dealing, American Quakers soon found themselves prosperous members of the New World's expanding economic life. As such, they might remind themselves frequently that they were only stewards of their wealth and that they had a calling beyond the temporal and material, yet all the while be drawn away from their original orientation to plainness and simplicity. By 1750 Quakers were the dominant population in Philadelphia's mercantile aristocracy and its richly endowed social life, and a similar pattern had evolved in other areas with a heavy concentration of Quakers.[6] By itself, the enlarged outward estate of so many Quaker businessmen suggests that the habit of inwardness, through which George Fox and his followers strove to discern the Spirit of Truth, had somehow been lost, and in fact a great autobiographical silence characterizes these "Quaker grandees," as Frederick Tolles calls them.

A more public trial of Quaker principles had meanwhile been moving toward a decisive stage. The history of early Pennsylvania, whoever tells it, records the failure of Penn's Holy Experiment. In the atmosphere of antagonism that developed between Penn and his Assembly, any hope of

[6] Frederick B. Tolles, *Meeting House and Counting House: The Quaker Merchants of Colonial Philadelphia, 1682-1763* (Chapel Hill, 1948), pp. 116-117.

6

applying the Sermon on the Mount to the governing of men was steadily dissipated. The Assembly succeeded early in garnering powers for itself while steadily diminishing those of the proprietor, and was able to increase its acquisitions in the years following Penn's death in 1718. The leaders of these assaults were Penn's co-religionists, an allegiance which failed to diminish their fervor against him but which came to the fore when issues confronted the Assembly affecting such traditional Quaker testimonies as the refusal to swear oaths or to carry on war. Citing the Quakers' experience, Daniel Boorstin has argued both the futility and the injuriousness of attempting to govern by absolutes.[7] The argument can be overstated, particularly in any estimate of the motivations of individual Quakers, but it is certainly true that from an attitude of unswerving loyalty to group convictions there easily arose a dangerous confusion between the preservation of Truth and the preservation of political power. The burden of Quaker perfectionism, moreover, fell on the community at large when settlers were left unprotected against Indian attacks through the failure of defense appropriations in the Assembly. Pragmatic adjustments favored by more compromising elements of the Society were, on the other hand, injurious to principle. When Quakers knew that funds approved "for the King's use" would be used for guns and ammunition, they established a precedent for blinkered assent to warfare in any cause: better to accept the advice of English Quakers, whose distance gave them clearer sight, and resign from government entirely. And so, in the clamor for arms that followed the severe Indian attacks of 1755-1756 most Quaker assemblymen either quit their seats or refused to stand for re-

[7] *The Americans: The Colonial Experience* (New York, 1958), pp. 63-69.

7

election. The testimony of peace could then be articulated in its full purity, but no longer from a position of power.

Quaker journals reflected these events directly in a few instances.[8] More important, they contended in autobiographical form with essentially the same problems. To what extent could the journal serve the aims of the Society of Friends alone, defending its doctrines, setting forth an exemplary autobiographical life of strenuous preaching and travel, while resigning from the larger society it so frequently indicted? Or, taking notice of "the world's people," how was the Quaker autobiographer to present his confrontation with them? Such questions face any writer engaged in the autobiographical acts of self-characterization and the depiction of other actors, especially antagonists. For the Quaker they were especially searching questions because they probed among the contrary tendencies of the doctrine of the Inner Light.[9]

The notion that all men possess something of divinity within themselves laid a strong base for democratic political ideas and for the development of the Quaker testimony against slavery. From the Society's beginning, however, the same doctrine had harbored a potential for self-righteousness and complacency in the way of Friends. In the vocabu-

[8] John Churchman and John Woolman together observed a group of settlers who demonstrated through the streets of Philadelphia, pulling a wagon which contained the bodies of victims of Indian raids. Churchman, however, in recording the incident, seems not to recognize the act as a reproach to Quakers for refusing to grant defense funds. *An Account of the Gospel Labours, and Christian Experiences of a Faithful Minister of Christ, John Churchman* (Philadelphia, 1779), pp. 175-176.

[9] Drawing chiefly on Robert Barclay, the seventeenth-century Quaker theologian, Brand Blanshard isolates four distinct meanings in the doctrine of the Inner Light. See "Early Thought on the Inner Light," *Byways in Quaker History*, ed. Howard H. Brinton (Wallingford, 1944), pp. 153-178.

8

lary of their didactic literature, "the Truth" was Quaker truth, though it might come to any man, as it came to George Fox, by inward divine revelation. Through such "openings" Fox came to know that attendance upon the inward voice was a more certain and direct guide than either reason or hypocritical priests could provide. To the orthodox such a claim was blasphemous. At worst the claimant to special revelation might proclaim new doctrines or offend against sexual morality by thinking himself above the law. At the very least, hearing the tones of divinity in one's own voice might lead to the use of extraordinary models for autobiographical self-characterization: "And a report went abroad of me that I was a young man that had a discerning spirit; whereupon many came to me from far and near, professors, priests, and people. And the Lord's power brake forth; and I had great openings, and prophecies, and spake unto them of the things of God, and they heard with attention and silence, and went away, and spread the fame thereof."[10]

Fox's text makes clear what a flat statement of the doctrine of the Inner Light does not: to the extent that the narrator's voice is divinized, those who hear it may be reduced to a scriptural multitude. If the speaker's words are proclaimed to be full of Light, the multitude is likely to be depicted lying in darkness. The autobiographical act clearly involves moral choices as real as the decisions made by Quaker merchants and legislators. Failure to establish a peaceable kingdom in Pennsylvania only shifted the trial of Quaker principles to the kingdom within, the original site of the struggle.

The journals produced by Quakers in colonial America comprise an extension of the Holy Experiment which is

[10] *The Journal of George Fox*, p. 21.

worthy of scrutiny in several representative selections. Each of these selections to be studied obeys conventions established for the journal in seventeenth-century England, in content and vocabulary, and in the vindication of Quaker habits and beliefs. Any individuality displayed in the journals of John Churchman, Thomas Chalkley, David Ferris, and Elizabeth Ashbridge results from choices made among various ways of setting forth Truth in the autobiographical life. The first two journalists, Churchman and Chalkley, though about equally didactic in temperament, exemplify first a simple then a slightly more complex autobiographical argument. Classified by subject matter, the narratives of David Ferris and Elizabeth Ashbridge might rest side by side as exemplary recitals of conversion to Quakerism. Neither work generates much suspense as to whether the protagonist will escape the darkness of former beliefs, but in each there is a present contention whose outcome is not certain. The narrator's struggle against self-righteous autobiography absorbs the reader as more immediate drama and submits less easily to categorical judgment.

John Churchman's *Account*

The most regular feature of the Quaker journal is the purposeful statement which, in an opening paragraph, declares that the writer, wishing to give thanks for God's gracious dealings with him, has gathered together these records of a life lived according to the Light for the instruction of others. To capitalize on the force of a living example, many journals were printed even before the death of the writer, and Quaker committees for publication lost little time rushing into print the memoirs of a departed "ancient and esteemed Friend." Manuscripts which had earlier escaped the notice of publishing committees eventually reached the public through such collections as the early nineteenth-century *Friends' Miscellany*: "Being a collection of essays and fragments, biographical, religious, epistolary, narrative and historical; designed for the promotion of piety and virtue, to preserve in remembrance the characters and views of exemplary individuals, and to rescue from oblivion those manuscripts left by them, which may be useful to survivors."[11]

Few journalists surpassed John Churchman[12] in attending earnestly and explicitly to the edification of survivors. Like nearly all Friends who wrote journals, Churchman was a "public Friend," or minister, unpaid, and ordained only by the Spirit; that is, the local Meeting had recognized and certified him for his demonstrated ability to articulate what the Spirit had revealed to him inwardly. Naturally enough, the sermonizing habit carried over into didactic autobiography, where entirely mechanical adjustments accomplished the integration. Relating that in his youth he examined his conscience nightly, Churchman concludes by recommending the practice as "a great help to sleep sweetly, and by

[11] Title page, *Friends' Miscellany*, ed. John and Isaac Comly (Byberry, 1831). By the time the Comlys published this collection, general interest in Friends' journals seems to have declined somewhat. The editors felt called upon at one point to answer "the sentiment alluded to by Job Scott, that 'some think there are journals enough printed.'"

[12] John Churchman was born and died in Nottingham, Pennsylvania. He began to preach at twenty-five, and as a public Friend traveled to Great Britain, Ireland, and Europe. Chosen a justice of the peace in 1748, he declined the honor, but in the same year came before the Pennsylvania Assembly to speak on the war tax and slavery. Churchman sometimes traveled with John Woolman, accompanied him in 1749 on visits to slave-holding Friends in Pennsylvania and New Jersey. See Amelia Gummere, ed., *The Journal and Essays of John Woolman* (New York, 1922), pp. 542-543.

long experience I can recommend it to children, and those also of riper age."[13] A wrathful outburst from an affectedly religious man so shocked Churchman as a boy that he is anxious to include the incident and to draw the appropriate moral: "I relate this instance, that it may be a warning to all, that they be careful of giving offence to little ones" (p. 4). Churchman recalls the first occasion on which he took a "concern" directly to the offender (who was in the habit of falling asleep at meetings), then goes on to underline his purpose in describing the incident: "My intention in writing this, is to encourage the humbled, carefull traveller in the way of his duty" (p. 14).

A good life preaches its own sermon, Churchman seems to say; the autobiographer has only to set its lessons in relief. For the Quaker, however, the figure who delivered the sermon could not escape inspection, because his various acts of articulation were an important part of his experience. The habit of self-scrutiny arose directly from the Quaker form of worship. Theoretically the Quaker who felt himself prompted to speak in meeting did so, not as an individual subject to praise or blame, but as the medium of the Spirit. If his delivery was well received, the words were probably of God. If the speaker did not touch the condition of his auditors, if his message was not a solid one or seemed objectionable to the group for some reason, it would seem that the Spirit had been thwarted in the dense medium of the speaker's concern for self. In practice, however, it must often have been difficult to escape the impression that one's own faculties had something to do with the excellence of an articulated concern. John Churchman's

[13] *An Account of the Gospel Labours and Christian Experiences of a Faithful Minister of Christ, John Churchman* (Philadelphia, 1779), p. 3.

handling of several anecdotes suggests how exposure in the medium of autobiography could accentuate this feeling.

On one journey, a Friend at Bordentown expressed his admiration for Churchman's stern admonishment of the meeting, and Churchman includes the words of the tribute: " 'Well my lad, I perceive thou art born for a warrior, and I commend thee' " (p. 43) . A Presbyterian elder in New England, complimenting Churchman on the extent of his knowledge, supposed that he had been educated at college. Churchman takes some pleasure in replying that beyond "reading to the weaver, his master," he has had only three months of higher education, and he goes on to report the elder's amazed reply (p. 57) .

Churchman's self-consciousness becomes all the more evident when his eloquence leaves him. Thinking on one occasion that he had "considerable matter" before him, he had risen to address the meeting: ". . . and after speaking three or four sentences which came with weight, all closed up, and I stood still and silent for several minutes, and saw nothing more, not one word to speak; I perceived the eyes of most of the people were upon me, they, as well as myself expecting more; but nothing further appearing I sat down, I think I may say in reverent fear and humble resignation . . ." (p. 64) . The embarrassment of the incident persists in its autobiographical retelling. Still bothered that some may have thought him "a silly fellow," Churchman attempts to defend the troubled speaker of his narrative by observing that the few sentences he managed were "self-evident truths" (thus perhaps locating the difficulty) , and were therefore "to the advantage of Friends, and did no dishonour to the cause of Truth" (p. 65) .

Churchman's case is typical for the Quaker autobiographer in its tension between the personal and the didactic

13

impersonal. Ideally "the Quaker autobiographer was a Friend first, and an individual penning his memoirs second."[14] As instructor and knowledgeable guide Churchman thus conducts the reader to selected actions in a life—his own—and calls attention to their lessons, which appear like titles beneath tableaux. Several of the scenes interest him more personally, however, and draw him in—to participate again in a victory for Truth or to render a past imprudence harmless. In both passages the subject is John Churchman, but the journalist maintains that the only subject is Truth. Quaker piety encouraged the subordination of the individual will to the Light, and Churchman accepts this morality in autobiography as in life. But two important questions were thereby neglected. Could the self ever be successfully banished from first-person narrative? And was the cause of Truth really advanced if it depended upon a sacrifice of self-knowledge? John Churchman was not the last autobiographer to make the implicit decision that in an important cause the materials of one's life are best used to affirm an obvious truth, not as the basis for the narrator's self-interrogation.

Regardless of Churchman's awareness of these problems, they inhere in his journal, and nowhere more clearly than in his didactic use of dreams. Reporting of supra-rational experiences such as dreams and visions was fairly common among Quakers, whose belief in an intuitive access to divine Truth allowed for the possibility that God might choose such a medium for revelation. The Quaker's narration of a dream thus establishes a meeting ground of the personal and impersonal. Dreams came unbidden, and their enigmatic qualities frequently puzzled the writer himself; yet in fairly obvious ways they tended to allegorize his preoccupa-

[14] Wright, *The Literary Life of the Early Friends*, p. 156.

tions. A deeply personal concern might in this way be presented as the least personal of testimonies, an authoritative confirmation of Truth which had no dependence on self. In one such testimony John Churchman depicts himself encountering a great light as he rode out in the early evening. At rest in the midst of "many curious stacks of corn," the light takes shape as an angel. After awakening, Churchman declares, he suddenly recalled that "the complexion of the angelic apparition . . . was not much different from one of the Indians clear washed from his grease and filth" (p. 185). The Spirit dwells in men of all colors, Churchman concludes; we should examine deeper than outward appearance.

Quaker piety did not, then, require the journalist to write about his life as if he had not lived it. Churchman's strong feelings about the plight of the Indian in Pennsylvania emerge from the passage, and his experience of unwashed Indians is implied by the incandescent variety he encounters in his dream. The Quaker autobiographer enjoyed a relative freedom; he was allowed to move about in the terrain of his past experience looking for likely places for sermons. Churchman had an especially sharp eye for the likely places and numbered his dreams among them. He once dreamed of two armies, one without weapons, arrayed against each other. One of the unarmed soldiers, as his side advances, extends an arm menacingly, only to have his finger sliced off by an enemy sword. "I cried out, if that hand had not been so stretched out, this wound would not have been received. . . ." The lesson was an important one in a society preparing for war, but the total passage can also stand as a parable for the spiritual autobiographer. Churchman's dream, a sufficient argument in itself, is dissipated by the intrusive sermon; "and so I awakened" (p. 132).

15

The *Journal* of Thomas Chalkley

Conventional statements of purpose made by spiritual autobiographers often fail to describe the variety of concerns and conflicts brought into play by the act of autobiography. Thomas Chalkley, for instance, can summarize the common method and intention of Quaker journalists while giving no hint of individual emphases that develop in his own writing: "And the Accounts here given, have been mostly general, not descending into many Particulars; tho' the adding some Things might have been instructive and agreeable: The whole being intended as a Motive to stir up others to serve, love, and faithfully follow, and believe in Christ."[15]

In describing his *Journal* as a motivating agent to Christian life and belief Chalkley appears to share John Churchman's impersonal didacticism, but to accomplish his intention he will be forced to confront himself much more directly than Churchman. His double life as a merchant sea-

[15] *A Journal, or, Historical Account, of the Life, Travels, and Christian Experiences, of that Antient, Faithful Servant of Jesus Christ, Thomas Chalkley* (Philadelphia, 1749), p. 76. Chalkley (1675-1741) was born in England and, after a missionary voyage to America in 1698, brought his family to settle in Maryland in 1700. He soon moved to Philadelphia and in 1723 settled on a plantation in nearby Frankford. Chalkley made numerous trading voyages to the West Indies. Late in his career he suffered losses of about $10,000, but worked strenuously in the years 1726-1731 to pay off his debts. Chalkley never set aside his calling as a public Friend; he combined business and the ministry on many of his voyages, preached for three years in England and on the Continent, and also preached to the Susquehanna and Shawnee Indians in Pennsylvania. Whittier mentions Chalkley, "Gentlest of skippers, rare sea saint," in "Snow-Bound," and in "Chalkley Hall" memorializes the Frankford home as a retreat from "the market" and "the world's madness." Details drawn from the *Journal* are the basis of the entry on Chalkley in the *Dictionary of American Biography*. His collected *Works*, of which the *Journal* forms the first part, include sermons, essays of advice to young people, and a friendly letter to Cotton Mather clarifying points of Quaker doctrine.

captain and traveling Friend led eventually to scandal and charges of hypocrisy. Willing enough to conform his *Journal* to the common didactic purposes of the Society, Chalkley finds himself continually distracted by the necessity to answer critics. More is involved, however, than the writer's defense of his past, for the present effectiveness of his *Journal* will be seriously compromised if Chalkley cannot demonstrate his consistent acquaintance with Truth. Autobiographical argument succeeds or fails initially with the autobiographer's attempt to demonstrate his authority. In autobiography as in fiction the plausibility and consistency of the narrator must be validated.

Thomas Chalkley, therefore, seeks the reader's assent to the proposition that his life as minister and his life as merchant were one in Truth. In this attempt he has the good fortune to gain credence without seeking it by giving the impression that although he belonged more to the world than most traveling Friends, he suffered no debilitating increase of worldly wisdom. With unintentional humor, he reveals his essential innocence when he sets down the remarks made to him once by a West Indian governor: "He said, 'Whoever lived to see it, *Pennsylvania* would be the Metropolis of *America*, in some Hundreds of Years.'—He said, 'He loved down-right, honest Men; but he hated Deceit and Hypocrisy.' *A great Man, and a great Expression!*" (p. 232.) The Governor, a type of the eternal politician, was quite evidently aware of both Chalkley's origins and his religion, but Chalkley seems too enthused by the Governor's attack on deceit to suspect being patronized. With no such end in mind he manages to suggest that he lacked guile and self-awareness in equal amounts.

For both reasons, perhaps, Chalkley found it impossible to understand accusations that cited his practice of holding

17

meetings and transacting business on trips to the West Indies and to England. How could he grow rich by his preaching, as some claimed, when the remuneration of ministers was against Friends' principles? Chalkley was sure enough in his own mind that in distinguishing between earthly and heavenly things, he had been "careful how they mix the one with the other," and it was difficult to avoid irritation at critics who seemed to have forgotten that the Apostles were, after all, fishermen, "and Fishing being their Trade, no doubt but they sold them, for it was not likely they could eat 'em all themselves" (p. 98). Far from increasing his wealth, Chalkley points out, the work of the traveling ministry had required of him not only his money but his time, "which was, and is, as precious to me, as to other People"—to say nothing of attendant physical discomforts, "very laborious and hard for my Flesh to endure (being corpulent and heavy from the 27th Year of my Age)" (p. 53).

There was in his defense another matter which Chalkley wished to have understood. Through "many losses," not further detailed, he had contracted sizable debts, which he had resolved to pay "or else to die in the Pursuit of it; in which Resolve I had inward Peace and Satisfaction; though such Labour, Travel, and Separation from my Family, was a great Cross to Nature" (p. 217). The claim of "inward Peace" in these activities would have helped justify Chalkley to critics within the Society, for the experience of such peace resulted only from a strict adherence to the dictates of the Inner Light. Other readers, detecting in Chalkley's tone as much as in his words the voice of a man at peace with himself and docile to Truth, could have been no less thoroughly convinced:

18

"I met with some who untruly censured me, as covetous of the Things of this World, or to be rich; and that for the sake of these outward Things, I might venture my Life until I might lose it: Really, as to my Life, it hath long been my Desire to be ready to resign it and is so still: And, as to those outward Things, so far as I know, my Heart is clear; Food and Raiment, and to be clear and even with the World, having rather to give than receive, is all the Grandeur I desire, and if that be not granted, I hope to be contented without it, and to be thankful." (p. 258)

It is not likely that Chalkley regarded occasional references to his family as part of his defense. Nevertheless, his professed endeavor to maintain the priority of things of the Lord by weaning himself from the world seems genuine beyond question when tested against the attitude of resignation he developed toward the numbingly regular deaths in his family. However extraordinary the infant mortality rate of this period may have been, it was surely exceeded in the household of Thomas Chalkley. In 1733, one daughter remained of twelve children born to him by two wives, and his first wife had died in 1711.

The death of his tenth child and namesake humbled Chalkley to understatement: "It was some Exercise to me thus to bury my Children one after another" (p. 107). When his eleventh child was born, Chalkley decided to name him George, after his father, brother, and nephew. George was also the name of the king, and therefore "a great Name among Men," but Chalkley's instruction on the transience of happiness fixed on earthly things had been too thorough to permit the hope that his son's name might preserve him to maturity: "I consider'd that no Name can preserve Life, so I gave him up to the Will of him who gave him to me, and desire, if I have no Name thro' Children to Posterity, I may have a name in the Lamb's Book of Life" (p. 108). For Chalkley to remark, then, that "as I had freely received from him, so I freely gave" (p. 71), but in reference to the loss of income resulting from his travels in the ministry, was only to extend the lesson inculcated over the years at the graves of his children.

Concentration on Chalkley's efforts to answer his critics could give the impression that self-justification was the only concern of his *Journal*. Rather, his concerns were as inclusive as those of most other Quakers and differed from them very little. The task of setting the record straight on his alleged avarice did not distract Chalkley from being consciously instructive, even in small ways, for the benefit of traveling Friends. When travelers by sea found their provisions low, it might have been helpful for them to know that to Chalkley the liver of the porpoise "was well-tasted, and eat more like fresh Beef than Fish. . . . they may eat freely without Danger, according to our Experience" (p. 99).

Quaker journals frequently threaten to dissipate themselves in such miscellaneous advice as this and in the changes of time and place and activity they recorded, following notes jotted down along the way. But in Chalkley's autobiography a larger coherence draws together several of the author's purposes. He expresses a strong concern for the "young and rising Generation," whose vices at one point arouse him to uncharacteristic ire. In judging these ungodly youth and in prescribing for them Chalkley dips back into the matter of his self-defense. To settle doubts about the morality of business, Chalkley had expounded a business morality. In doing so he adhered to the so-called Protestant ethic by assigning to his outward calling a religious sanction. The habits of a strenuous and exacting spiritual life applied equally well to the affairs of business; "for I was not easy to be idle," he says, "either in my spiritual or temporal Callings." An important dimension of the Quaker dilemma in America appears when Chalkley ceases to treat his attention to business as a matter for apology, but as the basis of a secure conscience: "I had not been extravagant, but frugal; not covetous, but charitable; not idle, but industrious; not willing to be such an *Infidel* as not to take care for my Family" (p. 213).

Out of the autobiographical peril in which he found his authority weakened by scandal, Chalkley has constructed a new basis for authority from which he surveys the phenomenon of moral laxity among the young. From this perspective he can discern root causes; young men who have inherited wealth as the fruit of their parents' "Labour and Industry, Frugality, Care and Watchings," and not as the reward of their own endeavors, are thereby encouraged in habits of "wasting and spending" (p. 226). The sins of the young ("these spending, drinking, Company-keeping, gaming, chatting, tippling Youngsters, . . . those topping, beggarly Beaus, and Spenders") derive primarily from the imprudent liberality of parents, from which children acquire a deep prejudice against sober practicality. Chalkley prescribes his antidote, then, not from the *Journal* of George Fox or any handbook of Quaker piety, but from Proverbs: "Wherefore I would advise them to regard what the wise King *Solomon* said, *Go to the Ant thou Sluggard, consider her Ways, and be wise; she gathereth her Food in the Summer* (i.e. *she prepares against the Winter*)"

21

(p. 227). Put a young man behind the counter, keep him at his business, and, Chalkley suggests, the Christian virtues will be revived in him.

No seamless garment, Chalkley's *Journal* nevertheless harmonizes its various elements with relative success. It is doubtful, of course, that Chalkley foresaw working out an autobiographical argument in which he would replace the figure of a profiteering minister with that of an exemplar to youth, but the reader must still be impressed by the sincerity and vigor of his testimony, which are firmly established in the length of the *Journal*. So vigorously, in fact, did he condemn the "Tyranny and Cruelty" of Barbados slave-holders in one meeting that several local planters protested, and another later expressed his dissent more forcefully by shooting at Chalkley and wounding him. What Chalkley did lack, however, was a sense that the journal was an appropriate place to relate the mistreatment of slaves to the economic motives for keeping them, motives which involved him as a merchant doing trade with the West Indies. To this extent the success of the autobiographical argument has depended upon a diminishment of the autobiographer's self-inquiry.

The *Memoirs* of David Ferris

By its attention to economic virtues and experience associated with his outward calling, Chalkley's *Journal* seems less oriented than others to the doctrine of the Inner Light, which gives so many other Quaker journals a source of energy and thematic coherence. At another extreme, David Ferris[16] reveals in his journal how pervasively the doctrine

---

[16] David Ferris (1707-1779) was born in Stratford, Connecticut, and when he died was attached to the Wilmington, Delaware, Meeting. Ferris's grandfather was an early settler in the Massachusetts Bay

could affect a Quaker's experience and how fundamental were its relations to autobiography. This is not to say that Ferris expounds the doctrine at great length. In actual or in autobiographical experience, the Inner Light was less a meaning than a source of meanings. The belief that for every man God is accessible within has clear mystical import, as well as moral implications. An inward consultation may be an act of conscience or an attempt to discern spiritual truth not available to reason or even a kind of clairvoyance, the extraordinary knowledge of natural fact.[17] The intuitive potential of the doctrine of the Inner Light had been well explored by seventeenth-century Quakers, but their "enthusiasm" was beginning to be replaced by a new mood of quietism in the Society.[18] Disregarding these changes, David Ferris sought refuge among Quakers for an enthusiastic disposition no longer in accord with his inherited Presbyterianism, and by the impetus of divine revelation was able to surmount theological differences with relative ease. Had his decision come a few years later, Ferris might as conveniently have followed George Whitefield on the trail of the Great Awakening. In fact, observes Frederick

---

Colony, and his mother was described as "of the Puritan sort of people" by his brother Benjamin. Ferris was probably well on his way to becoming a Quaker when he and about sixty others were accused of heresy in the aftermath of a revival in New Milford, Connecticut, in 1727. The charges were dismissed, and Ferris went on to enter Yale, already convinced, he says, that human learning was insufficient to prepare for the ministry of the Gospel. His mother and four other children in the family followed him in his conversion to the Quakers.

17 Blanshard, "Early Thought on the Inner Light," p. 153.

18 Frederick Tolles, *Quakers and the Atlantic Culture* (New York, 1960), p. 112. From its Greek origin, the term "enthusiasm" had meant to be possessed by a god. The doctrine of the Inner Light conformed literally to this definition, so that any Quaker might strictly be called "enthusiastic." From approximately 1650 to 1750, however, the term acquired a range of meanings, including particularly the claim to extraordinary revelations and implying disordered religious emotion in general.

Tolles, "When Whitefield appeared on the scene, his doctrine was at once recognized as a resurgence of the enthusiasm of Fox."[19]

Hence the severity of Charles Chauncy's attack on Ferris in his *Seasonable Thoughts on the State of Religion in New England*. Chauncy, a Presbyterian and a rationalist, bolsters the case against the enthusiastic among his own co-religionists by demonstrating that at Yale certain of them had been infected with the "Quakerish tenets" of Ferris. Since Chauncy's real purpose is to discredit the current wave of revivalism, he assembles evidence to demonstrate Ferris's ideas heretical and then associates Ferris with the most radical fomenters of emotional religion. One of Chauncy's witnesses, a former classmate of Ferris, supports his charge that Ferris "was the greatest *Enthusiast* I ever knew" with accounts of extravagant claims to personal sinlessness and direct communications from the Holy Spirit which Ferris had confided to him. He sums up with the observation: "He was, to be short, filled with *imaginary Revelations.*" Another member of the same class told Chauncy that the "religious Club" Ferris gathered around himself "pleaded for the SPIRIT'S *immediate, extraordinary Guidance* in the Manner 'tis now pleaded for."[20]

The telling of this story from Ferris's point of view differs very little from the account given by his critics. Ferris makes no effort to minimize his revelations. Rather, they become the essential structuring device of his journal, occurring at decisive periods of his life, and providing an ideal demonstration of the pilgrimage to the Quaker meeting house. Not through the power of his own reason, nor as a result of

[19] *Ibid.*, p. 111.

[20] Charles Chauncy, *Seasonable Thoughts on the State of Religion in New England* (Boston, 1743), pp. 210-213.

the arguments of others, but "experimentally" Ferris arrives finally at the Truth: "I had before this period heard of a people called Quakers, but was unacquainted with any of them. As I had never seen any of their writings, I knew not what doctrines they held, but ascribe all my knowledge in divine things to the inward manifestations of grace and truth, the teaching of the Holy Spirit."[21]

Covering his life only to age twenty-five, Ferris first wrote an autobiographical draft in Latin, because doubts that he would "hold out to the end" induced him to conceal experiences which might have proved illusory. This kind of uncertainty, more familiar in Puritan spiritual narratives, suggests the doctrinal ambivalence of Ferris's *Memoirs*. The Quaker, after putting away the vanities of youth and resigning himself completely to the direction of the Inner Light, came into the possession of a lasting spiritual peace. And for the Quaker there was the further possibility "that a man who yielded himself to the working of the divine in him might cast off the incubus of sin completely and thus become perfect while yet on earth."[22] Ferris, then, writes in the tradition of John Bunyan's *Grace Abounding* when he admits the Adversary to his journal as a dramatic character, "continually present, whether I was awake or asleep, disquieting my mind as much as possible" (p. 22). Satan tempts Ferris to despair, telling him, as he told Bunyan, " 'that as there was a day or time, in which men might be saved; so if they let that opportunity pass away unimproved, it would be in vain to attempt it afterward' " (p. 19). Believing that Satan has described his case, Ferris so far despairs that he fears he will do away with himself, until the voice that spoke to Bunyan now speaks to him of pardon

---

21 *Memoirs of the Life of David Ferris* (Philadelphia, 1855), p. 32.
22 Tolles, *Quakers and the Atlantic Culture*, p. 107.

and mercy. When, however, his assurance is followed by another, that " 'the God of peace would bruise Satan under my feet shortly' " (p. 23), Ferris has begun to pass beyond the doctrinal limits of his Presbyterianism. When he proclaims, "The power of the enemy to assault, or in any wise to disquiet me, was now taken away; neither was he able to lay any temptation before me" (p. 23), Ferris writes as a Quaker, though a very different sort of Quaker from Churchman or Chalkley.

Within a few pages, Ferris is making the enthusiast's claim to special revelation, although at the time of the experience he disclosed the news only to his mother. A severe illness had weakened him and brought him close to death, Ferris recalls: ". . . my soul (as I apprehended) departed from the body . . . and as I departed I thought I saw my body lying a lifeless lump of matter. But as I went forward, I was met by some excellent person whom I took to be the Son of God; and who informed me that I must not go; saying 'Thou must return to the body; thou shalt not die but live, and declare the wonderful works of the Lord' " (pp. 26-27).

John Woolman recounts a similar experience,[23] but he draws from it a conclusion exactly opposite to the assurance of special favor that Ferris sees embodied in his vision. Ferris characteristically emphasizes, not the instruction that has come to him through such an experience, but the privilege of being singled out for the communication of a divine imperative. It becomes, in fact, the ironic lament of his journal that a vitiating weakness of flesh prevents him from fulfilling the role God intended he should play.

In the first section of the *Memoirs*, which Ferris translated from the secret account in Latin, the future appears

[23] See below, pp. 71-72.

26

to hold great promise for the work of the Lord and for one divinely commissioned to labor at the very head of the ranks. It had been revealed to Ferris that God "was about to bring the church out of the wilderness, or wandering state in which she had long been destitute of a true leader. And he made it clearly known to me that it was his will that I should go forth, and be an instrument in his hand for the accomplishment of this design" (p. 38). But in the continuation of the journal into later life, the note of special favor blends with one of reproach when, in a dream, Ferris is shown a "large, spacious building," and, noticing that one of the supporting pillars is missing, asks for an explanation from the "master-builder." "He replied, it was left for me; and that I was specially designed and prepared for the place, and showed how I fitted it. . . . But notwithstanding all this, I objected to my capacity and fitness to fill the vacancy, and was therefore unwilling to occupy it" (p. 62).

On lesser matters, Ferris accepts divine direction unquestioningly and to the letter. He discontinues the courting of "a comely young woman" when a voice, quoting Jeremiah, advises him: " 'Seekest thou great things for thyself?—seek them not' " (p. 49). Dining at a Friend's house shortly afterward, Ferris notices a young woman, "a goodly person," seated opposite him, and is told, " 'If thou wilt marry that young woman, thou shalt be happy with her.' " When his destined wife arises from the table, however, Ferris realizes that she is lame. "The cause of her lameness I knew not; but was displeased that I should have a cripple allotted to me" (p. 50). Displeased though he may be, Ferris does not question the origin of the voice or the finality of its proclamation, at least not in his account of the incident. This image of absolute obedience may have helped to offset the larger self-portrait he was drawing of a man derelict in the duties of his calling. Forty years after the event, at any rate, Ferris was able to report the reward of obedience; his marriage had been a happy one: "There was no woman on earth so suitable for me as she was" (p. 52).

Ferris again benefited from the advice of a heavenly adviser when he embarked on a career as a merchant: "Being unacquainted with the merchants, and ignorant of the quality of goods, I felt my need of an instructor, to whom I might safely apply for direction; and as I looked to my divine Guide, I found to my admiration that He was near to help me" (p. 57). Although the editors of Ferris's manuscript allowed this passage to stand—and Quaker censoring committees took their task very seriously—an application to divine guidance for education in business would surely have seemed to many a perversion of the doctrine of the Inner Light.

As the sequel to another self-incriminating dream in which an eminent captain refuses to accept a position of leadership, Ferris describes the successful result of his first concern to speak in meeting, after which he gradually assumed the responsibilities God had designated for him in his youth. Subsequent entries in the journal[24] reveal him in his proper role, engaged in the long and difficult travels of a ministering Friend. Personal reflections no longer appear, and Ferris seems to have come to terms with the essential agony of his life, the certain knowledge that God had chosen him for an American Moses, "to bring the church out of the wilderness," together with the growing realization that he had no power to pass beyond Moses' objection— "O my Lord, I am not eloquent."

24 Only the final portion of the *Memoirs* consists of periodic entries.

Ferris made a final entry in his journal at the age of seventy-two. Looking over the narrative of his early life, he might have noted the irony of one passage in particular. In the description of his departure from Yale, where he could no longer remain to accept a meaningless degree, Ferris had dwelt rather gloatingly on the farewells he exchanged with a close friend and classmate. As they parted, the friend disclosed that he was nearly in agreement with Ferris's principles and pledged to follow his example if his duty should become more clear. Ferris had concluded his relation of the incident with a suggestion that economic motives later inhibited his friend. The absence of charity in this judgment was particularly conspicuous in view of discoveries Ferris was coming to make about himself: "I afterwards heard that to follow my example was a cross too heavy for him to bear. He took to preaching for a living among the Presbyterians; and never left them to my knowledge" (p. 40).

It may have been with this incident in mind, and with a sense of his own difficulties in taking up a cross, that Ferris recalled the pattern of his life, commending it, somewhat ambiguously, to the attention of posterity: "Although I had been called out of the world and uncommonly favored, as before related; . . . yet, after all this, I was so forgetful to my heavenly Benefactor, that it is a wonder I was ever restored. . . . This I have written for a warning to others" (p. 82). The same autobiographical evidence argues either an exemplary attentiveness to the Inner Light or the grave necessity of returning from a journey into self with human as well as divine revelation. The latter theme deserves to be inscribed over the entrance to Quaker autobiography, but in Ferris's *Memoirs* it is at most a dim final perception.

29

Elizabeth Ashbridge's *Account*

Only by a complete recasting of the provisional auto-biography he wrote as a young man could David Ferris have produced a narrative which integrated the perspective of his later years with the matter of his earliest experience. The autobiography of Elizabeth Ashbridge[25] attains unusual coherence by its convincing demonstration that the earliest part of the life of the writer may adequately represent the whole and that its two centers of interest, the narrative of her conversion to Quakerism and the characterization of her surly and dissolute husband, are integrally related. Superficially, the *Account* of Elizabeth Ashbridge appears to borrow coherence through its resemblance to a secular counterpart, the confessions of "injured females," which Donald Stauffer has described in his history of eighteenth-century English biography.[26] Though more subdued in the telling than the sensationalistic memoirs of English heroines, this autobiography shares several of the same features: a "foolish passion" and elopement at the age of 14; widowhood; kidnapping; discovery of a mutinous plot on board the ship which takes her, as an indentured servant,

[25] Elizabeth Sampson Ashbridge (1713-1755) was born in England, and came to America when she was nineteen. Her second husband, who plays such an important role in the autobiography, was named Sullivan. Her third husband, Aaron Ashbridge, relates in an epilogue to the *Account* that by sewing and "school-keeping," she paid off an eighty-pound debt Sullivan had left when he deserted her to enlist in the British army. Aaron Ashbridge and Elizabeth Sullivan were married in 1746, and in 1753 Elizabeth secured permission from the local meeting to preach to Friends in England and Ireland, where she died two years later. References to Elizabeth Ashbridge, drawn from the records of the Goshen, Pennsylvania, Meeting, may be found in Wellington T. Ashbridge, *The Ashbridge Book* (Toronto, 1912), pp. 24, 46, 47.

[26] *The Art of Biography in Eighteenth Century England* (Princeton: Princeton University Press, 1941), pp. 69-70.

to America; cruel treatment from her master; and a second precipitate, unhappy marriage—in short, the kind of experience that led many eighteenth-century women to relate the story of their lives, purportedly as a caution to others. Thus to her pious statement that she wishes to record "the dealings of Divine Goodness with me," Elizabeth Ashbridge adds: "And I most earnestly desire, that whosoever reads the following lines may take warning and shun the evils that through the deceitfulness of Satan I have been drawn into."[27]

More appropriately, the *Account* of Elizabeth Ashbridge may be seen as a moral action in which the narrator retraces her questing progress toward the Society of Friends only to encounter in the challenge of characterizing her wayward husband the same obstacle which, in life, had tried her new faith so severely. By comparison with the journals of Churchman, Chalkley, and Ferris, her narrative demonstrates that autobiography need not investigate the self overtly in order to demonstrate self-knowledge. At the same time, her *Account* serves as a useful introduction to the consummate Quaker rhetoric of John Woolman's *Journal* by showing that the selected exemplary actions of the life

[27] *Some Account of the Fore-Part of the Life of Elizabeth Ashbridge . . . Wrote by Herself* (Nantwich, 1774), p. 3. There were numerous reprintings of the *Account*, abridged and "improved" in varying degrees, through the first half of the nineteenth century. My references are to the first edition, printed at Nantwich, near Elizabeth Ashbridge's birthplace, but two twentieth-century editions may be consulted: *Quaker Grey* (Guildford, 1904) printed by A. C. Curtis from an early transcript which already embodies the more fluent syntax of later versions, though Curtis believed it had been taken from the original manuscript; and *Remarkable Experiences in the Life of Elizabeth Ashbridge* (Birmingham, 1927), edited by Edmund Hatcher from an 1847 edition, with additions from a transcript in the Bevan Naish Library, Birmingham, "which appears to be her husband's original copy of her own accounts."

argue less convincingly than the more immediate acts of the autobiographer.

The heterogeneous experiences which open the *Account of the Fore-Part of the Life of Elizabeth Ashbridge* do not immediately disclose a potential Quakeress, save in the young girl who grieves that only boys can become ministers and who, observing "that there were several different religious societies," weeps secretly for direction to the Truth. Miscellaneous adventures, which include Elizabeth's emigration to America, fill out the introductory portion of the narrative, but gradually the protagonist becomes identified as a religious seeker. By the time she arrives in New York, Elizabeth Ashbridge has already denied, by neglect, her Anglican upbringing, and has refused to subscribe to the articles of faith read her by a Catholic priest, including as they did recognition of the Pretender and the damnation of all—even her mother—who died outside the Church. In America, she begins to doubt all religion under the cruelty of a hypocritical master, whom she had taken to be "a very religious man." Observing the worldly clergymen her master entertains, she feels a miserable and "atheistical" frame of mind gaining in her, and is tempted to suicide. But after a voice warns her of hell, Elizabeth dreams she has been visited by "a grave woman," who promises mercy and future enlightenment, signified by a brightly burning oil lamp. At this point she was able to buy her freedom, and within a few months had entered into what she describes as another form of servitude, by marrying a young man "who fell in love with me for my dancing" (p. 14).

For a time, Elizabeth's quest for the Truth brings no opposition from her new husband; she worships with Baptists and Presbyterians and, though she finds no satisfaction, is made to see that her duty to God involves the love of her husband: "he saw I grew more affectionate to him, but I did not yet leave off singing and dancing so much, but I could divert him whenever he desired it" (p. 16). The beginning of discord comes when she takes leave of her husband to visit relatives in Pennsylvania and discovers not only that her relatives are Quakers, but "what was worse of all, my aunt was a preacher." Once before she had visited a Quaker meeting, and had heard a woman preach; her reaction, she notes, was one of contempt mixed with pity.

Prejudice fades, however, in the home of her aunt and uncle. She had heard that Quakers "deny the scripture," and that they recognize "no other bible but *George Fox's Journal*"; but curiosity proves stronger than bias and she casually picks up one of her aunt's books: "I . . . had not read two pages before my very heart burned within me, and tears came into my eyes, which I was afraid would be seen. I therefore walked with the book into the garden, and the piece being small, read it thro' before I went in . . ." (p. 23). The quest has ended. Conversion follows shortly, though not instantaneously. At the first meeting she attends with her relatives, she finds that the custom of silence conduces only to sleep. But several weeks later she hears a Friend preach the gospel with such power "that I was forced to give up, and confess it was the TRUTH" (p. 25).

With the recall of this conviction, Elizabeth Ashbridge begins the account of her sufferings for Truth. She portrays herself as unwilling at first to acknowledge the change that has taken place, yet attached deeply enough to the scene of her illumination that she must send for her husband. An itinerant schoolteacher, much given to "rambling," he joins her readily enough, but as she later discovers, rumors had reached him of her conversion. Her greeting to him— "My dear, I am glad to see thee"—confirms the rumors and

33

elicits a reply that signals the beginning of an entirely new domestic relationship: "at which he fell in a great passion, and said the devil THEE thee, don't THEE me" (p. 27).

Wittingly or not, and with what purpose in mind one cannot be sure, Elizabeth Ashbridge here initiates the dramatic process by which her husband becomes the chief character in her autobiography. His abuse of her, after she acquainted him with her intention to become a Quaker, deserves inclusion under the heading of "sufferings," the impressive testimony Quakers had used from the beginning to illustrate the power of pacific truth against militant error. She would also have been intent on tracing God's dealings with her husband just as she had noted the actions of Providence in her own life. But nothing in the tradition of the Quaker journal encouraged quite so vivid a portrait as she provides of her moody, complex, and irresolute husband. The "affection" which she had cultivated for him under the pressure of a theoretical consideration lay deep enough at least to inspire a sympathetic portrayal of his character, most striking when she passes over an opportunity for moralistic revenge in favor of a more charitable reflection. One of their frequent migrations had exhausted Elizabeth so thoroughly that her husband sought to revive her energies with a drink of mulled cider; but the cider only made her sick and faint, and she fell down; "which my husband observing, tauntingly said, what's the matter now, what, are you drunk? where's your religion now? He knew better, and at that time I believe he pitied me, yet was suffered grievously to afflict me" (p. 33). The narrator's use of incident and dialogue pleases by its vividness, and Elizabeth Ashbridge may well have hoped to gain credence for her themes by realistic depiction of her experience. The larger advantage, however, is the increasing respect her autobiographical choices elicit as she develops the character of her husband. Having recorded the worst, she nevertheless attempts to believe the best of him.

The husband's objection to Quakerism was not, apparently, theological; he might have tolerated his wife's conversion had it not involved a change in her habits. A scene in a Philadelphia tavern, which Elizabeth Ashbridge renders from her husband's point of view as well as her own, makes his feelings evident. Denouncing his wife's conversion to those around him, he paints a melancholy contrast between her present sobriety and her former willingness to dance and sing. Someone brings out a fiddle, and he has occasion to test the conversion he has just been describing:

"He came to me and took me by the hand, saying, come my dear, shake off that gloom, let's have a civil dance, you would now and then, when you were a good Church-woman, and that is better than a stiff Quaker; I trembling desired to be excused, but he insisted on it, and knowing his temper to be exceeding choleric, I durst not say much, but would not consent; he then pulled me round the room till tears affected my eyes, at sight of which the musician stopped, and said I'll play no more let your wife alone, of which I was glad." (p. 30)

The dramatic situation itself tests the autobiographer's conversion. In such scenes as this, Elizabeth Ashbridge can legitimately demand increased sympathy from the reader with the negligible sacrifice of her husband's character. He, after all, plays the lion, she the Christian; or more proximately, he stands for all the persecutors of Quakers in England and America. "If you offer to go to meeting to-morrow," he shouts threateningly, "with this knife I"ll cripple you, for you shall not be a Quaker." Yet she will not allow him to become the stock villain of a pious melodrama and

35

instead sympathetically establishes an essential but pardonable weakness of character beneath his violent appearance. Despite his threat, she continues to attend meetings without hindrance.

Soon it becomes possible to depict a divine ordering of these conflicts toward some higher end. Relying upon her husband's description of a sobering revelation, Elizabeth Ashbridge reconstructs the scene of his lying in bed one morning when she had gone to meeting. Inexplicably, the words "Lord where shall I fly to shun thee?" cross his mind. He sets out immediately to join his wife, and arrives soon enough to gather, as the meeting breaks up, that she had preached that morning. There is a noticeable change of tone in the plea he addresses to her as they ride back: "What do you mean thus to make my life unhappy? Could you not be a Quaker without turning fool after this manner?" After receiving a firm but sympathetic reply, he concludes, "Well, I'll even give you up; for I see it don't avail to strive, if it be of God, I cannot overthrow it, and if it be of yourself it will soon fall" (p. 39).

In continued deference to the integrity of her husband's experience, Elizabeth Ashbridge rejects on his behalf the convenient but at this point inappropriate shape of reformed persecutor, emphasizing instead the more painful problems brought about by his uncertain reformation. "Melting into tears," he would acknowledge the truth of her beliefs, she remembers, and would then proclaim his weakness and inability to tolerate the scorn of his drinking companions. It occurs to him that "if he was in any place where it was not known that he had been so bitter against Friends, he could do better. . . ." He teaches briefly in Bordentown, then moves on to Mount Holly. Removal to unfamiliar circumstances, however, only serves to obliterate the memory of his earlier resolutions. Elizabeth Ashbridge describes his deterioration from the period when he "would often in a broken manner condemn his bad usage of me" to a new stage of hostility and depression:

". . . my husband coming home a little in drink, in which frame he was very fractious, and finding me at work by a candle, came to me, put it out, and fetching me a box on the ear said, you don't earn your light, which unkind usage, for he had not struck me of two years before, went hard with me, and I uttered these rash expressions, thou art a vile man, and was a little angry, but soon recover'd and was sorry for it; he struck me again, which I received without so much as a word in return, and [he] went on in a distracted manner, uttering several rash expressions that bespoke despair, as that he now believed he was predestinated to damnation, and he did not care how soon God would strike him dead and the like." (p. 43)

Briefly in this passage, Elizabeth Ashbridge and her husband are at war, but it is the autobiographical character rather than the narrator who expresses disgust, and the husband is damned only by his own despairing rashness. Although the exemplary restraint of the Elizabeth Ashbridge who endures suffering "without so much as a word in return" strikes one as a most provocative sort of patience, her narrative restraint, at least, is admirable. Elizabeth Ashbridge thus reinforces her argument, which is also the assumption of Quaker autobiographical writing, that the experience of Truth can be shared and extended. In a fallen world, conversion must be a narrative which has no conclusion. Ideally, the pattern of the narrator's conversion should blend imperceptibly, as this one does, into the pattern of another. In the closing paragraphs of her *Account*,

Elizabeth Ashbridge recalls her horror at discovering that another rash act, a final plea for deliverance "by some means or other," had deprived her of her second husband. While "in drink" he had enlisted with the British army for duty in Cuba, and although he never returned, Elizabeth was able to recover satisfactory evidence of his arrival at Truth: "When they came to an engagement he refused to fight, for which he was whipped, and brought before the general, who asked him why he inlisted, if he would not fight. I did it, said he, in a drunken frolick, when the devil had the better of me, but my judgement is convinced that I ought not neither will I, whatever I suffer. I have but one life and you may take that if you please, but I'll never take up arms." (p. 44)

A final paragraph gives Elizabeth Ashbridge the opportunity to sort out her feelings about her husband and to reflect that by using his character in a Quaker autobiography she has subjected him to a variety of "hard usage" not unlike his surliest treatment of her. It seemed a duty, therefore, "to say what I could in his favour," and dutifully she adds the hope that she has been improved by the adversity he so amply provided. Her language is equable, not warm, when she adds that "altho' he was so bad, yet had several good properties, and I never thought him the worst of men." Indeed, the only statement that tells the reader explicitly what has been implicit in the narrator's conduct seems distant and impersonal: "he was one I loved," she observes, "and had he let religion have its perfect work, I should have thought myself happy in the lowest state of life. . . ."

But the words of a single paragraph are less indicative than the total weight of the narrative, especially when they must express the feelings of the wife of Aaron Ashbridge about a man named Sullivan. The moral action of the *Account* must be measured in the distance between an "unaccountable" marriage to "a man I had no value for" and her reverential handling of the climactic scene in which her husband becomes the exemplary Quaker, testifying for peace against a cruel antagonist, persevering despite being "used . . . with much cruelty." By this sharing of identical roles with her former husband, Elizabeth Ashbridge accomplishes a unity which had not been available in their lives.

The sense of having completed a coherent narrative persisted for her, apparently, beyond these closing paragraphs. Aaron Ashbridge, replying to news of his wife's death in Ireland in 1755, recalled that she had intended to set down additional "hints of her experience" but, being drawn to Friends abroad, could never complete the writing.[28] Any autobiographer may be reluctant to conclude his autobiographical life. Elizabeth Ashbridge chose as well as more sophisticated autobiographers in allowing a passage of her life to define the whole and in making a single character, never individualized by a name, the representative of the world she needed to triumph over for Truth's sake, first by endurance and finally by love.

Autobiography and the Inner Light

By most criteria the literary value of early American Quaker journals must be judged very slight. Commonly, one's most favorable impression of a journal begins with the autobiographer's departure from the language and patterned experience of other Friends. Of necessity such outbursts of originality were incidental, brief, and contained

[28] Hatcher, ed., *Remarkable Experiences in the Life of Elizabeth Ashbridge*, p. 49.

39

within the larger structure of the journal, which was already well established by 1700. Conformity to this structure resulted from a group mentality, but also of course from the common experiences of traveling Friends. With few exceptions, Quaker journals were the autobiographical expression of Quaker ministers, and taken as a whole they display the same tendency toward repetitive experience as might the autobiographies of buffalo hunters or retired generals. The *Account* of Elizabeth Ashbridge can vary so interestingly from the usual pattern partly because it concludes before the standard experiences of the Friends' ministry might have been taken up. Had she written later, her early experiences might have suffered considerable foreshortening as no more than a prelude to the serious labors that followed. By this standard, most of an early life was expendable, with the single important exception of that process by which the autobiographer attained peace through submission to the Light, the Quaker equivalent of conversion. In the narration of this experience, too, uniformity prevails. The operations of the Spirit prove so regular that one hesitates to commend a given writer for whatever coherence he achieves.

Imposed autobiographical unity can be expected only from a relatively brief work, like that of Elizabeth Ashbridge, composed at a single point in time. Striving to discharge the duties of his inward and outward callings, meeting responsibilities not only to his family but to Friends in remote areas of the wilderness, the Quaker autobiographer had little time for studied composition. John Woolman exercised unusual care in making revisions through a succession of manuscripts. Most journalists probably organized and rewrote their jottings only once. Unable to sift through the periodic entries made over an entire career, the writer surrendered to chronology and the record of his travels, perhaps digressing occasionally into special concerns. Hugh Judge no doubt voiced the experience of many when, having begun a unified narrative, he concluded that his purpose could be achieved just as well in a disconnected form: ". . . my main end in writing is to let my children and others see a little how I have got along in my religious concerns. This, I think I have felt it right for me to do, whether I shall have put it in better order to be read or not."[29]

The authors of Quaker journals never consciously aimed at "fine writing"; most were incapable of it and, unlike some prominent Philadelphia Quakers, would have been unacquainted with any literary models on which to pattern themselves. Moreover, the vocabulary of Quaker spiritual experience had been standardized since the time of George Fox, and it resisted firmly any infiltration of the journalist's secular reading experience. Thomas Chalkley's reading of Addison, for instance, must be learned from his own admission rather than by inference from his prose. The diction and cadences of the Old Testament and the Pauline epistles were of course always on the lips of Quakers, but this kind of borrowed eloquence frequently becomes egregious with the narrator's movement back and forth between scripture and the ordinary level of his own expression. Disdaining the world's literature, a Quaker journalist too often neglected as well an immediate and natural source of imagery in the wilderness through which he traveled from meeting to meeting. The ordinary but undeniable pleasures of travel narrative are sacrificed to the autobiographer's single-minded concentration on his mission and itinerary.

[29] *Memoirs and Journal of Hugh Judge* (Byberry, 1841), pp. 261-262.

Even the hardships he endured must ordinarily be imagined by the reader. Only his sympathy with settlers on the frontier occasionally drew him into a description of the living conditions he shared with them. Hugh Judge describes himself crossing flood-swollen rivers, sitting down to a dinner of mush and milk, and resting one night in a cabin with no windows and no light, save from a smoke hole in the roof. But Judge is a more interesting observer than most, instinctively assimilating his external observations to his inward disposition:

"We dined in the same room that George Fox dined, and where he used to hold meetings; but the walls could not tell us on what subjects he treated. . . . The aspect of the trees, both fruit trees and forest, wears a serious appearance, and speaks in a solemn language to thoughtless man; as if to show to him who is not deaf to instruction what the Almighty can do." (pp. 323-324)

As a member of a later generation of Quakers, Judge (1750?-1834) no doubt received a superior education in the language of Nature, but any traveling Friend might have fashioned metaphors for his experience out of the materials around him. Well acquainted with the instructive nature of adversity, he needed only to consult his surroundings for an image responsive to his condition. Few did so, although John Woolman effectively set meditations on man as a primitive warrior and as a son of Adam in the wilderness. Perhaps only for the sea-captain Thomas Chalkley was there an inevitable figurative comparison: "I may say without boasting, I have witnessed the Rage and Noise of mighty Waves and Waters, both natural and spiritual; the one, as tho' it would swallow up my Reputation among

Men, and the other, as tho' it would swallow up my Person, in this my watry Peregrination" (p. 100).

But questions of language and narrative are not, by themselves, the most important questions to ask about autobiography. One wishes to know of an autobiographer what he can contribute to one's estimate of the nature of human experience. The reader interrogates an autobiographer on this point not in the autobiographer's summary statements —not for instance in John Churchman's expository rendering of Truth—but in the total autobiographical phenomenon, including especially its formal aspects. What difference did their belief in an Inner Light make for Churchman, Chalkley, Ferris, or Elizabeth Ashbridge as autobiographers? Obviously any conviction makes a difference for subject matter. In the journals of Churchman and Chalkley, Quaker beliefs make no other important difference, although Chalkley's writing has rhetorical interest for the autobiographer's attempt to harmonize experience and stated belief. The *Memoirs* of David Ferris begin to suggest the autobiographical implications of the doctrine of the Inner Light by shifting the focus of the life from outward experience to a pattern of inward revelation. As autobiographer, Ferris must then measure the discord between the life of his visions and the life in which he acted, or failed to act. Elizabeth Ashbridge's narrative suggests the greatest potential of the Quaker autobiography even though her writings explore very little of the inward space implied by illuminist belief. Her testimony for peace is the moral rather than the epistemological application of the Quaker belief that something of God dwells in every man. Like any autobiographer, she argues her convictions from the example of herself, and in this respect differs not at all from the other Quaker autobiographers. But she has begun

43

to demonstrate some of the possibilities of a rhetoric appropriate to autobiography. The homilist too uses exemplary characters, and there is no rhetorical difference between his argument and Elizabeth Ashbridge's observation that when the character, "my husband," struck his Quaker wife she suffered "without so much as a word in return." Instead, it is the narrator's decision not to retaliate which constitutes the specifically autobiographical argument. By her selection of incidents, by allowing her husband his own voice in frequent passages of dialogue, by characterizing what she understood of the tensions underlying his behavior, Elizabeth Ashbridge testifies for a loving sympathy through means appropriate to autobiography. Her husband's dramatic prominence in the last scene of the *Account* argues that he had found a basis of strength in himself, as any man could who submitted to the Light.

The early Quaker journal deserves attention, then, less for its intrinsic merit than as an introduction to the problems of spiritual autobiography as argument. None of the Quaker autobiographies so far studied attains a thoroughgoing adherence to the informing principle of the Inner Light, and they generally fail to bring the reader within the autobiographer's vision of Truth. David Ferris's illuminations regarding his own destiny are automatically exclusive. Elizabeth Ashbridge communicates well the fruits of her inwardness but not the phenomenon itself. John Woolman's definitive achievement as a Quaker autobiographer was to realize fully in his autobiographical argument the epistemological and moral implications of the Inner Light. For Woolman, as we shall see, the autobiographical act was indivisibly a kind of sight and a moral challenge.

CHAPTER TWO

THE *JOURNAL* OF JOHN WOOLMAN

Alone among Quaker journalists in America, John Woolman has the ability to convince his reader that he began life as a *tabula rasa*, and that as his experience grew there was written on that slate, with remarkable pureness and clarity, the instruction of divine Truth. Two kinds of activity are recorded in Woolman's *Journal*, then; and the act of making this record is itself a third kind. Woolman describes, first of all, the manner in which he came to apprehend the Truth; principles thus arrived at required an appropriate action in his life, which must also be set down; and because the journal was of little value if it did not move others to conform more perfectly to these principles, Woolman describes his experience so that it becomes an argument.

An autobiography is probably the last form of literature Woolman would have attempted, although technically and superficially his *Journal* may be so classified. Self-revelation, the frankly egocentric attempt to promulgate oneself, would have seemed to Woolman an ambition that led directly away from Truth. The self is indeed at the very center of his *Journal*, but as a topic, or as an entity to which Truth must be related, not as a personality to be expressed or anatomized.

I

Whatever the distinction that has set the *Journal* of John

Woolman above the numerous performances of other Friends in the same genre, his first words do little to indicate. So conventional had the journal's statement of purpose become by the middle of the eighteenth century that a modern reader finds it difficult to distinguish any difference among three such statements. The last, however, prefaces a narrative which has been read and republished by generations never reached by the first two.[1]

"I have, for some years, had thoughts of writing an account of the tender dealings of the all-wise Being with me from my youth up."[2]

"It has been repeatedly revived in my mind, to leave some hints of the gracious dealings of the Lord my Creator with me from my youth."[3]

"I have often felt a motion of Love to leave some hints of my experience of the Goodness of God: and pursuant thereto, in the 36 year of my age, I begin this work."[4]

The choice of words that distinguishes Woolman's sentence from the other two is the "motion of Love" he cites as disposing him to make his record. That the choice was carefully made becomes clear in the textual notes provided by Amelia Mott Gummere in her edition of the *Journal*. Woolman first wrote, "I have often felt a desire . . ."; but in his first revision of this early manuscript, he substituted the

[1] In her Introduction to Woolman's *Journal*, Amelia Mott Gummere estimates that "there are half a hundred editions of the Journal. . . ." *The Journal and Essays of John Woolman* (New York, 1922), p. x. All references are to the Gummere edition, which makes available variant readings from the three successive manuscripts of the *Journal*, as it was lengthened and revised by Woolman.

[2] "A Narrative of some of the Exercises and Christian Experiences, in the early part of her life, of JANE REYNOLDS . . . ," *Friends' Miscellany*, XI (1838), p. 49.

[3] *Memoirs of Elizabeth Collins* (Philadelphia, 1833), p. 15.

[4] Woolman, *Journal*, p. 151.

phrase, "a motion of Love," retaining the substitution in the folio manuscript from which the first edition of the *Journal* was printed.[5] Although "desire," in the sense in which Woolman first used the word, appears a harmless enough choice, his sensitivity to connotation had been so stimulated by his first act of extended personal narrative that he feared the word might convey something exactly opposite to his mature intention. Whereas "a motion of Love" placed the origin of action in a will submissive to God, "desire" conveyed an unfavorable association with the creaturely will. The revision directs the reader's attention away from the journalist and toward God, just as in speaking of "my experience of the Goodness of God," Woolman himself withdraws in order to emphasize the divine attribute experienced. In contrast, the phrasing of Jane Reynolds and Elizabeth Collins maintains their own prominence as objects of God's attention.

This single revision helps to illustrate the two most striking features of Woolman's *Journal*: its essential statement that, as self diminishes, the experience of divine love increases; and Woolman's habitual conscientiousness of expression, which strives to reveal Truth without distortion or dilution. As a primary theme and an ideal of form, these are general concerns of the Quaker journalist. "Practically every narrative contains a detailed account of the spiritual struggle involved in the surrender of the individual will to the leadings of the inner Light, and of the resultant peace which followed."[6] The purity of the Word was maintained only when it passed through a medium which was itself purified through submission. Woolman's literary testimony achieves more than pious passivity, however. By stressing

5 *Ibid.*, p. 151n.
6 Wright, *The Literary Life of the Early Friends*, pp. 156-157.

the continuity of the operations of divine love beyond the stage of conversion, into later experience, and into the widely conceived environment of his experience, Woolman manages better than other Quaker journalists to unify the narrative of his conversion and the narrative of his labors in the ministry. And by regarding autobiography as an extension of the conflict between self and selflessness he made a single act of the life and its articulation.

The process that brought Woolman "low enough to find true peace" differed not at all from the experience of other Quakers and not in many respects from that of Puritans like Jonathan Edwards. The narrative covering the early part of Woolman's life presents the familiar stages of youthful delight in scripture, "Gracious Visitations" of memorable "sweetness," early waywardness, and, in adolescence, estrangement from God through associating in "Vanities and Diversions" with a set of "wanton young people." For a period, strong resolutions—such as the one prompted by a nearly fatal illness—were succeeded in a recurrent pattern by relapses into vanity. When peace finally came, it represented the end of one stage of spiritual life and the beginning of another. Woolman is careful at this point to indicate two important relationships which, once established, dominate the theme and expression of the entire *Journal*. Experiential knowledge of a "Heavenly Principle" made possible, indeed demanded by its very nature, the dissemination of that principle: "And now, as I had Experienced the Love of God, through Jesus Christ, . . . and as my heart was often enlarged in this Heavenly Principle, so I felt a tender compassion for the youth who remain'd entangled in the same snare which had entangled me. From one month to another, this Love & tenderness increased, and my mind was more strongly engaged for the good of my fellow-creatures."[7]

While Woolman's concentration on his outward engagement accounts for the apparent impersonality of the *Journal*, it should be noted that the roots of this engagement lie in a deeply personal experience. From this experience Woolman derives a criterion for every judgment significant enough to be recorded in the *Journal*. He will make no decision and no observation, will neither perform nor refrain from any action, without considering how the self will be inclined as a result: toward Truth, when attentive to the principle that resides within; toward vanity and its effects, when the self is allowed to become its own principle for action.

Having established this paradoxical relationship—the greater the attendance upon an inwardly revealed principle of love, the more powerful the movement of love outward and away from the self—Woolman goes on immediately to relate purity of expression to the same kind of discipline. Not yet schooled in the rigors of "keeping close to the Divine opening," he had one day in Meeting "spoken more than was required. . . ." So great was his affliction following this error that Woolman found himself deprived for weeks of "any light or comfort." But the experience proved requisite to a second one in which, he reports, "I said a few words in meeting in which I found peace; this I believe was about six weeks from the second time, and as I was thus humbled and disciplined under the Cross, my understand-

[7] *Ibid.*, p. 159. In the earliest manuscript of the *Journal*, Woolman had described his sense of the proliferating nature of love. The final clause in the quoted passage read: "and I found it too strong and forcible to be much longer Confined to my own breast" (p. 159n). In revising, he apparently felt it less important to express the sensation of love than to name the object toward which love had moved him.

ing became more strengthened to distinguish the language of the pure Spirit which inwardly moves upon the heart . . ." (p. 159). The understanding, Woolman says, must first be made docile and purified of vanity's predilections before it can receive light undistorted. Knowing is related to interior disposition, as he had suggested in the term "intellectual deep" that originally stood for "heart" in this passage; and lucid prose becomes a moral and spiritual achievement.

II

Struggles of conscience comprise much of the usual content of Quaker autobiography. The record of Woolman's attempts to determine whether he could feel "easy" or "clear" to follow a course of action resembles in a general way the testimony of many other journals. In addition to the regular quest for a certain conscience, however, Woolman narrates an equally strenuous search for evidence that will define the moral situation externally. Within the circumscribed limits of life in Mount Holly, New Jersey, traditional Quaker testimony would indicate an appropriate course of action. If the patrons of a local tavern "spent their time in drinking and vain sports, tending to corrupt one another" (p. 160), the owner should be spoken to. When it became clear that the life of a merchant would be "attended with much cumber, in the way of trading in these parts" (p. 164), a simpler way of life, like tailoring, would have to be taken up.

But the quest that occupies most of the *Journal* began in unpreparedness. The man directing Woolman to draw up a bill of sale for the Negro woman was his employer; the man waiting for the bill of sale, an elderly member of the Society. Partly because of these circumstances, partly because he had not had time to relate his general position, that slave-keeping was "a practice inconsistent with the Christian Religion," to his responsibility as an individual, Woolman wrote the bill of sale. From Woolman's later point of view, the act was not exemplary even of a man's duty to his employer. But as the beginning of an attempt to see his social environment in the light of Truth, the incident required telling: "As often as I reflected seriously upon it I thought I should have been clearer, if I had desired to be Excused from it, as a thing against my conscience, for such it was" (p. 161).

The autobiographical record of Woolman's lifelong concern with slavery testifies to the variety of his approaches to a problem in social justice. To discuss first his attempt to gather evidence, to understand the forms which darkness assumed in the world, is to follow Woolman's own method. The Quaker could know Truth by looking inward, in a proper spirit of humility and resignation, but he could not relate Truth to an imperfect world without understanding deeply the problem he addressed. Even for the practical efficiency which Quakers sought and achieved, informed opinion was a necessity. As Woolman remarked after sitting through a series of eight-hour business meetings, "except our minds are rightly prepared, & we clearly understanding the case we speak to, instead of forwarding, we hinder business, and make Labour for those on whom the burden of the work is laid" (p. 219).

It was likely, too, that the effectiveness of the autobiographical argument Woolman was constructing would depend upon his ability to fill the reader's vision with all that he had seen. As in his own experience he moved deeper into the problems of slavery and war and poverty, Woolman no doubt hoped that he was bringing readers along with him, just as in narratives of their conversion, Quaker journalists wrote so as to involve others in their experiential discovery of Truth. William Penn made this purpose explicit when he addressed the non-Quaker reader in his preface to *The Written Gospel Labours of John Whitehead*: "Thirdly let him read, therefore, with an inward as well as an outward Eye and Read no Faster than he feels and understands in himself, and brings things to the inward Test and Touchstone. And if he has not attained to the Experience of these Truths, he may by the Spirit's Mirrour in himself or the Glass of Righteousness see so far as to give an assent to the Truths therein Discovered. . . ."[8]

Woolman's probing of darkness began always in his own experience. He journeyed into the South to sow the seeds of Light among slave-holding Friends through "close laborings" which brought out the inconsistency of their practice with their professed religion. The travels also provided an opportunity to validate and leaven with sympathy his more theoretical labors. Love demanded not only that he object, and remonstrate, and write essays and epistles, but that he signify his unity in the Light with slaves by experiencing, if only at second hand, their condition of life.[9] "Understanding the case we speak to," understanding what was signified by the abstract word "oppression," for instance, required a foundation in seeing: "Many whose labor is heavy being follow'd by a man with a whip, hired for that purpose, have in common little else allowed but Indian corn and salt, with a few potatoes; the potatoes they commonly raise by their

---

[8] Quoted in Wright, *The Literary Life of the Early Friends*, p. 71.
[9] Dissatisfied with merely vicarious participation, Woolman began in 1766 to make these trips on foot, "that by so Traveling I might have a more lively feeling of the Condition of the Oppressed Slaves, and Set an example of lowliness before the Eyes of their Masters" (p. 271).

52

own labour on the first day of the week. The correction ensuing on their disobedience to overseers, or Sloathfulness in business, is often verry severe, and sometimes desperate" (p. 194).

Unlike many subsequent censurers of the evils of slavery, Woolman does not lose himself in the sensationalism of what he has to report. He feels it important to sketch the conditions of life for the slave, but his language is restrained to the simple statement of fact. Physical suffering had always and everywhere been the lot of man, whether slave or free; and while God was always indignant, as Woolman noted, "against Oppression and Cruelty," the conditions of slaves, or Indians, or sailors, were most lamentable because they placed hindrances in the path of righteousness. These difficulties were what Woolman wished sympathetically to understand and alleviate: "Love was the first motion, and then a Concern arose to Spend Some time with the Indians, that I might feel and understand their life, and the Spirit they live in, If happily I might receive some Instruction from them, or they be in any degree helped forward by my following the Leadings of Truth amongst them. . . . I looked upon it as a more favourable Opportunity to season my mind, and bring me into a nearer Sympathy with them" (p. 254).

That Woolman looked forward to the prospect of receiving instruction from Indians regularly leads his admirers to comment on the evident humility of such an expectation. Yet Woolman regarded such instruction as indispensable to a full comprehension of the object of his concern. To be directed rightly and effectively, the concern needed to be based in understanding, and understanding began, not in theory, but in "seeing, hearing, and feeling, with respect to the life & Spirit" (p. 291), as Woolman insisted once again, this time with reference to the sailors he lived with in his passage to England.

He began to understand, for instance, the relation between several sets of problems. A mind seasoned with sympathy could begin to see that the evil of selling rum to Indians was more extensive than its immediate result in spectacles of drunken frenzy and quarreling. Woolman observed that to indulge themselves repeatedly in the habit taught them by white men, Indians sold their furs "at a low rate," and then suffered for lack of clothing and other "necessaries of life." Inevitably, their anger at being cheated resulted in strife and bloodshed. But this was not all: "I allso remembered that the people on the frontier among whom this evil is too common are often poor people who venture to the outside of a Colony that they may live more independent on such who are wealthy, who often set high rents on their Land. . . ." Driven away by landlords' "inordinate desire after wealth," these settlers, by their own similar desires, were often under the temptation "of being drawn into schemes to make settlements in Lands which have not been honestly purchased of the Indians, or of Applying to that wicked practice of Selling rum to them" (p. 252). And yet—though Woolman does not say it—both settlers and landlords would reproach the Quakers for refusing to defend the frontier.

Woolman does not argue that Indians who drank and quarreled and answered injustice with bloodshed were blameless; he simply prefers to illuminate motives and to seek out ultimate causes rather than to make a superficial condemnation. Nor could charity have been partial to deserve the name. Woolman never fell prey to a counterfeit of love which would deny sympathy to the "oppressors." He attempts to understand the case of the settlers themselves, who, "with a small stock . . . have houses to build, Lands to clear and fence, Corn to raise, Clothes to provide, and Children to educate" (p. 165). In remonstrating with slaveholders, he kept in mind that "deep rooted customs though wrong are not easily altered," and that in good conscience a "Charitable, benevolent man" might keep a slave "on no other motive than the Negros good" (pp. 179-180). He took note of history, observing on one journey "the different circumstances" of Friends in southern colonies. He had read "of the warlike disposition of many of the first settlers in those provinces, and of their numerous Engagements with the Natives, in which much blood was shed." There had been few Friends among those original settlers, but those who later entered the Society carried their past with them, and as a result "had a great work to go through" (pp. 272-273). Their mode of life was cause for even greater concern than that of the slave, for evil, Woolman believed, tended to multiply itself, and future generations would bear the burden of a final reckoning: "I saw in these Southern Provinces, so many Vices and Corruptions increased by this trade and this way of life, that it appeared to me as a dark gloominess over the Land, and though now many willingly run into it, yet in future the consequence will be grievous to posterity" (p. 167).

III

There is more than joyless puritanism, then, in Woolman's contention that "the least degree of luxury hath some connection with evil" (p. 184). By observation and by experience, he had found that the first departure from the "Purity of Righteousness" made successive departures less easy to resist and even contained within itself an act more vicious than the first.[10] When Woolman recalled an incident in his childhood which had given him much pain, he was setting down the origin of his ability to make such connections. At the very beginning of the *Journal*, Woolman writes of the time he had thoughtlessly been throwing stones at a robin until, to his horror, one struck and killed her, depriving her young of nourishment. Since he had already condemned them to death by starvation, he could only extend a grim sort of mercy: "I climbed up the Tree, took all the young birds, and killed them supposing that better than to leave them to pine away and die miserably" (p. 153). The boy could not have seen that the second act was contained in the first, but his ignorance was of incalculable value to the man, who never stopped making applications of the lesson he had learned: compliance with a desire for wealth merely increased the desire; there was a series of connections between the avarice of landlords and Indian raids on settlers, and another between the practice of slavery and the customs of using "Spiritous liquors" and of "wearing too costly apparrel." Having analyzed the parts so thoroughly, Woolman was able to say of the whole that all these evils were manifestations of "that Spirit which leads to Self-exaltation and strife, . . . which frequently brings Calamities on Countries by parties contending about their claims" (p. 246).

Once he had understood by experience and direct observation, had weighed motives and considered the relation between immediate circumstances and ultimate causes, Woolman could express himself without the hesitation that accompanied his writing the bill of sale for his employer's

[10] Woolman found a simile for this discovery in his essay, "A Plea for the Poor." He observed: "This is like a Chain, where the end of one link encloses the end of another. The rising up of a desire to obtain wealth is the beginning." *Journal and Essays*, p. 419.

slave. To the arguments of a group of slave-holding Friends, he answered confidently and without pause, "The love of ease and gain are the motives in general of keeping Slaves, and men are wont to take hold of weak arguments to Support a cause which is unreasonable" (p. 192). Once he had made the connection between evil and "the least degree of luxury," Woolman also found himself in possession of a criterion by which to judge his own actions. Interpreted positively, the criterion required that he attend diligently to the "Principle of Divine love," which excludes the selfish spirit and directs the use of things "to the purposes for which they were intended" (p. 184). The number of Woolman's testimonies by denial tends to imply that the principle could be interpreted only negatively. On the contrary, Woolman affirms most strongly when he refuses to assent in the spread of the selfish spirit. His reasons for deciding not to perform a given action are always accompanied by a meditation on the course he prefers. And his "negative" testimony takes on significance from its origin in his comprehensive and thoroughly integrated understanding of moral problems.

The *Journal* cannot be read in its depicted actions alone, nor merely for the ideas it elaborates, when Woolman has argued so carefully the unavoidable relation between what a man knows and what he must do. His refusal to wear dyed clothes or to use silver vessels seems an entirely negative response to the problems of a society bringing calamities upon itself through its desire for luxuries. But he maintained that an act derived its significance from the considerations which motivated it. One need not judge success or failure simply by results. Woolman reviewed his decisions, "looking less at the Effects of my labour, than at the pure motion and reality of the Concern as it arises from Heavenly Love" (p. 201). A man as prudent as Benjamin Franklin might object that to ignore results as a criterion for judging the wisdom of an act was to lessen individual responsibility. Practically speaking, no act then would matter any more than another, and men would be deprived of their sense of duty. On the contrary, Woolman saw individual responsibility as co-extensive with one's total experience, and his emphasis on duty actually increases as the efficacy of his actions appears to diminish.

In what way could an individual challenge something so intangible as the spirit of selfishness and self-exaltation which lay behind the evils of war and oppression? Was not one's duty to Truth discharged by rejecting all customs that tended to indulge and exalt self and by exhorting others to do the like? Woolman thought not, and put arithmetic to service to demonstrate how evil could subtly involve Friends complacent in their righteousness. He spoke, as always, from experience, and was able to accuse others only because he had discovered that he must accuse himself—of abetting the practice he had labored against.

Woolman had observed in his visits to slave-holding Friends that among the annual expenses which made it "impracticable" for them to free their slaves was the "verry considerable" cost of entertaining traveling Friends and of caring for their horses. Consider then, he asked his reader: "In Fifty pounds are four hundred half Crowns. If a slave be valued at Fifty Pounds, and I with my Horse put his Owner to half a Crown Expence, and I with many others for a Couple of Years repeat those Expences four hundred times, Without any Compensation, then on a fair Computation this Slave may be Accounted a Slave to the Publick, under the direction of the man he calls Master" (pp. 268-269). Woolman was here computing his guilt as a slave-holder some time after the discovery had made him carry with him on his journeys a supply of silver coins, to be given either directly to slaves in payment for their services to him, or to his hosts, who could "give them to such of their Negroes as they believ'd would make the best use of them" (p. 189). When he decided to make these travels on foot, he aimed in part to "be less expence mongst them."

The same relentless pursuit of his responsibilities led Woolman to wear only garments of undyed cloth, since dyes were available in Pennsylvania and New Jersey through the labor of slaves in the West Indies. He gives the reader almost no details to explain his adoption of this singular habit (a source of great affliction for him and of bewilderment to many Friends), just as he had declined to acquaint Friends with "the manner of my being led into these things." It seems likely, however, that in 1761 reports had reached him of the latest battles between France and England for control of the West Indian trade. Woolman records the decision, at any rate, with a meditation on the sufferings of those who must prosecute wars:

"Being most Sorrowfully affected in thinking on the unquiet Spirit in which wars are generally carried on & with the miseries of many of my fellow-creatures engaged therein, Some suddenly destroyed, Some wounded and after much pain remain crippled, Some deprived of all their outward Substance & reduced to want, & some carried into captivity, thinking often on these things the use of hats and garments died with a die hurtfull to them, & wearing more cloaths in summer than are useful grew more uneasie to me, believing them to be customs which have not their foundation in pure Wisdom." (p. 246)

Since Woolman gives no evidence of cherishing a naive expectation that the economic impact of his gesture would be felt at the courts of England and France, it would be entirely natural for his twentieth-century readers to view this as at least an act of protest, a demonstration to kings and ministers and merchants that the trade for which they fought wars was superfluous to the real needs of men. It seems unlikely, however, that he imagined so distinguished an audience either for his acts or his autobiography. His actions were directed, not toward correcting the waywardness of rulers, but toward awakening a sense of responsibility in the ruled by indicating the extent of that responsibility. One of the last of such testimonies that Woolman included in the *Journal* was his refusal to take passage in the ship's cabin on his voyage to England. He chose instead to lodge in the steerage with the crew because, as he told the ship's owner, ". . . on the outside of that part of the Ship where the cabbin was, I observed sundry sorts of Carved work and Imagery, and . . . in the Cabbin I observed some superfluity of workmanship of several sorts, and . . . according to the ways of mens reckoning, the Sum of money to be paid for a passage in that Appartment hath some relation to the Expence, in furnishing the room to please the minds of such who give way to a conformity to this world. . . ." (p. 290)

If at first the ship's owner thought this only the puritanical objection of an extraordinarily austere man, Woolman was willing to disclose the total context of his objection to mahogany cherubs and grape clusters. From his view of the "great oppressions on this continent," he had concluded that "it was with a view to get riches, and provide estates for Children to live conformable to customs" that men were "entangled in the Spirit of oppression." A ship's cabin that preserved in its comforts and decorations some of the smaller luxuries of the plantation house was just such a custom.

For Woolman, his present responsibility was as great as if he had been offered the plantation and all its slaves. It was a question of living in the "Spirit of meekness" or in the "Spirit of oppression," a decision made by individuals, and in practically every act of their lives. As for himself, "the exercise of my soul had been such that I could not find peace in joining with any thing which I saw was against that wisdom which is pure" (p. 290).

To Woolman, it seemed that either a pure or a perverse spirit would dominate the land. At one point, he speaks of "the spreading of a wrong Spirit" as though, like a communicable disease, it would afflict all but those who were vigilant in self-examination, persistently asking themselves "whether I as an individual kept clear from all things which tended to Stir up, or were connected with wars" (p. 255). By his diagnosis, "Luxury and Covetousness" were the causes of the disease, and he characterized them as "the Seeds of great Calamity and desolation . . . Sown & growing fast on this Continent," adding a prayer that faithful workers would be given strength to check their growth, "that they may not ripen to the Ruin of our posterity" (p. 256). He counted most on the uprightness of Friends, and was dismayed that the testimony of many now lacked the purity it had in times of persecution.

A greater trial was obscuring the Friends' vision in this "Newly Settled Land of America," the trial of "favour and prosperity": "Being thus tryed . . . this world hath appeared inviting; our minds have been turned to the Improvement of our Country, to Merchandise and Sciences, amongst which are many things usefull, being followed in pure wisdom, but in our present condition that a Carnal mind is gaining upon us I believe will not be denied" (pp. 206-207). Any number of explanations are available to the student of this period for the failure of Penn's Holy Experiment. Woolman is here suggesting another; or rather he suggests as many causes as there were departures from the "standard of Pure Righteousness." In the sufferings of posterity would be felt the effects of what he took to be the compromiser's slogan, "I must needs go on; and in going on I hope to keep as near to the purity of Truth as the business before me will admit of" (pp. 298-299).

IV

When Woolman remarked, "Conduct is more convincing than language" (p. 188), he admitted the limited efficacy of the journal as an incentive to Truth. He did not dismiss the form as useless, however, but attempted to realize the unique potential of autobiographical testimony. In the numerous essays and epistles he composed, Woolman organized and extended his meditations on concerns that had occupied his life. Each form of expression possessed its own virtues and imposed its own conditions. The essay form allowed for concentration on a specific topic and for an expository development not hampered by the continual necessity to return to a chronological narrative. The autobiographical form had the advantage of grounding meditation in experience, and permitted the kind of vicarious participation in Truth which William Penn had recommended to readers of Quaker journals.

Some features are common to both forms of expression. Personal reference sometimes occurs in the essays to indicate that the writer's observations have arisen from an experienced concern. In *A Plea for the Poor*, Woolman acknowledges, "My heart is affected with sorrow while I write on this Subject. . . ."[11] And in the *Journal*, he shifts regularly

11 *Journal and Essays*, p. 435.

to an objective emphasis in passages which can be regarded as brief versions of certain essays. The form of his *Conversations on the True Harmony of Mankind,* between a laboring man and, successively, "a man rich in money," and a "thrifty Landholder," may be the result of Woolman's somewhat wider reading experience in comparison with other Quakers; yet the journals of the Society in this period are full of conversations between the author, who argues for Truth, and an opponent, often the advocate of another faith, who attempts to support the cause in error. In these conversations, the Quaker always clearly triumphed, so that by recording them a journalist availed himself of yet another device suited to the task of convincing readers that the way of Friends was the way of Truth.

Woolman's conversations with slave-holders provided abundant material of this sort, but his use of it is characteristically economical. Only once does he record such a conversation, but there, in the space of a few pages, he manages to refute nearly every known argument in favor of the oppressive treatment of Negroes: that Scripture justified it, that the Negro had a naturally "Slothful disposition," that Negroes lived better as slaves in America than as free men in Africa. Woolman seized the opportunity to enlighten others who used these arguments by setting down his unanswerable replies, observing, among other things, ". . . there's great odds in regard to us on what principle we act. . . . If compassion to the Africans, in regard to their domestick troubles, were the real motives of our purchasing them, That spirit of Sympathy being Attended to, would Incite us to use them kindly, that as Strangers brought out of Affliction, their lives might be happy amongst us. . . ." (pp. 190-191)

The record of conversations of this sort, revealing dia-

63

lectically that arguments for slavery were unreasonable, might accomplish something. Woolman seemed to feel, though, that argumentation as such had limited uses. Perhaps because the same arguments rose up again and again, necessarily eliciting from him the same replies, Woolman recorded no other conversations on slavery in the *Journal*. Perhaps, too, he became convinced that reasoning was lost on those who lived in the spirit of selfishness. Wide experience in individual dealings with slave-holders had preceded the observation that men commonly offer arguments which will support a cause in which they have a selfish interest. This could be the only answer to the impenetrable "darkness of their Imaginations" that blunted the edge of "reasons" as a weapon against error.

Instead, it would be necessary in some way to bring readers of the *Journal* to the same conclusions he had reached by the same path he had followed. He had not been argued into the positions he maintained; he had been brought to see, with an absolute clarity of vision in the Light, that the forces contending for supremacy in the world were divine Love, selfless and expansive, and self-love, a counterfeit of the other, a disease that lived but gave no life, and that nourished and extended itself by absorbing what there was of life around it. What Woolman wanted, even more than notional agreement with his arguments, was the reader's attainment of an equal clarity of vision. He hoped that the purity of Truth, once clearly seen, would dissolve opposition, and that from the ardor of a man's embrace of Truth would follow compliance with its demands.

Speaking as the laborer of his *Conversations on the True Harmony of Mankind*, Woolman had pointed out to the rich man, his opponent, that the differences between them might be resolved if their positions could be stated with sufficient clarity, and in a loving spirit (p. 462). Incidents described in the *Journal* suggest that this was, in fact, Woolman's habitual manner of settling differences. He had been able, in one case, to alleviate a "Shyness" between himself and some "Friends of considerable note" (the result, presumably, of his inflexible interpretation of the demands of Truth) when, meeting with one of them, "things relating to that Shyness were Searched to the bottom" (p. 220). A similar conversation had removed the difficulties surrounding a question of "outward business," which had arisen through matters "not being clearly stated, nor rightly understood by all" (p. 163). His approach would be the same, then, as he confronted in his *Journal* the problem that superseded all others: "The standard of Pure Righteousness is not lifted up to the people by us as a Society in that clearness which it might have been" (p. 278).

The literary art of Woolman's *Journal* consists largely in the author's essential act of clarification, the attempt to make every word, every image, every relationship between ideas, as faithful a reflection of the pure standard as language can achieve. To this attempt, Woolman brought the advantage of long experience in meetings striving to preserve the purity of the "divine opening," and the inheritance of a plain style whose virtues were simplicity and clarity. Before him, the greatest obstacles to perfect illumination of Truth were the limits of language and autobiography's unlimited appeal to vanity. He might at any time be subject to the spirit of self-exaltation, inclining him to exaggerate, to grow intemperate, or to characterize his struggles egocentrically, as though they involved only a personal success or failure.

At its best, Woolman's simplicity of style, wedded to a view of his subject that excludes personal inclinations and prejudices, gives the impression of remarkable freshness and timelessness, as though a problem in values were being estimated for the first time, and a judgment passed which could be for all time. Consider, for instance, Woolman's characterization of the American Indian. Other descriptions of Indians in our early literature—as both an agent of Satan and a noble savage, an enemy to civilization, yet the tutor of civilized man—often tell more about the observer and the audience to which he spoke than they do about their subject. John Woolman comes to the Indian with none of the assumptions of his period, and renders him in universal terms, explicable not by reference to contemporary culture but by reference to the nature of man. His Indian warrior could as well be an Anglo-Saxon, an Athenian, or a Rogers Ranger:

"Near our Tent on the sides of large Trees peeled for that purpose, were various Representations of men going to, and returning from the wars, and of Some killed in Battle, this being a path heretofore used by warriors. And as I walked about viewing those Indian histories, which were painted mostly in red but some with black, and thinking on the Innumerable Afflictions which the proud, fierce Spirit produceth in the world; Thinking on the Toyls and fatigues of warriors, traveling over Mountains and Deserts, Thinking on their miseries & Distresses when wounded far from home by their Enemies, and of their bruises and great weariness in Chaseing one another over the Rocks and Mountains, and of their restless, unquiet state of mind who live in this Spirit, and the hatred which mutually grows up in the minds of the Children of those Nations Engaged in war with each other: The desire to cherish the Spirit of Love and peace amongst these people, arose very fresh in me." (p. 253)

It would still be necessary to compose essays, to admonish slave-holders, and to bear testimony continually to the love of fellow-creatures, but in the vision of this passage Woolman had stated in essence his entire understanding of man's inhumanity to man—its causes, its effects, the response of love it demanded when viewed in the eternal light of Truth. Appropriately enough, another of Woolman's pristine visions of man in his relation to Truth occurred in the wilderness. Removal from society and immersion in a primitive and apparently unchanging environment stimulated him to contemplate man in his original and universal condition:

"Thus lying in the wilderness and looking up at the Stars, I was led to contemplate the Condition of our first Parents, when they were sent forth from the Garden. And considered that they had no house, nor tools for business, No Garments but what their Creator gave them, no Vessels for use, nor any fire to cook roots or herbs. But the Almighty Being, though they had been disobedient, was a Father to them, and way opened in process of time for all the Conveniences of Life. And he who by the Gracious Influence of his Spirit, Illuminated their understanding, and Shewed them what was Acceptable to Him, and tended to their true Felicity as Intelligent Creatures, did also provide means for their happy living in this world, as they attended to the manifestations of his Wisdom.

". . . But some not keeping to the pure gift, have in the Creaturely Cunning & Self-exaltation, sought out many Inventions, which Inventions of men, as distinct from that uprightness in which man was created, as in the first motion it was evil, so the effects of it have been, and are evil. That, at this day it is as necessary for us constantly to Attend on the heavenly gift, to be qualified to use rightly the good things in this life amidst great Improvements, as it was for our First Parents, when they were without any Improvements, without any Friend or any Father but God only." (p. 202)

In both of these passages, Woolman sketches the setting and origin of his meditations with suggestive brevity. Both are distinguished by a highly developed sense of phrasal rhythms, an ability to move with interesting variety toward an inevitable climax of sound and statement, and to sustain emphasis in the anticlimactic close, as through the gradual shortening of sentence elements at the close of the second passage. In each, there is the same elementary denomination, and acceptance, of certain material facts of existence: "Toyls and fatigues," "miseries & Distresses," "bruises and great weariness" in the first; "no house nor tools," "No Garments . . . no Vessels," "fire . . . roots . . . herbs" in the second. Woolman assigns names with equal simplicity when he deals with abstractions, yet the force of his logic and moral earnestness, particularly in the second passage, must strike any reader who suspects oversimplification.

Passages of illumination such as these could not be called mystical; yet mysticism is a strong undercurrent in Woolman's thought, and he scrupulously records such special visitations of Truth as dreams and visions.[12] At the conclusion of the folio manuscript of his *Journal*, which he had prepared to be published after his death, Woolman entered

[12] Their epistemology disposed Quakers to take dreams seriously, though with caution. Woolman testifies to the nearly equal status of dreams and visions in a phrase commonly used by other journalists, "Dream or Vision of the Night" (p. 322). For a survey of the handling of dreams in Quaker journals see Howard H. Brinton's essay in *Byways in Quaker History* (Wallingford, 1944), pp. 209-231.

the title, "The Fox and the Cat: A Dream," and then proceeded to describe as accurately as he could recall them the sights and speeches of the dream and the emotions aroused in him as a witness.[13] "A man had been hunting," he began, and had brought back to Mount Holly a strange animal, part fox and part cat: "it appeared active in various Motions, especially with its Claws and Teeth." From the conversation of a company of people gathered in the house to which the animal was brought, Woolman gathered that to feed it, "an old Negro Man," past his usefulness, had been hanged. More horrible even than the act itself was the indifference of the witnesses: "One woman spoke lightly of it, and signified she was seting at the Tea Table when they hanged him up, and though neither she nor any present said anything against these proceedings, yet she said at the sight of the Old Man a dying, she could not go on with Tea Drinking" (p. 116).

Silent before, Woolman now began "to Lament bitterly, like as some Lament at the Decease of a friend. . . ." His sorrow was not shared by the group; some smiled at his outburst, "but none mourned with me." When he attempted to answer a man who had given reasons to justify the hanging—"not only that this Creature might have plainty, but some other Creatures [hunting dogs, Woolman guessed] also wanted his flesh"—he discovered that the power of speech had been taken from him, his muteness persisting "till I began to wake, and opening my Eyes, I perceived it was Morning."

Perhaps it is meaningless to praise a man very highly for his dreams, although Coleridge has so been praised for "Kubla Khan." Still, it is obvious that the material from

[13] Gummere prints the dream in her Introduction to the *Journal*, pp. 115-117. See also her editorial comment following the text of the folio manuscript, p. 287.

which dreams are fashioned is waking experience, and that
the recording of a dream involves certain acts no different
in their nature from those of the poet or novelist giving
shape to his experience, real or imagined. The dream may
have been, in a sense, a gift to Woolman for which he can
take no credit. Yet he drew on his own resources to indicate
deftly and devastatingly the character of the woman who
drank tea, and to arrange the first paragraph, in which we
have, successively, the ominous figure of the fox-cat, whose
rapacity Woolman suggests in observing its claws and teeth;
a suspenseful transition that, while offering the information
of an old Negro's death, conceals the manner of his dying;
and a concluding sentence that fashions horror out of understatement—the barbaric yet casually stated motives for
murder, and the abrupt description of the act itself: "So,
raising a long Ladder against their house, they hanged the
old Man."

The dream is so effective a commentary on Woolman's
entire experience with slavery and slave-owners that even
the key he left for its understanding seems inadequate, especially since he neglects to comment on the symbols of his
moral isolation—weeping alone—and of his lingering sense
of frustration—the inability to articulate his protest. "A
Fox is Cuning; A Cat is often Idle; Hanging represents
Vain Delights; Tea Drinking, with which there is Sugar,
points out the Slavery of the Negroes, with which Many are
oppressed to the Shortening of their Days" (p. 117). The
dream says more than this. It says that vanity and idleness,
under the practice of slavery, are nourished on the flesh of
human beings; it accuses slave-owners of murder; and it reveals that the consciences of members of this society have
grown immune to shock under the numbing influence of
self-indulgence. It was, in short, Woolman's strongest state-

ment on the subject of slavery, and the likelihood that God had chosen a familiar means of communication to indicate divine displeasure at so perverse a departure from Truth moved him to record the dream with detailed fidelity.

The last vision Woolman described in his *Journal* had taken place nearly three years earlier, during an attack of pleurisy. Why he delayed recording the vision until August of 1772, little more than a month before his death, does not emerge from the brief prefatory statement, "I feel a concern to commit to writing that which to me hath been a Case uncommon" (p. 308). Part of the uncommonness of this vision derived from its being more obviously than any other a direct visitation from a heavenly messenger. He had been granted the vision, not in sleep, but in a waking state, although the severity of his illness may have left him only partly conscious.

Brought to the very "gates of death," Woolman thought he had forgotten his name: ". . . being then desirous to know who I was, I saw a mass of matter of a dull gloomy collour, between the South and the East, and was informed that this mass was human beings, in as great misery as they could be, & live, and that I was mixed in with them, & henceforth I might not consider myself as a distinct or Separate being" (p. 308). Remaining in this state for "several hours," he then heard "a soft melodious voice," the "pure and harmonious" voice, he believed, of an angel speaking to other angels: *"John Woolman is dead."* Before he could resolve the mystery of these words, he was transported "in Spirit" to the mines, "where poor Oppressed people were digging rich treasures for those called Christians. . . ." The words Woolman then had to write must have given him as great pain as his experience of the conditions that gave rise to them. Informed that their oppressors were followers of Christ, the workers had said among themselves, "If Christ directed them to use us in this Sort then Christ is a cruel tyrant" (p. 309).

The vision evaporated, but the enigma of the angel's words remained with Woolman until, after a period of stillness, he was brought to see that they "meant no more than the death of my own will." In realizing this, Woolman had moved back to the point at which the *Journal* had begun, and through the description of his vision had restated succinctly the *Journal's* central emphasis on the recession of self that allows participation in and identification with the experience of fellow-creatures. If his other visions, of the day or night, could stand for whole chapters of experience and reflection, this one represented the discoveries of a lifetime. As one of the last things Woolman wrote, it stands in its proper relation to the rest of the *Journal*, at the end of the book.

One is tempted to credit Woolman with a premonition of his death in the portion of the *Journal* kept in England. The last entry in his own hand, a reflection of several pages "Concerning the Ministry," could have been written, however, only before the onset of the smallpox from which he died.[14] In the final pages of the *Journal*, Woolman writes as if aware of a need for summing up. By deciding to include at this point the remarkable vision of his illness two years before, he called the reader's attention to the principle by which his life had been governed, to the application of it in the major concern of his life, and to the scandal of Christians failing to make a similar application. In the autobiographical essay, "Concerning the Ministry," he turned to the subject of eloquence in a passage representing

[14] See Amelia Gummere's note on the probable time and place of composition, p. 313.

72

THE JOURNAL OF JOHN WOOLMAN

his nearest approach to literary theory, and thus indicated the ideas that had governed his composition of the *Journal,* now coming to a close. Recalling first the caution he had learned to exercise in determining whether to speak in meeting, Woolman moves into a general description of his manner both of perceiving and articulating Truth: "I have gone forward, not as one travelling in a road cast up, and well prepared, but as a man walking through a miry place, in which there are stones here and there, safe to step on; but so situated that one step being taken, time is necessary to see where to step next" (p. 315).

Woolman's simile, the choice of a man who had traveled much in the wilderness, expresses perfectly his lifelong effort to make out the way of Truth in a deceptive (and self-deceived) world, and the reflective, deliberate quality of his logic. There is something here, as well, of Woolman's expository manner—its restraint, its recognition of difficulties and obstacles, its relentless pushing on to the next area of a comprehensively viewed terrain. To bring others along the same path was, of course, a guiding purpose of the *Journal.* Long experience in meetings and wide acquaintance with Friends' journals had convinced Woolman that Truth could not be magnified through the world's rhetoric. To stand up in Meeting and to venture into print were essentially the same act. In both acts, one hopes that what God has given man to see will be attended to strictly, and thereby will be seen as clearly by one's audience. Too often, Woolman observed, the purity of this gift is sullied, its burden of Truth obscured, by the speaker's mistaken love for the sound of his own voice:

"The natural man loveth eloquence, and many love to hear eloquent orations: and if there is not a careful attention to the gift men who have once laboured in the pure gospel ministry, growing weary of suffering, and ashamed of appearing weak, may kindle a fire, compass themselves about with sparks, and walk in the light,—not of Christ who is under suffering,—but of that fire which they, going from the gift, have kindled: And that in hearers, which is gone from the meek suffering state, into the worldly wisdom, may be warmed with the fire, and speak highly of these labours, 'and thus the false Prophet in man may form likenesses. . . .' " (p. 315)

Conversely, Woolman implies, the true prophet may also form likenesses through a "careful attention to the gift," that is, by illuminating Truth, not with the distracting fires enkindled by the self, but through a submission to the Light that clarifies the more perfectly as self recedes. Woolman's understanding of the requirements imposed on the prophetic autobiographer must be the basis for a literary study of his *Journal*. His attempt to maintain the purity of "the gift," as it came to him in dreams and visions, accounts for the vividness of their narration, their fidelity to all remembered detail, the absence from his waking vision of the Indian warrior of all local or temporal presuppositions. For the same reason, certain dreams are incomprehensible, either totally or in part. Woolman discharged his responsibilities to Truth not only by narrating his dreams, visions, and "openings" as clearly and vividly as they had come to him, but also by refusing to embellish them, or to supply deficiencies of coherence from his own imagination.[15]

[15] Woolman describes one dream in scrupulous detail, even to the drawing of an illustrative diagram, but although the dream relates generally to the military preparations of 1754, it defies coherent interpretation. See pp. 175-176.

V

Most often in the early part of the *Journal*, which Woolman twice had the opportunity to rewrite, his thinking on the dangers of natural eloquence and on the ideal manner of adumbrating Truth makes itself felt in numerous revisions. Woolman's two most recent editors have commented on the loss of a certain youthful "spontaneity" in his rewriting of the earliest portion of the *Journal*.[16] Woolman himself, however, must have welcomed the opportunity to substitute more considered phrasings for the exaggerations of youth, to put out the occasional sparks of self that immaturity had allowed to be kindled. In fact, Woolman revised most heavily in passages of self-comment, guided primarily by a desire to say only what had been literally true of his spiritual condition and to emphasize aspects of the soul's relation to God that were taking on added significance as he began to diagnose the world's ills.

Woolman's standards for revision can be illustrated in a general way from a comparison of the first and last descriptions he gives of a dream that occurred when he was about nine years old.[17] The habit of attending closely to "the gift"

[16] Gummere, "Introduction," *Journal and Essays*, p. xi, and Janet Whitney, "Introduction," *The Journal of John Woolman* (Chicago, 1950), pp. xii-xiii.

[17] Amelia Gummere incorrectly states of this dream, "It is given in full in all three of the manuscripts, with no change except the omission of the last line in A and B" (p. 152n). Compare her text with that given in the Whitney edition (p. 2), where the C, or first quarto, manuscript is followed. Some confusion also arises from Gummere's contradictory labeling of the first quarto manuscript as B, and the second quarto as C, in her Introduction, p. xviii. For enlightenment on both these points, I quote from a letter to the writer, dated March 22, 1962, from Dorothy G. Harris, Acting Director of the Friends Historical Library, Swarthmore College: "Janet Whitney placed a pencil notation at the end of the Friends Historical Library copy of Gummere calling attention to this: 'Evidence of the footnotes is that the small quarto, above called B, is referred to invariably in the foot-

fostered in Woolman an increasing literalness of statement. Transcribing his earliest relation of the dream, he modified the first description of his vantage point within the dream from the flatly objective "door of my father's house in which I stood" to the subjectively valid "in which I thought I stood."[18] And because the moon of the dream was not actually the moon Woolman saw at night, he ought not to have said that it "ran on with equal swiftness," but that it "appeared to run on" in this way. He had first described a tree in the dream as "blooming." But on second thought he could only say it was a "little green Tree." The mysterious "Sun Worm" that entered the dream at its conclusion had given him the impression earlier of "a being small of size full of strength and resolution." Although at a later date Woolman still remembered the smallness of the Sun Worm, the reasons for its having seemed "full of strength and resolution" had faded, and he deleted the words, along with the afterthought, "Tho' I was A Child, this dream was instructive to me." The moral qualities of the Sun Worm would seem to have been related to the meaning of the dream, and Woolman could not refer confidently to the instruction he had received if those virtues had faded from memory.

Woolman's labors over the wording of this passage seem pointless in view of the enigmatic nature of the dream. Yet he is upholding the same standards of revision he applies to passages of self-analysis. He had read enough narratives of conversion, for instance, to realize that spiritual

---

note quotations herein as *MSS. C.* By no means all the variations are given, either in the text or in the footnotes. J. P. W.'" For this reason, I shall cite the Whitney edition for variant readings not available in Gummere.

[18] For the following variations in Woolman's description of the dream, cf. Gummere, p 152, and Whitney, p. 2.

autobiographers tended to deal in extreme statements. A man's sense of his own sinfulness could not, of course, be stated mildly; but there was the possibility, too, that the facts might be overstated lest the writer's experience appear the less valid for its lukewarmness. Woolman seems to have discovered that he had occasionally succumbed to this temptation. If it had been literally true that at one stage, "I let go my hold of God's covenant," and that subsequently, "the tempter when he came, conquered me," then Woolman ought to have been bound in darkness forever. It was more accurate to say instead, "I lost ground," and "the tempter when he came found entrance."[19] And there was certainly too much self-conscious contrition in the phrase, "for these things I weep; mine Eye runeth down with Water." Better to moderate one's tone by saying simply, "my heart is affected with Sorrow."[20]

As he returned to this early narrative of his struggle to achieve peace through self-abnegation and an acceptance of divine love, Woolman carried with him the concerns of his ministry. The seasoned observer of slavery, an institution founded in and nourished by selfish desires, was quick to substitute "a motion of Love" for "desire" in the first sentence of the *Journal*. More convinced than ever that love was the power that united mankind in its divine source, Woolman could see that unity on any other basis was apparent only. A group of young people banded together in the pursuit of "Vanities and Diversions" was not a unity at all, as he had at first carelessly stated. There was a contradiction in the statement, "We were united in that which is reverse to true Friendship," and so Woolman began instead, "We associated. . . ."[21]

19 Cf. editor's notes and text, Gummere, pp. 154-155.
20 Cf. editor's note and text, Gummere, p. 154.
21 Cf. editor's note and text, *ibid.*

Woolman's thinking on another of his concerns—the entanglements of merchandise as a worldly vocation—drew most of its forcefulness from a description of his own difficult victory over the "creaturely" desire for wealth and success. Yet the structure of meditation and argument he was erecting on this subject could be no stronger than its base, and he needed, therefore, to be especially careful in stating the motives that had influenced him. Taken out of context, some of these explanations, as he had phrased them originally, might signify the opposite of what he intended. What causal relationship might a reader infer from the statement, "Having now been several years with my Employer, and he doing less at Merchandize than heretofore, I was thoughtfull what way I should take for a living In Case I should settle [marry]"?[22] The wording of a similar sentence might also be misleading: "My business in the Shop growing Slack, it came to my mind to learn the Taylor's trade." In the first sentence, Woolman acted against a possible misreading by deleting the statement of his concern for the future, explaining only that he was "thoughtful of some other way of business," and adding an observation that the life of the merchant was "attended with much cumber, in the way of trading in these parts." By replacing the second sentence with an explanation that his employer's keeping a tailor had led him to consider that occupation for himself, he prevented the inference that tailoring appealed to him as a more lucrative trade. The opposite had, in fact, been true, and because the new trade appeared to him a more humble one, Woolman had not reached his decision easily. Originally, he had said of this struggle that although he learned to be content in the business Provi-

[22] For Woolman's revisions in this passage, cf. editor's notes and text, Gummere, pp. 164-165.

dence had pointed out for him, "it was reverse to the creaturely will." He meant, of course, that the way of plainness
had been opposed by his own unsubjected will, an idea
conveyed obscurely by the impersonality of his wording.
Stepping forward, then, to accept the guilt and imperfection that were his, he wrote instead, ". . . though I felt at
times a disposition that would have sought for something
greater."

It was always possible that in claiming divine authority
for what he urged on others, a man would also be claiming that he spoke Truth as an unusually favored emissary.
Self-characterization of this sort would also have been to
walk in the light kindled by oneself. In the earliest form
of the *Journal*, Woolman described his first, impetuous
words in meeting in a manner suggestive of David Ferris—
as though, personally ordered to speak for God, he had
betrayed his command: "Not keeping close to the True
Opener I said more than He directed me to say."[23] His
revisions replace the figure of a special emissary with that
of the humble servant: "Not keeping close to the Divine
opening, I said more than was required of me. . . ."[24] It
would have been like Ferris to say, as the younger Woolman did, "I found help in my distress, and through faith,
Mountains were removed" (p. 156n). The mature Woolman, having reminded himself of the *Journal's* initial statement of purpose, and fearful that so magnificent an image
of his faith might obscure this "hint" of the "Goodness of
God," improved the sentence, though not its grammar,
when he substituted, "Thus being brought low he helped
me. . . ."[25]

[23] Whitney, p. 11.
[24] Gummere, p. 159.
[25] Cf. Gummere, text and editor's note, p. 156, and Whitney, p. 7.

A similar but more extensive reworking shows Woolman erasing a self-complimentary reference to his sincerity and further quelling the spirit of self-exaltation by expressing a desire for greater humility. The first quarto reads: ". . . my cries were put up in sincerity and contrition, and in the multitude of his mercies he heard me; my hope was renewed and I found his favour to be more than life. I was strongly engaged in mind that if He was pleased to restore my health I might serve Him faithfully."[26] Woolman's final wording is: ". . . and then my Cries were put up in contrition, and in the multitude of his mercies I found inward relief, and felt a close Engagement, that if he was pleased to Restore my health, I might walk Humbly before Him."[27]

Having viewed at first hand the evils resulting from the spread of a spirit of self-exaltation, Woolman was not about to cancel the effect of his autobiographical argument against it by setting forth a "character" of himself "as a Religious man." (He thoughtfully substituted "reputation" for "character" in this context.)[28] It is not difficult to believe that Woolman viewed autobiography as a kind of writing uniquely capable of exploiting men's vanity. He thus disqualified himself from consideration among the world's great autobiographers, strictly defined, but he was about other business. In directing attention away from himself and toward his vision of Truth, Woolman does not come forward to his reader with the exhortation, "Do as I, a model for action, have done"; he simply insists, "Do as you must, seeing what I have seen." In his own words, "The gift is pure; and while the eye is single in attending thereto, the understanding is preserved clear; self is kept out" (p. 315).

The recording of his ministerial labors presented especially tempting opportunities to nourish past discomforts

---

[26] Whitney, p. 5.   [27] Gummere, p. 154.   [28] *Ibid.*, p. 228n.

with the fruits of autobiographical victory. An incident that clearly merited description as a personal triumph came as the sequel to a meeting of slave-holding Friends which Woolman had gathered at Newport, Rhode Island. Woolman recalls being gratified by the "tenderness" with which his words were received there, and by the intention expressed by several Friends of "disposing of their negroes after their decease." But from his narration of the incident, it is impossible to determine either what he said or how forcefully he said it. In fact, Woolman is scarcely in the picture at all:

". . . after a short time of retirement, I acquainted them with the Steps I had taken in procureing that meeting, and Opened the Concern I was under, and so we proceeded to a free Conferrence, upon the subject. My exercise was heavy, and I was deeply bowed in Spirit before the Lord, who has pleased to favour [us] with the Seasoning Virtue of Truth which wrought a tenderness amongst us; and the subject was mutually handled in a Calm and peaceable Spirit." (p. 237)

Once Woolman had "opened the concern," a reader might gather, his effective participation in the meeting ended. More probably, he exposed the same unanswerable arguments, made the same logical connections, and dwelt fervently on the same vision of Truth that one finds in his *Journal.* Many autobiographers might incline toward a more personal account, but to write of oneself, Woolman knew, is to follow a line of gratifyingly weak resistance. He achieves another effect by again immersing himself in the spirit of the group, refusing credit for what he regarded as the work of "the Seasoning Virtue of Truth."

When Woolman decided to act on the news of a juggler's

arrival in Mount Holly, a man who "did by Slight of hand, sundry things; which to those gathered, appeared Strange," he involved himself in a somewhat different situation. The customers who were assembling at the tavern to be entertained were not the members of a Friends' meeting, nor were they coming to be lectured on how to spend their time and money. Woolman's chances of persuading such a group to his opinion were very slim, and it would have been entirely natural to draw consolation from righteousness where success had not been attainable, to judge the folly of those who remained after he left, or to dilate on the single victory of the evening, over a man who argued the case of the audience. Woolman adopts none of these courses in narrating the incident; he wishes only to extract the essential issue:

"I had conversation with them in the fear of the Lord, and Laboured to convince them that thus Assembling to see those Tricks or Slights of hand, & bestowing their money to Support men who in that capacity were of no use in the world, was Contrary to the Nature of Christian Religion.

"There was one of the Company who for a time endeavoured by Arguments to show the reasonableness of their proceedings herein: but after Considering some texts of Scripture, and calmly debateing the matter he gave up the point. So I having spent, I believe, about an hour amongst them, & feeling my mind easie, departed." (p. 266)

On a first reading the passage arrests one by its unconscious humor: the picture of Woolman, stationed strategically "on a long Seat by the Door," soberly attempting to turn away the juggler's business. When Woolman divulges his objection, however, the humor begins to evaporate. There was far too much serious business to be performed, he thought, in a world preferring darkness to light, to sub-sidize useless occupations; amusement too was a luxury that assisted the growth of a wrong spirit. Woolman's phrasing here continues to prove utterly charitable and selfless. He condemns, not the juggler, but the capacity in which he was then operating. And in the final paragraph, he so well sustains the prominence of his opponent that one hesitates for a moment before assuming that it was Woolman him-self who offered certain "texts of Scripture" for the man's consideration.

Just as, in life, it had been necessary to humble himself in order to be properly receptive to the leadings of Truth, so in the *Journal* Woolman chastised the actor who might have performed his duties as if they were personal accom-plishments. One phrase used repeatedly, like a scourge, represents a triumph over the impulse to self-righteous characterization. The reader's impression of Woolman's boldness in interfering with the tavern's business must be modified when he explains that he "had conversation with them in the fear of the Lord" (p. 266). Woolman's first pub-lic concern had also drawn him to a tavern, where he spoke to the owner about the "disorder" (in the earliest manu-script, "uncomon Reveling") of his house, expressing him-self "in the Fear and Dread of the Almighty" (p. 161). And when he tells of remonstrating with a Friend who held slaves, Woolman balances the stern approach of his having used "much plainness of Speech" with the recollection, again, that he spoke "in the fear of the Lord" (p. 190).

The central idea of Woolman's *Journal*, then, fully in-forms its style: the self must recede, must be denied, so that Light may enter and Truth be affirmed over personality and individual inclination. From his continual striving for self-abnegation come Woolman's objectivity and simplicity and the habit of understating himself so that Truth may be fully and clearly articulated. And because Truth was not only a concept, but the relation of divine love to the condition of men, Woolman's prose can be not only ordered and logically consecutive, but fervent and moving as well. Making less careful distinctions perhaps than Woolman, we should have to describe his prose as occasionally eloquent. In one such passage, he appealed to the whole man in his reader, moving from the phenomenon of injustice, through the argument from natural reason, to the ultimate democracy of men under God. And as the level of Woolman's appeal rises, so does the stature of the Negro slave whose case he argues; the succession of sentences transforms an oppressed "people" into "souls":

"These are a people by whose labour the other inhabitants are in a great measure Supported and many of them in the Luxuries of Life. These are a people who have made no agreement to serve us, and have not forfeited their Liberty that we know of. These are souls for whom Christ died and for our conduct toward them, we must answer before that Almighty Being who is no respecter of persons." (p. 194)

It would not have occurred to Woolman that in his prose, here and in other passages we have considered, he revealed himself as fully as later autobiographers more enamored of their individuality. His efforts to withdraw from the reader's view result finally in a self-portrait whose art is its transparency; the central actor of his narrative is no less compelling a figure for his reluctance to take the stage. What Woolman excludes, after all, he had defined as nonessential, exaggerated, or self-exalting; and few autobiographers have written whose knowledge of their subject was more honest or complete.

PART TWO

PURITAN SPIRITUAL NARRATIVES

CHAPTER THREE

TRADITIONAL PATTERNS IN PURITAN

AUTOBIOGRAPHY

In a lifetime of spiritual turbulence, John Bunyan, the quintessential Puritan autobiographer, became accustomed to the heavenly voices that conveyed pertinent words of monition or reassurance to him. Perhaps the most influential voices Bunyan heard, however, did not come as sudden darts from heaven but from a group of "three or four poor women sitting at a door in the Sun, and talking about . . . the work of God on their hearts."[1] Previous to this episode, *Grace Abounding to the Chief of Sinners* has detailed the experience of a "poor painted Hypocrite." Now, listening to the women, the hypocrite becomes suddenly aware of the difference between his superficial religiosity and a graciousness in them which he recognizes but does not comprehend, "for they were far above my reach."

Even as Bunyan's anecdote sets in place the thematic cornerstone of seventeenth-century spiritual autobiography by its basic distinction between easy self-righteousness and the new birth of saving grace, it also exhibits the fascination of the narrator with the very act that occupies him. Bunyan's mind would hereafter be "fixed on Eternity," and it would be drawn on, at least in part, by the memory of these voices, not only by what they told each other, but by

[1] *Grace Abounding to the Chief of Sinners*, ed. Roger Sharrock (London, 1962) , p. 14.

87

the telling itself. "And me thought they spake as if joy did make them speak: they spake with such pleasantness of Scripture language, and with such appearance of grace in all they said, that they were to me as if they had found a new world, as if they were people that dwelt alone, and were not to be reckoned among their Neighbours."[2]

From the point of view of history, nothing in this experience should have astounded Bunyan. Since Paul and Augustine, indeed since Pentecost, Christians had evangelized in the first person. Englishmen, in particular, began to adopt a habit of introspection and to speak about what they discovered when Calvinist theology suggested to them that the clue to their eternal destination lay in the furthest recesses of their own hearts. In the seventeenth century, in both Old and New England, great numbers of Protestants were probing the darkness in their hearts for the gleaming nugget of grace and shouting "Eureka!" in a variety of communicative modes, at a sunny doorway, from a prison cell, and out of a savage wilderness.

Although Bunyan was the pre-eminent spiritual autobiographer of his time, he was of course neither alone nor original in what he did. One of the fruits of his long imprisonment as a Dissenter, *Grace Abounding* (1666) seems to have been written without the aid of personal memoranda; Bunyan depended more on the storehouse of his own mind than on the kind of spiritual account book some Protestants had been keeping since the time of Elizabeth. One can only guess how widespread the practice was, remembering too that diaries were, by definition, private records. Through the early decades of the seventeenth century, their currency must be inferred largely from biographies that used them as a primary source in reconstruct-

[2] *Ibid.*, p. 15.

ing the piety of an exemplary Puritan. "Not otherwise could we have had such vivid and detailed accounts of the inner religious experiences of such persons."[3]

Beginning about the time of the Civil War, a large number of first-person narratives appeared which were written by Quakers, Baptists, and Seekers,[4] the uneducated social inferiors of such ordained clergymen as Richard Baxter, whose even-tempered *Reliquiae Baxterianae* stands as England's other classic Puritan autobiography. Baxter yielded to no one in urging the importance of "holy passions" in religion, but he found it "somewhat unsavoury" to give any very "particular account of heart occurrences" because he felt God's dealings were much the same with every man. By contrast, the prophetic and pentecostal autobiographies of enthusiasts implicitly advertised the author's visitation by the Spirit and the gifts he had as a result.[5] The writer thus validated his authority to teach even as he taught, by example, the way of salvation.

Even a brief comparison of Bunyan and Baxter, then, suggests the kinds of sharp differences to be found in English spiritual autobiography. In New England, however, a seventeenth-century autobiographer would produce a fairly predictable variety of the genre, at least in its broad outlines. Only with the flourishing of numbers of American sects and following internal changes in American Puritanism would there come, in the eighteenth century, as vigorous and motley an assortment of spiritual autobiographers as seventeenth-century England could claim. There is no American *Grace Abounding* in this period for the simple

3 William Haller, *The Rise of Puritanism* (New York, 1938), p. 98.
4 Roger Sharrock, "Introduction," *Grace Abounding*, p. xxix.
5 William York Tindall has isolated this intention in *Grace Abounding* and other enthusiastic autobiographies. See his *John Bunyan: Mechanick Preacher* (New York, 1934), pp. 22-41.

reason that Puritan Boston would not have accepted so vocal a heretic as Bunyan in its midst.[6] Around 1660, the ministers and magistrates who hanged four Quakers would not have been so inconsistent as to allow the publication of a personal narrative whose pages glowed with communications from the Spirit. The "particular faiths" which Cotton Mather recorded in his diary amounted to no less, but even among a more tolerant generation Mather was prudent enough to leave his revelations for the astonishment and edification of posterity rather than submit them for immediate publication. As long as the Puritan magistracy held sway, enthusiastic autobiography was for the closet only.

Relatively temperate and subdued, the typical seventeenth-century spiritual narrative written in New England tends more toward formalistic recitation and mechanical pattern than do contemporary English counterparts. John Bunyan, too, followed convention in his autobiography by employing the form and idiom in which so many "mechanick preachers" advertised their warrant to handle soul concerns. Yet the very impulsiveness and wild fluctuation of emotion he reports tend to distract attention from the framework within which they take place. New Englanders, on the other hand, had the abstract pattern always in mind, giving them an early reputation as English Protestantism's most sophisticated students of the process, the signs and stages, of conversion. So well known were they as detectors of hypocrisy and devisers of trustworthy criteria for graciousness, Perry Miller tells us, that William Chappel, Milton's tutor, listed only New England writers when

---

6 Although *Pilgrim's Progress* had an American printing (Boston, 1681) only three years after its publication in England, *Grace Abounding* was not published until 1717 (Boston). See David Smith's checklist of Bunyan publications in America, *New York Public Library Bulletin*, LXVI (December 1962), p. 641.

recommending treatises on conversion to his students at Cambridge.[7]

The ability to make incisive distinctions in spiritual experience appears not to have been limited to the clergy. Almost from the beginning, New England Puritans regularly stipulated a qualification for church membership which their English brethren did not generally require. Beyond the usual confession of faith, the applicant was required to give a satisfactory narrative of his experience of grace.[8] These narratives hardly deserve to be considered as autobiography, not simply because their subject matter is restricted, nor even because their vocabulary is uniform and impersonal, but because their authors' designated purpose was to convince the elders that the presence of grace was evident in their experience.[9] The issue, whether or not conversion had taken place, is never in doubt. The autobiographical act is reduced to testifying that one's experience has conformed, with allowable variations, to a certain pattern of feeling and behavior. Yet these narratives must be kept in view by the student of more remarkable products of the Puritan autobiographical tradition, for they indicate how limited the Puritan's freedom of movement could be as he prosecuted his inward exploration. They are the only appropriate measure of independence and originality in the genre.

[7] *The New England Mind: The Seventeenth Century* (Cambridge, 1954), p. 27.

[8] Congregations grew to be so thoroughly knowledgeable about matters of conversion that the question has been raised whether over-scrupulous self-analysis did not tend to reduce the number of church members and thus, ironically, play a part in the general decline of piety in the seventeenth century. See Edmund S. Morgan, "New England Puritanism: Another Approach," *William and Mary Quarterly*, Ser. 3, XVIII (1961), pp. 236-242.

[9] Michael Wigglesworth transcribed several of these "relations" into his diary manuscript. See "The Diary of Michael Wigglesworth," ed. Edmund Morgan, *Publications of the Colonial Society of Massachusetts*, XXXV (1942-1946), pp. 426-444.

Edward Taylor's "Spiritual Relation"

As witnesses to the mass acceptance in our time of emotions dispensed through entertainment media, we should not be surprised at the conventionality of many Puritan spiritual narratives. It is disappointing, nevertheless, to discover that the convention can best be illustrated by the autobiography of a poet. Of surviving spiritual autobiographies by the more eminent Puritans, Edward Taylor's is the most regular, the least interesting on its own merits, a narrative which is unusually successful in suppressing evidence of the character and personality of its author—and in a genre known for its paradoxically impersonal self-analysis. The publication of Taylor's poetry in 1939 revealed unsuspected dimensions in the Puritan aesthetic; yet in 1679 Taylor drafted a textbook conversion which allows only a fleeting glimpse of the rich meditative life regularly encountered in his poetry.

The reasons appear to be several. Taylor drew up his "Spiritual Relation" for a specific purpose and on a particular occasion. Eight years after coming to Westfield, Massachusetts, he decided finally to settle there, enabling the community to make plans for the formal gathering of a church. An important part of the foundation ceremonies was the recitation by Taylor and the other "foundation men" of their experience of grace, which would serve, Taylor observed, "as a foundation for the Charitie of Gods people to act upon, in order to the inroling of us in their Soule as Suitable Matter for Such a glorious Structure in hand."[10] In fact, the "inroling" had already taken place:

[10] The "Spiritual Relation" was edited by Donald Stanford, with a brief introduction, in *American Literature*, xxxv (January 1964), pp. 467-473. Brackets in quoted passages enclose the editor's emendations .

Taylor and the other men were simply giving formal proof of their worthiness to assume a calling for which they had already been judged worthy. Necessarily, then, Taylor demonstrated his spiritual fitness by an unambiguous appeal to signs which his congregation would immediately recognize. This was not the occasion to explore minutely and exhaustively a single condition of the soul, as he would do later in the *Preparatory Meditations*. Here the total sequence and its result were of primary significance. In a brief preface Taylor made the distinction clear: "I did not go to gather up the Speciall workings onely of one Season but of what I can through the grace of God assert to be what I have and in some measure do injoy at present" (p. 468).

Delivering his "Relation," Taylor was bound by physical restrictions not present even in Bunyan's prison. Taylor's was not the only narrative to be given on Foundation Day, and the narratives formed only a portion—his own long sermon was another—of the ceremonies. Although he had written out his statement in advance, Taylor noted in the Church Record, he found the sentiment of his visitors, "the Elders and Messenger[s] of Northampton and Hadly," was against reading the manuscripts; they "drove on to the contrary," he said. Differences between the spoken and written versions were minor: "some small variations in the words, and phrases. And that something briefer." In any case he was obviously not free to dwell at length on seasons of joyful transport or perplexing aridity.

The highly formal character of Taylor's "Relation" may owe less, however, to Puritan ecclesiology and the circumstances in which Taylor spoke than to the necessity that his narrative be instructive and exemplary. Theoretically, Taylor's evidence might have been rejected when he submitted his declaration "unto the judgment of Gods people whether it will hold a touch in the Scales of the Sanctuary, by the judgment of Christian Charity." But in eight years Westfield had enjoyed ample leisure to determine whether it found Edward Taylor a gracious and godly man. By now he could speak to them not as a supplicant for their good opinion, nor as one dubious about his place among them, but as their pastor and spiritual guide. His mild discontent with the expeditious temper of the gathering seems to stem from his desire to read exactly what he had written; "doubtless," he wrote, "it would have been to more edification." Taylor might only have been thinking of the unseemliness of the minister's stumbling over terrain he knew better than anyone, but personal considerations seem to be irrelevant when he explains that he schematized the Spirit's "gracious workings" in his soul so that "they might be given as much to edification as might be. . . ." Then follows his remark that he wrote to display a prevailing pattern rather than isolated "Special workings" (p. 468).

By choosing to reduce his spiritual experience to a logical exposition of the "order" of the Spirit's working on his soul, Taylor transformed a first-person statement into a brief sermon on conversion. The question implicit in most spiritual narrative glares at the reader from Taylor's account; how far does autobiography of any sort allow itself to be put to specialized uses while remaining autobiography? Most American autobiography from Taylor through Franklin to Henry Adams has aimed at some form of edification. At least it has framed an argument, a recommendation, a special plea of some sort. Indeed, ours has been a notably sermon-ridden literature from the beginning. One thinks not only of those Puritan histories which were in large part sermons on Providence but also of Emerson's sermon-essays and Thoreau's attempt to awaken slumberers; of Father Mapple's warnings thundered from the prow of the world and Ishmael's explication of a text from Job; the sermon-confession of Dimmesdale and the Easter morning sermon of the St. Louis preacher in *The Sound and the Fury*; the varieties of misanthropic sermon preached by Colonel Sherburn and Gail Hightower.

Still, these sermons have their place in unique imaginative contexts, while the sermon of a seventeenth-century spiritual autobiography is likely to occupy all available space. The question is not so much whether some kind of argument is discernible in the work—it is no praise to say of a writer that he has been able to tell the story of his life only for the love of narrative[11]—but whether the argument has been wrested from the life in a manner analogous to the moment-by-moment struggle to refine brute experience into something other than itself. In this there is both art and human achievement. One can reject on critical grounds the autobiography whose argument is imposed entirely from without, or which fails to create an illusion to the contrary. But to reserve praise only for the autobiographer who writes in complete freedom is to await an autobiography free from order and coherence.

Taylor's pastoral obligations, then, forced an adjustment between patterns uncovered by private self-analysis and the design of his autobiographical argument. Presumably, though, even in church-gathering testimonies, no inevitable form prevailed. Taylor chose a rigorously deductive approach, describing objectively what the operations of the

11 In response to the publication of Ernest Hemingway's *A Moveable Feast*, Alfred Kazin described a kind of autobiography "very characteristic of our period and usually written by novelists or poets, that has no other aim, whatever the writer may think he is doing, than to be enjoyed as narrative." "Autobiography as Narrative," *Michigan Quarterly Review*, III (Fall 1964), p. 211.

Spirit consisted in and then giving instances of each work from his own experience. He thus demonstrates himself indubitably gracious, despite conventionally modest expressions of uncertainty. John Bunyan was no less concerned to demonstrate to the people of Bedford the validity of his call, but his method was principally to assault his audience with the weapons of spiritual melodrama. Taylor chooses to convince by means of the logic of Peter Ramus.

The Ramist approach to knowledge, which was generally the approach of the educated Puritan in the seventeenth century, was characterized by the habit of making dichotomies as a means of exhibiting a subject matter and by the use of a major dichotomy between artificial and inartificial arguments. In a sense, the artificial argument was experientially oriented, for in its simplest conception it offered "such truths as a man may see by himself." Yet no extraordinary empirical emphasis differentiated these truths from Aristotle's self-evident axioms. A man seized the truth of an inartificial argument through "another man's eye," accepting on trust and testimony what had not been available to him at first hand. Finally, there was an order of priority between the two kinds of arguments "because none can testifie of a thing before he have seen it himself, *ergo, artificiale* is before *inartificiale*."[12]

In Taylor's "Spiritual Relation," the "order of the Spirit in his work upon the Soule" is made to conform to the order of Ramist logic, a progression by dichotomies. The first sentence of the "Relation" announces: "The work of the Spirit of God bringing a poor Sinner unto Christ consists in Con-

---

[12] Quoted in Miller, *The New England Mind: The Seventeenth Century*, p. 129. Within the traditional Puritan format of text, doctrine, reasons, and application, this was also apparently Taylor's habit of exposition in sermons. See *Edward Taylor's Christographia*, ed. Norman S. Grabo (New Haven, 1962), p. 77 and *passim*.

viction and Repentance"—scarcely an autobiographical statement. Taylor then pursues the dichotomies that fan out from the stem of conviction, illustrating from his experience each stage in the process. He next turns to the process of repentance, which has conversion as its final component. His organization is also roughly chronological. Taylor first describes the memories of youth with which a Puritan's mind seems inevitably to have been furnished: a youthful awakening to the heinousness of sin and to the gloriousness and sufficiency of salvation by Christ, and a brief recitation of the vanities of his youth and the reproofs they elicited. Taylor's mother apparently had a sharp eye for youthful vanities and an unerring sense for prescribing the appropriate scriptural horror. These images continue to be vivid for Taylor, as his precise recall of certain passages indicates. In one, the eye of the disobedient son is picked out by ravens and eaten by eagles; in another the liar is punished by brimstone and fire.

Generally, however, chronology recedes as a pattern of organization in favor of a pattern that would make the speaker's experience rationally available to his audience. We get only brief glimpses of an individual idiom when the expanded description of a particular work momentarily creates an expectation of more personal language. Taylor attributes the early stages of conviction to his sister's narration of the fall of Adam and Eve and the birth, death and resurrection of Christ. Her narrative is introduced by a sketch of its circumstances, imperfectly remembered: "when I was but Small: viz. upon a morning a Sister of mine while she was getting up, or getting me up, or both. . . ." Taylor recalls that it took his sister two mornings to complete her account, but he presents her less as a person than as a means of grace, important for what she said rather than for how she

97

said it: "these things I well remember she spoke but cannot say she spoke them in this exact order, or words." What Taylor sets down, in fact, is not his sister's language but Luke's, which he reproduces at leisure ("there being Shephards in that Country keeping watch over their flocks at night an Angel of the Lord appeared unto them"), until forced into a hurried concluding summary (pp. 469-470). In his public and pastoral role, Taylor is scrupulously instructive, even to the point of retelling a thoroughly familiar scripture narrative.

This is not to say that Edward Taylor the poet goes undetected in his "Spiritual Relation," but any such discovery benefits greatly from hindsight. One might offer, for instance, the poet-mystic's familiar exasperation with the inadequacy of words to articulate a transcendent experience: "I was musing every way [when] alone how to get Suitable expressions to carry up the [lov]e of my Soule unto God through Christ in prayer. . . ." Thinking back to the "Strange frame that I was rapt up in" on the morning he awakened to his sister's evangelizing, Taylor confesses, "I know not how to express it." The complaint is more than familiar; it is so conventional in the literature of spiritual experience that distinction becomes possible only for such singular expressions of inadequacy as we meet in Taylor's Prologue to the *Preparatory Meditations.* Any number of Puritan preachers might also have mined scripture for figurative vehicles which would convey mere obedience as "a dead carkass good for nothing without [Faith]," or graceless works as "dung and dogs meat," or might also imagine the Saints shining "a[s] Sparkling Diamonds in the Ring of Gods glory." Certain passages exhibit an admirable control of periodic rhythms and climax, though not beyond the art of Puritan preachers like Hooker or Shepard:

98

"Oh the sight of [it,] oh a lost State, oh a deceitfull heart, a Colde heart, a [har]d heart, a formall heart, neglect of Christ, deadness in duty, [lov]e of vanity, and the like: how did and do these Stare in my face— . . . and altho I prayed, this nei[ther] availd: but Still deadness, dulness, unspiritualness. Watch[fulne]ss would not do, heart examination oftimes ended in a [dete] station: hence an universall weriness of myselfe, disqui[et] with myselfe, judging of myselfe, Battlings of myselfe, [follo]wed, and I find with the Apostle Phil 3.8. all things of mine dung and dogs meat." (p. 472)

The poet of the *Preparatory Meditations*, which date from three years after the gathering of the Westfield church until 1725, makes his appearance only at the end of the "Spiritual Relation." Taylor begins the final category of his examination by indicating an awareness that he has been called upon not only to give evidence of his graciousness but also to assess his faithfulness in discharging the duties of the ministry. He will not praise himself: "In this respect modesty commands my Silence"; but he replies indirectly with an implicit pledge of continual self-scrutiny: "The time was that I never looked within doore, but now by meditation and heart Examination I finde it a harder matter to keep Rule than the victor hath in taking a City."

By sealing up the door to his soul, and tacking on it this narrative of conversion, the minister would bequeath his congregation a superficially edifying façade of successful piety. Taylor chose instead to wear the black veil. He began to do so, he recalls, at the time he heard the sermon of a "godly able Minister in England" who "press[d] all to try whether they were in the way of heaven, and that from the hardness of the way." He had been startled to find that "no such hard work" had been part of his experience until the minister began to specify the trials he had in mind and "laid down one from the deceits of the heart and Sinfulness thereof." Introspection itself was the trial, with its constant psychological reversals, the continual enmity it laid bare between rationalization's promise of an inexpensive peace and the suspicion that a creature who had traded his "brightest diamond" for a "coalpit stone" could not be trusted to judge what was most valuable in himself. In as many words, the minister was promising continued vigilance over his soul in place of a recital of his gifts and deeds. Memory had renewed the initial impact of the English minister's sermon: "And then me thought I founde myself deeply engaged in the war" (p. 475). Out of this engagement came the most striking poetry of its time and place.

John Winthrop's "Christian Experience"

Any Puritan autobiography exhibits its author's awareness of the traditional stages through which a man passed as God brought him to grace.[13] But some narratives serve as paradigms in their adherence to textbook descriptions of the order of grace. Edward Taylor's "Spiritual Relation" is one of these. Another, the "Christian Experience" of John Winthrop was written more than forty years before Taylor's "Relation," and yet there is little substantial difference between them. Taylor's diagram of his experience can be applied to Winthrop's relation with little difficulty. Taylor divides the whole process of conversion into two parts, conviction and repentance. As it relates to the understanding, conviction is more precisely termed illumination, "but as

13 Edmund Morgan describes the "morphology of conversion" developed by two generations of Puritans like William Perkins, William Ames, and Ezekiel Culverwell in the early seventeenth century. *Visible Saints: The History of a Puritan Idea* (New York, 1963) , pp. 66-73.

it affects the Conscience whereby it turns its Checks upon the Will, and affections its properly called Conviction . . . and is a Singular Spur unto Repentance." In turn Repentance divides neatly into Aversion, "whereby the heart is broken of[f] from Sin," and Conversion, "whereby the Soule is carried to God in Christ." Conversion then flowers triply into Love, Hope, and Joy while Obedience works daily to carry on "the work of Repentance unto perfection."

John Winthrop dated the beginning of his progress in the Spirit from the time he came under the ministry of Ezekiel Culverwell, a prominent explicator of the ways of grace to non-separating English Puritans. Winthrop gives Culverwell's preaching as the means by which he moved, in Taylor's terms, from illumination to real conviction: "living there sometimes I first found the ministry of the word to come to my heart with power (for in all before I found onely light). . . ."[14] Thereafter the stages succeed one another so nearly according to ideal form that a modern historian of the Puritans can safely offer Winthrop's narrative as representative of "hundreds of others."[15] The typicality of the Taylor and Winthrop narratives, then, provides a basis for discussing later developments in Puritan spiritual autobiography while indicating the pervasive uniformity of its structure and vocabulary in the seventeenth century.

It would be difficult, nevertheless, to find autobiographical compositions which are wholly barren of individuality. Taylor's definitive articulation of his spirit in another form is hinted at in some of the language of the "Relation" and in his closing affirmation of the significance of the meditative act. Winthrop's narrative, although it lacks the names

<hr>

[14] "Christian Experience," *Winthrop Papers*, Massachusetts Historical Society (1929) , I, 155.
[15] Morgan, *Visible Saints*, p. 72.

and dates that make his *Journal* the indispensable primary record of the Massachusetts Bay Colony, shows the impact of events and controversies in which the writer found himself engaged as a public magistrate.

For Winthrop, the winter of 1636-1637, during which the "Christian Experience" was composed, was a period of reassessment. Although he would soon be governor again, resuming the leadership he had exercised over the Bay Colony from 1630 to 1634, he was now in the third year of his exile from power. As an assistant, and more recently as deputy governor, he commanded influence, but was still denied executive power. Although he had not sought office energetically, rather had "earnestly desired, at every election, to have been freed,"[16] he would nevertheless be driven to seek an explanation for his eclipse, alternatively in the "jealousy" of the freemen or in some shortcoming of his own. Immersion in the affairs of the colony had left little time for introspection. In England, Winthrop had kept a diary, his "Experiencia," which contain several extended passages of self-analysis. Since arriving in New England, he had made no additional entries. Now, on January 12, 1636 / 37 he was beginning his fiftieth year of life and it was time for an accounting.

Impetus for autobiographical composition did not come from the calendar alone. In the previous October, Winthrop had received a letter from Roger Williams in Providence. Since Winthrop's timely and prudent suggestion that Williams might avoid deportation to England by setting his "course to Narragansett Bay and Indians, for many high and heavenly and public ends,"[17] there had developed a

[16] "Financial Statement to the General Court," *Winthrop Papers,* Massachusetts Historical Society (1943), III, 173.

[17] These are the words of Roger Williams, paraphrasing a letter which he said Winthrop sent him privately. Quoted in Edmund S. Morgan, *The Puritan Dilemma* (Boston, 1948), p. 219.

warm and mutually respectful correspondence between the two men. From his frontier outpost Williams was able to convey a good deal of useful information to Winthrop, especially concerning the movements and disposition of the Indians. A kind of dialogue developed between them, ranging over the issues on which Williams had been found to hold heretical opinions.

Assuming reciprocal understanding on Williams' side, despite his reputation for intransigence, Winthrop apparently felt no need to suppress the topics on which they were divided or to veil them in gentlemanly obscurities. In a letter whose contents are known only through Williams' reply of October 1636, Winthrop had posed six questions intended finally to wring an admission from Williams that he had caused a great stir over nothing. Williams' detailed reply argues that the dictates of conscience are unavoidable: "the stroke lies upon the very Judgment." Yet Winthrop had gone beyond frankness to call into question Williams' motives and spiritual estate. His sixth question implied that contentiousness as to doctrine was not the habit of the saints, that if Williams had grace he could not have set himself apart so easily from his fellow believers.

For the record, Williams repeated Winthrop's question to him: "You ask whether my former Condicion would not have stood with a gracious Heart etc.?" He then proceeded to emulate his own highest praise of Winthrop ("You beare with Fooles gladly because you are Wise") by drawing the most elementary of distinctions between reprobation and misjudgment. Surely Winthrop must be aware of the irony that he, and not Roger Williams, was espousing the perfectionism of the enthusiasts. "At this Quaerie Sir I wonder much because you know what Sinnes yea all manner of Sinnes (the Sinn unto Death excepted) a Child of God may lye in Instance I neede not." Too much the controversialist to forego examples, Williams then drove home his most telling point: "Instances I shall be bold to present you with: First doe you not hope Bishop Usher hath a Gracious Heart? and 2ndly Doe you not judge that your owne Heart was gracious even when (with the poysoned shirt on your back) you etc.?"[18]

In the breaking off of the last sentence one feels Williams' reticence to deal as sharp a blow as he had sustained. As a result the sense of the poisoned-shirt allusion is ambiguous, perhaps implying a comparison between Williams' position in the colony and Winthrop's as a Puritan in England, perhaps referring to the controversy over the Governor's authority that led to Winthrop's defeat in 1634. In either case, Winthrop would have to reply that he hoped his judgment had been right and his spirit gracious at the same time. Williams claimed no more for himself.

The Winthrop papers contain no reply to Williams' question unless it is the spiritual autobiography written three months later. Simultaneously, another question was taking shape, which Winthrop assumed responsibility for posing to himself before someone else could point out the necessity. The Antinomian controversy, an explosion into the horrified view of the Bay Colony Puritans of that enthusiasm which had always been implicit in their doctrine of election, claims John Winthrop as a leading though not decisive figure. At first he only observed, and recorded what he saw. He set down in his *Journal* such errors of the Church of Boston as "that the Holy Ghost dwelt in a believer as he is in heaven; that a man is justified before he believes; that faith was before justification, but it was only passive, an empty vessel, etc."[19] Soon Winthrop attempted to

[18] *Winthrop Papers*, III, 318.
[19] *Winthrop's Journal: "History of New England,"* ed. James Kendall Hosmer (New York, 1949), I, 206.

enter the controversy directly by means of two compositions, a "Declaration" to demonstrate that faith preceded
justification, and an irenic attempt at a "Pacification" between the parties. But in the review of his arguments which
he requested from Thomas Shepard, Winthrop faced the
charitably phrased question, "whether it will be most safe
for you to enter into the conflict with your pen (though the
Lord hath made you very able and fit for it)," followed by
a systematic baring of the flaws in his amateur's arguments.[20] This was in December of 1636. Five months later
Winthrop would be elected Governor once again and have
his chance eventually to sit in judgment of Anne
Hutchinson.

Whatever his limitations in doctrinal controversy, Winthrop knew two things for certain: that Antinomians encouraged impiety when they preached the dangerous doctrine that conviction, repentance, and other preparatory
stages of conversion had nothing to do with God's bestowal
of free grace; and that the doctrine of free grace, as a
cornerstone of Puritan piety, needed to be preached with
all the rigor of a John Cotton.[21] The very extremity of Anne
Hutchinson's position made it necessary to reaffirm an
undistorted yet untainted version of free grace and to allow, autobiographically, that he had just been rescued from
creeping Arminianism: "The Doctrine of free justification
lately taught here, took mee in as drowsy a condition, as I
had been in (to my remembrance) these twenty yeares, and
brought me as low in my owne apprehension as if the whole

[20] *Winthrop Papers*, III, 327.

[21] Cotton's preaching emphasized that no preparatory steps were
efficacious toward obtaining grace. Anne Hutchinson praised his doctrine for its freedom from Arminian taint. Shortly after he completed
his spiritual narrative Winthrop took notes on one of Cotton's sermons "about the worke of Conversion." *Winthrop Papers*, III, 35.

work had been to begin anew."[22] The "Christian Experience" of John Winthrop is evidence that the public figure who sternly judged heresy welcomed the therapeutic effect of the Antinomian controversy on his own spiritual condition. A perfectly ordinary Puritan statement of the author's private dealings with his spirit, it nevertheless implies everywhere an involvement in a complex outer world of issues and personalities.

The conventional features of Puritan autobiography appear early in the "Christian Experience." Winthrop's opening statement, "In my youth I was very lewdly disposed," could be transposed to any of hundreds of other narratives without notice and with no special discredit to its new owner. Puritan autobiographers also suffered chronically from an adolescent disease that masqueraded as true conviction until it disappeared and left good health and a heart more depraved than ever: "But so soon as I recovered my perfect health, and met with somewhat els to take pleasure in, I forgot my former acquaintance with God, and fell to former lusts, and grew worse then before." Given the constant recurrence of these conventional features, it is not too severe a judgment to say that many spiritual narratives of the period were not so much composed as recited. The luxury of reducing past experience to predictable ritual was denied Winthrop, however, by the impact of his present experience. The narrator of the "Christian Experience" has been stirred to validate in autobiography his conviction that faith precedes justification and is the free gift of God, even though man must reach out his hands to receive it; and in an implicit concession to Roger Williams, he comes to acknowledge that there are ways for the justified man to offend God which the natural man has not dreamed of.

22 *Winthrop Papers*, I, 160.

To begin, Winthrop describes the limited contributions made toward grace by his natural abilities. In his youth he had simply extended the application of certain "logicall principles" with which he was acquainted, and had achieved a better "understanding in Divinity then many of my yeares." Those years, which for many were "wild" and "dissolute," were somewhat less shameful for Winthrop because of the restraint he had felt imposed upon him by "natural reason" and the "sad checks of my naturall Conscience." This much, it could be admitted to the Antinomians, the Spirit had no part in. But through the means of Mr. Culverwell's ministry, grace began to make itself felt, "so as there began to bee some change which I perceived in my self, and others took notice of." How did these "strong excersises of Conscience" differ from the natural workings of conscience he had already experienced? Paradoxically, they prove themselves the work of the Spirit by leading to defeat rather than victory. Winthrop's irony gradually undermines the triumph that had seemed to proceed from his penitential fever at age fourteen: "I betook my self to God whom I did believe to bee very good and mercifull, and would welcome any that would come to him, especially such a yongue soule, and so well qualifyed as I took my self to be." Rather, the soul that would take its life from the Spirit of God first had to suffer total defeat. It was a battle, Winthrop saw, which he could not have won, whatever the strength of his depravity: "hee left mee not till hee had overcome my heart to give up itself to him, and to bid farewell to all the world, and untill my heart could answer, Lord, what wilt thou have mee to doe?" (I, 156.)

For a time, Winthrop remembers, his only solace in defeat was a measure of "peace and comfort"; then came a gradual onset of delight and zeal, but in unsettled patterns.

Could the autobiographer identify justification at the basis of these feelings? Had he consulted Anne Hutchinson, Winthrop would not have been assured by her probable reply. Whereas most Puritan ministers would counsel that a tree is known by its fruits, Anne Hutchinson maintained that "no sanctification can help to evidence to us our justification," as Winthrop reported in his *Journal*. For Mrs. Hutchinson, the soul knew of its graciousness by an "immediate revelation" or not at all. The full cruelty of this position was only too clear to one who had experienced repeated "tremblings of heart" and "plunges," who had feared he "was not sound at the root" and so received the praise of others as "a dart through my liver." In its naked irrationality, Mrs. Hutchinson's thinking was fearlessly consistent with the essence of the Puritan attitude toward conversion and divine sovereignty. Yet it would have had nothing to offer the self-accused hypocrite Winthrop described: "It was like hell to mee to think of that in Hebr:6," Paul's promise of damnation for those who fall away from repentance. Before he had ever heard of Anne Hutchinson, Winthrop implies, he had rejected the import of her thinking. Whatever uncertainties were involved in distinguishing God's determinations in the impalpable, a man pondering the fate of his soul preferred to scrutinize such evidence under the tutelage of Mr. Culverwell rather than wait for a thunderclap and bolt of lightning that might never come.

Hence the theological ambivalence of the John Winthrop we see portrayed in the "Christian Experience." Within the range of emphases which comprised Puritan orthodoxy, he appears first near the border which separated the impious doctrine of works from the legitimate search for evidences of salvation; then he appears as a bright embodiment of the doctrine of free grace, to be distinguished from the irrational intensity and lurid illuminism of the Antinomian. Of the two positions, the latter is more consciously assumed, in response, as Winthrop notes, to recent controversy. Even as one grants that the emphases may well have been compatible in the sequence of Winthrop's experience, one feels the strain of incompatible terminologies. Reviewing a period when grace was highly dubious, Winthrop is inclined to describe himself as "looking to my evidence more narrowly." He recalls being alerted by one of Perkins' works to a "better assurance by the seale of the spirit," and looking within was ashamed that "in all this time" he had "attained no better evidence of salvation." Even when Winthrop makes a point for free grace, describing a period of fruitless bondage to mere duties, he uses the legalistic term "evidence" uncritically. "I was held long under great bondage to the Law . . . yet neither got strength to my Sanctification nor betterd my Evidence. . . ."

Only when Winthrop begins to shape his autobiography as argument is there a noticeable shift in terminology. The idiom in which the Antinomian controversy was conducted penetrates to Winthrop's description of "the time that the Lord would reveale Christ unto mee whom I had so long desired." In the "Experiencia" he had kept in England, Winthrop located the cause of spiritual depression in his too great attachment to the world, and had attributed his experiences of divine favor to rejection of "earthly pleasures"; but in the "Christian Experience" he restates the essential struggle of this period in specifically doctrinal terms. After he had realized that his "greatest want was fayth in Christ," Winthrop recalls, "it pleased the Lord in my family exercise to manifest unto mee the difference between the Covenant of grace, and the Covenant of workes. . . . This Covenant of grace began to take great impression

in me. . . ." Now it was impossible to feel discontent "for
want of strength or assurance" because "mine eyes were
only upon his free mercy in Jesus Christ." This is scarcely
an Arminian position, yet Winthrop is anxious to demonstrate its compatibility with the assumption protested
against by Mrs. Hutchinson, that a process of sanctification
helps to reveal prior justification: "And the more I grew
thus acquainted with the spirit of God the more were my
corruptions mortifyed, and the new man quickened" (I,
159). In a closing paragraph describing how he learned
to value both justification and sanctification, the amateur
theologian has given way to an autobiographer who is the
sole authority for his argument. Shaped to the uses of the
present, experience gave the lie to both Antinomians and
legalists.

CHAPTER FOUR

OF PROVIDENCE, FOR POSTERITY

The most convenient image of the Puritan autobiographer which is presently available suggests complete meditative withdrawal: the dark figure is bent over a crudely fashioned writing table, barely warmed by the ill-supplied fire; his passionate introspection totally absorbs him, and he has filled a dozen pages with a crabbed, involute script that seems the material counterpart of his soul. Despite the vaguely Hawthornian charm of the image, it fails to convey, indeed denies, the numerous relations between the Puritan autobiographer and the concentric circles of his environment. As the member of a family, a church, and a body politic, he could never speak simply to hear his echo, nor was he free to consider his autobiographical reflection of himself totally apart from the faces that surrounded it. Edward Taylor, as we have seen, delivered his personal narrative as part of a public ritual inherent in the ecclesiology of the New England Puritan. And although John Winthrop composed and retained his "Christian Experience" in solitude, his writing was prompted and influenced by events and relationships in his public life.

Rather often the broader uses of personal narrative are indicated explicitly by the autobiographer in the very common dedication, "To my dear and loving children." The family is the ordinary and unspectacular context in which spiritual narratives are set in this period. If committing one's experiences to paper dissipated no enigmas for the writer, the work was supposed at least to be edifying for one's children.

Captain Roger Clap, who wrote from an obligation he felt imposed by scripture, closed his narrative with a lengthy exhortation that left no doubt what had kept him at the labor of extended composition: "I say, I do here *charge you solemnly,* and every one of you, as if I did Charge you every one by Name: *Sons, Daughters,* and *Grand-children,* . . . and Servants, or any other whom God hath placed within my Gates: I say, I *Charge you* that every one of you *Fear the Lord our God, and Obey his command-ments. . . .*"[1]

So great a devotion to the didactic must have its effect on the nature of autobiography. For while it is possible to defend an autobiographer who tells only the life of his soul by pointing to another who confines himself to reciting his sexual triumphs, there is a point at which the autobiographical intention has so narrowed itself to an exclusive interest that its product must be placed in another category entirely. Such is the case with autobiographical testimonies used to apply for church membership. Personal narratives addressed to the writer's descendants are also particularly liable to this difficulty. In addition to the usual complexities of self-definition, this writer struggles under the burden of domestic emotions which he understands, perhaps, only a little better than his intended audience. For the Puritan patriarch, it was not a question of hiding one's faults from the family; his grandchildren did not need his personal testimony to know that he had sinned miserably. But neither do any narratives survive in which the writer submits to posterity the evidence for his damnation. As always,

[1] *Memoirs of Capt. Roger Clap* (Boston, 1731), p. 26.

112

the next generation took its lessons from success stories, however violent the struggles they recited.

Anne Bradstreet's "Religious Experiences"

Curiously, Puritan writers familiar to us from other work, who might have been expected to articulate their spiritual lives with more verve and originality than usual, submit rather easily to practical didactic considerations when addressing their children. Cotton Mather, who deserves separate treatment, is largely content to collect the most instructive portions of his diaries in the autobiography he assembled for his son. Anne Bradstreet specifically rejects motives which guided her as poet when "in much sickness and weakness" she finds brief time to offer the "spiritual advantages" of her experience to her children: "I have not studied in this you read to show my skill, but to declare the Truth—not to sett forth myself, but the Glory of God. If I had minded the former, it had been perhaps better pleasing to you—but seeing the last is the best, let it bee best pleasing to you."[2]

Characteristically, Anne Bradstreet apologizes for the imperfections of her work; surveying her brief narrative at the end, she finds it "very weakly and imperfectly done." But the only failure for which there could be no apology was not to have spoken at all: "if you can pick any Benefitt out of it," she concludes, "it is the marke which I aimed at." The last metaphor suggests nicely the deliberate manner of Anne Bradstreet's succinct instruction. Cotton Mather attempted to warn his son against all sins individually and

[2] *The Works of Anne Bradstreet,* reprinted by Peter Smith (Gloucester, 1962), p. 40. The title "Religious Experiences" was supplied by John Harvard Ellis in the first (1867) printing of this edition. Anne Bradstreet addressed the composition simply, "**To my Dear Children.**"

to pass on intact his vast knowledge of devices for acquiring holiness. Anne Bradstreet had time and strength only for essentials, and from the rich detail of her life selected what had been crucial. Her children, she knew, would have to bear pain, would be tempted to unbelief, and would agonize over their graciousness, or lack of it. Until they were delivered into Christ, she said, her apprehension for them in these trials would be as great, "with great paines, weaknes, cares, and feares," as when she had delivered them into the world.

Scriptural as well as personal, the symbol of childbirth could sum up much of what Anne Bradstreet wished to say in her "Religious Experiences." On the literal level, she invests it with personal emotion when she recalls the years barren of children, which "cost mee many prayers and tears before I obtained one." The birth of her first son was therefore doubly significant of travail issuing in great joy. So much had this been the way of things, she finds, that the pattern tolerates enlarging to include all affliction. Pain that is the direct result and necessary "correction" of a "heart out of order" offends not even a child's sense of justice; and the memory of an "untoward child"—she speaks of herself—is "no longer then the rod has been on my back." For her own children, Anne Bradstreet set forth a lesson regarding affliction that required greater docility and a keener sense of paradox. A later, festering Puritanism would say: read joy as evil. This Puritan directs her children to read pain, the world's evil, as joy: "If at any time you are chastened of God, take it as thankfully and joyfully as in greatest mercyes." The Puritan inclination toward autobiographical hyperbole appears briefly when she goes on to claim "yea, oft have I thought were it hell itself, and could there find the love of God toward mee, it would bee a Heaven"; but her meaning has been strictly literal: "in Truth, it is the absence and presence of God that makes Heaven or Hell" (p. 8).

As she labored to make clear that pain was more than a matter of nerve endings and that fire could be felt as God's ardor, Anne Bradstreet could not be certain that she recommended anything more than a formula. Admittedly, the paradox was resolved only on a condition: "and could there find the love of God." Her own experience contained evidence that the basis of any such hope could disintegrate in an instant: "many times hath Satan troubled me concerning the verity of the scriptures, many times by Atheisme, how I could know whether there was a God." Reason suggested the necessity of a creator, but a part of her not touched by logic continued to refuse, not in an occasional crisis, but "thousands of Times," the idea of a triune God revealed in "such a Saviour as I rely upon." A half dozen rhetorical questions that follow embody the arguments that periodically rose up to meet her doubts. They are strenuously announced; yet they have not been so intricately fashioned as to suggest that Anne Bradstreet had hopes of preserving her children from atheism by her own irrefutable logic. The climactic passage of this sequence recalls a species of doubt against which logic seemed futile and irrelevant. "But some new Troubles I have had since the world has been filled with Blasphemy, and Sectaries, and some who have been accounted sincere Christians have been carried away with them, that somtimes I have said, Is there faith upon the earth? and I have not known what to think" (pp. 9-10). She will proceed to hymn "the King, Immortal, Eternall, and invisible, the only wise God," but only after confessing to her children her helplessness in a world in which not God, but faith itself was absent.

Do these well-intentioned but disjointed meditations constitute an autobiography? The "Religious Experiences" of Anne Bradstreet lacks even the staple of Puritan autobiography—a description of the emergence of grace in its various signs and stages—and instead appears to substitute a kind of rudimentary apologetics. Such an approach to autobiographical writing would suggest that experience can be gathered up into issues and ideas through which a man thinks his way to death. Without granting that this is Anne Bradstreet's assumption, one may ask how safe it is to assume otherwise, whether one makes a false distinction in demanding that the autobiographer relate his experience rather than his "ideas." The thread of an argument runs through almost any autobiography, justifying individual decisions or the total tendency of a life, defending by personal example the sublimest ideologies or the most vulgar of unspoken convictions. Anne Bradstreet's first-person testament to her children appears to be something less than autobiography as it is ordinarily defined, but it can be put down as mere apologetics only through a failure to distinguish between its stated and implied arguments. The writer does indeed give reasons for the existence of a providential God and feels it important to condemn the "vain fooleries" and "lying miracles" of the Church of Rome. But the essential argument which she addresses to her children never takes explicit form. The argument is based on the unstated premise that a mother cannot bequeath grace to her children or persuade them into heaven. Rarely does a spiritual autobiographer in this period fail to acknowledge the efforts of his pious parents to inculcate virtue and punish waywardness. Nevertheless, the remainder of a given narrative amounts to a confession that depravity is ineradicable and that, however saving grace came about, it did not follow automatically from parental solicitude and regular habits. Aware of these limitations on her verbal efficacy, writing in brief space and with physical difficulty, Anne Bradstreet saw that she would accomplish much if she only prepared her children to be lost by willing to them the example of a stoical and loving resignation to Providence. In the midst of the narrative's final affirmation, "upon this Rock Christ Jesus will I build my faith," she grants tersely, "and if I perish, I perish."

More pervasively, the argument is built into the pattern we have already seen operating in her selections from her total experience. By presenting her "life" largely in its afflictions, atheism, and temptations to despair, Anne Bradstreet works to dissipate illusion and to suggest an image of life as typically stern, barren, and hostile. Her argument for the validity of this image is not interrupted even when she reaches the emotional center of Puritan autobiography. She is able to say, "I have sometimes tasted of that hidden Manna that the world knows not," and she expresses confidence "that against such a promis, such tasts of sweetnes, the Gates of Hell shall never prevail." Yet she also confesses herself "perplexed" at not finding "that constant Joy in my Pilgrimage and refreshing which I supposed most of the servants of God have" (p. 7).

No pilgrim's progress, of course, was without its "sinkings and droopings," as Anne Bradstreet here describes those frequent withdrawals of light. Usually, however, narratives were organized to strike a more favorable balance between dry and fruitful seasons, or they described periods of spiritual transport with a devotional intensity that made up for their infrequency. Anne Bradstreet seems almost reluctant to claim that she has not been left "altogether without the wittnes of his holy spirit, who hath oft given mee his

117

word and sett to his Seal that it shall bee well with mee";
and she is unwilling to elaborate on her occasional taste
of "that hidden Manna." To deny her children the comfort
of a detailed enumeration of signs that it would be well
with her—signs which they might have applied with similar
success—was also to deny them the fatal luxury of mistaking
the sign for the reality and thus of being ambitious to acquire evidence rather than sorrow for sin. Understated as
her "Religious Experiences" are, Anne Bradstreet is not
surpassed by other Puritan autobiographers in harmonizing
the contrary demands of her occupation: to set an autobiographical example for her "dear remains" while avoiding,
even discouraging, illusions about the efficacy of parental
advice; and to set down affliction as the rule of life while
not stifling or distorting emotions that arose from "such a
promis, such tasts of sweetnes," as she saw fit to claim.

The *Memoirs* of Roger Clap

Severely restricted as it is in scope, Anne Bradstreet's
brief autobiographical narrative is related at every point to
the small audience it was intended to serve. Having been
formed for purposes outside itself, it is introspective without really being egocentric. There will always be enough
material to keep vivid the figure of the Puritan dissolved in
brooding meditation, foreshadowing Romantic descendants
who will carry on the tradition in dungeons of the heart.
Yet many Puritan autobiographies, seen at close range, add
little support to this thesis. The autobiographical search for
self, the self that would endure in the life of grace, very
often has a quite public purpose. In autobiography as in
life, seclusion was a luxury that could interfere with accomplishment in the society of other men.

118

Puritan history, too, was delivered publicly and told its audience what it meant to be a chosen people by revealing God's regular disposition of events in their favor. Less favorable events were not less instructive, since in them the historian could point out the chastisement of a forgetful people. As historian of himself, the Puritan autobiographer was engaged in essentially the same task, acknowledging divine blessings and providential intercessions and weighing the positive benefits of the most dismal calamities. Just as the historian tended less to describe events than the divine ordering of them, the autobiographer often made Providence the chief character of his narrative, his own life merely the setting for its actions. Few Puritan autobiographies embody this relationship in any extensive way, however, and those that do—the narratives of Thomas Shepard and Roger Clap for instance—do not always move coherently and comprehendingly from the smaller to the larger cosmos. Roger Clap struggles to articulate a relation between his migration to New England and his new birth in the life of the spirit, but while his spiritual history and the history of the colony are seen to overlap, their relationship is never precisely defined.

Unlike John Winthrop and Anne Bradstreet, whose prominence in New England was already assured, by birth or by marriage, before they left Old England, Roger Clap (1609-1691) rose to a level above middle station entirely within the new society. Elected a representative many times between 1652 and 1673, he served the colony less as a legislator than as a military man. Having joined the artillery company in 1646, he became its lieutenant nine years later and earned Edward Johnson's praise as the "stout and valiant Lieutenant Clapes, strong for the truth."[3] After his pro-

[3] *The Wonder-Working Providence of Sion's Saviour in New England*

motion to Captain he commanded the fortification on
Castle Island from 1665 until he resigned in 1686. As an
early arrival in the Bay Colony—he has a sharp recollection
of the constant hunger of his first year—and as its servant
for most of his life, Clap could rightfully expect an attentive audience in his children when he spoke of his concern
for them and for New England. But Clap relates his two
concerns imperfectly, and as a result divides whatever attention the best of his narrative should earn. Published
forty years after Clap's death, his *Memoirs* are introduced
by Thomas Prince, whose enthusiasm for historical and
biographical example led him to compile the *Annnals of
New England*. No doubt it was also Prince who gave Clap's
narrative a title, discovering as he did so that the author's
purposes were not easily summed up in a few phrases. The
title promised a narrative of these dimensions:

> Relating some of GOD'S Remarkable Providences to
> *Him*, in bringing him into *New-England*; and some of
> the Straits and Afflictions, *Good People* met with here
> in their Beginnings.

> ### AND

> *Instructing*, Counselling, Directing and Commanding his
> Children and Childrens Children, and Household, to
> Serve the LORD in their Generations to the latest
> Posterity.[4]

Fulsome by convention, the title still failed to mention
that Clap had also related evidence of his election, gaining
as a result the authority by which he advised his children

(New York, 1910), p. 229. Additional biographical information on
Clap, including the names of his children (e.g. Thanks, Desire, Unite,
Supply), can be found in James Savage, *A Genealogical Dictionary of
the First Settlers of New England* (Boston, 1860).

[4] *Memoirs of Capt. Roger Clap* (Boston, 1731).

on their souls' welfare. Similarly, Clap was able to describe the colony's struggle for existence from the point of view of a participant, and could thus suggest a representative quality in his personal experience. The hand of Providence had been as evident in his own passage to the New Canaan as it had been for William Bradford when he recorded the deliverance of the Plymouth settlers from trials of opposition, weather, and disease. Clap could not speak of persecutions by authorities or treacherous sea-captains, but there had been his father's opposition to the voyage. Since, however, "it was God put it into my Heart to incline to Live abroad," it was also God who "made my father willing" and two months later "landed me in Health at Nantasket."

More generalized descriptions of the initial hardships of settlement, even those of participants like Bradford and Winthrop, take on body in Clap's first-person account. At times during the first year, "the then unsubdued Wilderness yielding little Food," hunger and nostalgia assaulted him together, so that "I tho't the very Crusts of my Father's Table would have been very sweet unto me." Without divine support, Clap avers, he might easily have weakened and set his heart on returning home. Nothing revealed this support more clearly than the settlers' determination to persevere in their experiment. Indeed, "the Discourse, not only of the Aged, but of the Youth also, was not *How Shall we go to England?* . . . but *How shall we go to Heaven?*" In a time of material privation, God showered his greatest spiritual blessings on New England: "Many were Converted, and others established in Believing: many joined unto the several Churches where they lived, confessing their Faith publickly, and shewing before all the Assembly their Experiences of the Workings of God's Spirit in their Hearts to bring them to *Christ*" (p. 5).

Clap numbers himself among the many who were converted, noting that he joined the Dorchester Church "at our first beginning" in 1630. At this point his narrative scope constricts to an emphasis on his own spiritual experience in isolation from the experience of the group. In so doing Clap indicates the fulfillment of the divine plan in the case of an individual. If New England was blessed at all, it was in the graciousness of its individual souls, and Roger Clap was certain he had grace. The time and manner of his conversion were obscure, but assurance was not: "it did so transport me as to make me cry out upon my Bed with a loud Voice, *He is come, He is come.* And God did melt my Heart at that Time . . . Yea the Love of God, that He should Elect me, and save such a one as I was did break my very Heart" (p. 9).

Thus, either by plan or by an habitual association, Clap makes autobiography extend itself into the domain of history. Separately they set forth alternative views of God's providential disposal of human affairs. In the first half of his narrative, Clap merges the two perspectives: personal history takes on the significance of the larger pattern to which it belongs and which the reader is aware of as its context; and the larger pattern assumes a more concrete reality for its embodiment in the single instance.

Having carried his twin narratives to an early climax, Roger Clap abdicates his role as communal autobiographer to become another memoirist of New England's fall from grace. "You have better Food and Raiment," he tells his children, "than was in former Times; but have you better *Hearts* than your Fore-fathers had?" The present appears to him a vast spectacle of immorality: "Drunkenness, Adultery, Fornication, Oppression, and abominable Pride." His desire to evoke an earlier era of "Tranquility & Peace"

122

forces him into repetition and harangue. Returning to the hardships of the early settlers, Clap forces the metaphor of the chosen people into exotic shapes: "And in those Days in our Straits, though I cannot say God sent a *Raven* to feed us, as He did the Prophet *Elijah*; yet this I can say to the Praise of God's Glory, that he sent . . . poor *ravenous Indians* . . . (p. 14).

Redundancy, uncertain chronology, a tendency to stray from the subject, all these may be excused as exactly the kind of difficulty one expects in a garrulous old soldier reminiscing for his offspring in a genre notoriously attractive to amateurs. Clap is too vulnerable a target to make much of his failures. But the failures are instructive. More lively than many of its contemporaries, Clap's narrative is finally unsuccessful as autobiography—that is, it exhibits discord and disproportion between its argument and its freight of experience—not because its tasks were difficult but because they were too easy. The complexity of experience is inevitably simplified to some extent in autobiography, but the principles by which Clap organizes his experience and the terms in which he conveys it appear extraordinarily over-simplified, especially in comparison with other spiritual narratives of the period.

Clap's testimony nowhere suggests the rigor with which the early settlers are said to have examined one another in founding churches. A catechism definition exceeds in moral energy Clap's statement of the conviction with which he sensed his corrupt nature, "whereby I felt myself prone to sin." As illustration, he offers an incident in which his friends gave him "those Points which they played for, to hold for them until Game was out" (p. 6). There follows a comparison between this offense and Paul's holding the cloaks of the men who stoned the martyr Stephen. Beyond

123

the initial stages of conviction, Clap describes his spiritual experience only in the most general terms: "God has made me sensible That I am a Sinner, and Jesus Christ came to save Sinners, and why not me, tho' a very sinful Man." His principal assurance of grace derived from the quasi-mystical experience in which he shed tears and cried out, "He is come"; but the analytic device Clap relies on to discover more objective evidence is the widespread notion, derived from I John 3:14, that only the elect can truly love their brethren. Clap cites his love for a man, "a Stranger to me, and a very hard favoured Man," who had recently declared his own godliness. But, Clap avers, when he is thrown together with the ungodly, "so that I cannot avoid it," he finds himself lamenting, "Wo is me that I am constrained to be with such Persons" (p. 7).

Interpreting events outside his personal history, Clap encounters no greater difficulties than when he consults his feelings about strangers as a test of sanctity. The Puritans' view of themselves as a chosen people and of history as a providential design, shaped to their eventual triumph, regularly informs Clap's description of the colony's affairs. Anne Hutchinson and her followers are enemies "puffed up . . . with horrible Pride" by their leader Satan. Quakers were hanged "because God's people here could not Worship the true and living God as he hath appointed us in our publick Assemblies, without being disturbed by them." An adulterer who had threatened the authorities with recrimination from his friends in England illustrates by his violent death—he was reported roasted alive by Indians—divine solicitude for the reputation of New England: "Thus did God destroy him that so proudly threatned to ruin us by complaining against us when he came to *England*" (pp. 19-20).

124

These demonstrations of providential care for New England, like comparable passages reciting the speaker's evidence for his graciousness, benefit from an analysis which employs the principle it is supposed to illustrate. The result, in other words, is autobiography as circular argument. Necessarily, the autobiographer in reflecting upon his experience is guided by habits of vision and speech which are products of that same experience. However much this formula simplifies the autobiographical act, it serves quite adequately to describe the simplistic process by which Roger Clap "discovers" the significance of his own and the colony's experience. To his descendants, then, Clap passes on a self-portrait which he seems to have had some notion of labeling the representative New Englander, disciplined in self-denial and the rigors of first-generation piety. No doubt the portrait justified its title admirably for those who first beheld it; but change would assert itself without regard for what hung in the family gallery. Roger Clap's providential reading of his own and his society's experience was exercised on the data of success; yet his example is intended to forestall imminent failure, the involvement of his offspring in the widely lamented "declension" of New England. At the close of his autobiography, Clap expresses this intention, encouraging his children to build a millennial New England by recourse to a formula that explained only the past: "Since all the People of God in other parts of the World, that shall hear that the Children and Grand-Children of the first Planters of *New England*, have better Hearts, and are more heavenly than their Predecessors, they will doubtless greatly Rejoice and will say, *This is the Generation whom the Lord hath Blessed*" (p. 25).

What, conversely, would have to be concluded about a generation whose hearts proved less heavenly than those of their predecessors, a generation that committed no great scandal but that testified less and less to an experience of grace? Clap was hindered from approaching this question by the whole tendency of his narrative. The autobiographer is limited to a single performance, not subject to revision, and Roger Clap's formula, while it was capable of explaining calamities, could not make a meaning of indifference.

John Dane's *Declaration of Remarkable Providences*

Two other personal narratives from this early period add to the evidence provided by Anne Bradstreet and Roger Clap that divine Providence was a major character in any Puritan autobiography and received special emphasis in manuscripts directed to the attention of posterity. At the same time, John Dane's *Declaration of Remarkable Providences* and Thomas Shepard's "Autobiography" illustrate the Puritan conviction that Providence often manifests itself in men's experience in ways too mysterious to calculate. The trustworthiness of scriptural promises did not assure their fulfillment in the individual; notional certainty regarding the manner in which the divine will would execute itself in time could not rashly be translated into a triumphant first-person narrative. Of the four autobiographies grouped here, only Roger Clap's makes an easy analogy between the chosen people and a chosen self.

John Dane (1612?-1684) is the most thoroughly anonymous member of this group, but his narrative, like the others, is designed to be both exemplary and devotional. Dane's survivors are the recipients of such wisdom as he has been able to achieve in a lifetime and are also the audience before which he gives public thanks for the con-

126

tinual mercies of Providence. Dane, too, is an early (c1638) emigrant to New England, but with Anne Bradstreet he fails to see himself taking part in a geographical extension of the Reformation. At the prospect of removal from England, Anne Bradstreet recalls, "my heart rose," though a typically stoical resignation soon followed. John Dane hoped only for some relief from the apparent omnipresence of temptations which had assaulted him in his native country, but, he tells his heirs, conditions are the same everywhere: "I find here a devell to tempt and a corupt hart to deseve."[5] Plainly, the similarities between Dane's narrative and anything written by Anne Bradstreet end here. The natural phonetics of Dane's writing suggests his general artlessness and the unplanned, improvisational quality of his autobiography. As his title makes clear, Dane consciously attempts to portray the merciful role of Providence in his life. Having summed up as much relevant evidence as he can recall from his seventy years, he states his intended theme: "Thus god hath all along presarvd and cept me all my daies." His deliverances from sin and from physical danger have so obviously been recited with this conventional purpose in mind that execution alone, or rather the divergence of purpose and execution, constitutes the special interest of his narrative.

I

For the most part, Dane allows chronology to arrange his description of the acts of Providence in his life. Until he left

[5] *A Declaration of Remarkable Providences in the Course of My Life* (Boston, 1854), p. 12. This is a separate printing of Dane's narrative, which was edited by John Ward Dean for the *New England Historical and Genealogical Register*, VIII (1854), pp. 147-156. In a preface, Dean comments on the manuscript, which contains a rhymed version of the autobiography, and provides a pedigree of the Dane family.

England at about the age of twenty-five, Providence seemed to act primarily as a restraining force, checking those depraved impulses which sermons and attendant introspection had revealed to him. Later, his preservation through a series of economic reverses, illnesses, and dangerous incidents suggests to Dane that Providence may also have his material well-being in mind. Neither sequence shows Dane coping more successfully than other Puritan autobiographers with the problem of making Providence a more convincing cause of events in a narrative of individual experience. No New England Puritan quite equals or seems aware of Augustine's vividly dramatic habit of addressing God directly and almost continuously, so that the soliloquy of autobiography takes on the effect of dialogue. The latent sense of dramatic interchange in the *Confessions* gives Providence a reality within the narrative that justifies as it evokes the speaker's devotional outpourings. The *post hoc* logic of so much Puritan narrative, historical or personal, automatically and mechanically assigns Providence a role in past events which have displayed in some sense a "providential" tendency.

In John Dane's narrative, the disparity between the role ascribed to Providence and the role it plays dramatically can be traced directly to a habit of mind which emerges from the anecdotal progress of the work. In the first of several anecdotes sketching his childhood, Dane gives his parents conventional praise for the strict and pious upbringing he had from them. He admits that as an eight-year-old he "was given mutch to play and to run out without my fathers Consent and againe his command." Inevitably his father confronted him as he returned one day from his frolics, and "toke me and basted me." Our speculation on the boy's immediate reaction would be fruitless and irrelevant, especially since Dane recalls so positively, "I then thout in my

128

harte, o that my father would beat me when I did amis. I fard, if he did not, I should not be good." The anecdote makes no tribute to his father's educational technique, offers no moral that just punishment should never arouse resentment. In fact, Dane recalls being thoroughly angered ten years later when his father threatened him with another basting, this time for attending dancing school: "If I went agayne he would bast me. I tould him, if he did he should never bast me againe. With that, my father toke a stick and basted me" (p. 8). Convinced of his father's lack of sympathy and steadiness of purpose, Dane this time runs away from home. Already a dominant pattern has been set for the narrative. Dane is unable to find a disposition to regular conduct in his past experience. For any goodness he displayed on a given occasion he regularly tenders credit to an agency outside himself: his father's basting, his parents' prayers, and more frequently, God's "Restrayning grace."

The reader is not free to question the accuracy of Dane's report, but there can be little question that its precise form has been lately assumed and for the purposes of autobiography. Acknowledging an early preservation from sin, Dane takes note of "gods goodness in then giving me Restrayning grace to presarve from sutch a temptation, though then I slytly passed over many such provedenses." An initiatory experience occurring soon after he left home illustrated the same lesson; and the same distance obtains between the event and its defined significance. Dane had found work as a tailor and one night had been working late for his master. When he returned to the inn where he lodged, he encountered the hostess and her maids, the former disposed alluringly by the fire. Invited to "drink a pot" with her, Dane pleaded his weariness and promised to drink with her in the morning; "and so I hastend awaie to my Chamber." In his anxiety to avoid temptation, however, he had been ignorant of the real source of his strength. "Her I toke no notes of the goodnes of god in Restrayning me, but Ratther ascribd it to my self; all though I had as Retched a natter, as I have bene sens more sensable on then before" (p. 8).

The tension between a naturalistic narrative and its supernatural interpretation grows considerably more strained following a lengthy anecdote that deserves to be quoted in full:

"And upone a day, as I remember, thare came on from Starford [Stortford, Dane's home] that I was wonderfull glad to see, that I myt inquier of my frinds thare. I invited him to this in to drink; and thare was one of theas brave lases thare which dind at the table I dind at, and it is lykly that I myt drink to hur and she to me; but this I know, I never toucht hur. The nite after, I came to goe to bead and askt for a lite. My ostes sayd, we are busey, you may goe up without, the mone shines. And so I did. And when I cam in the chamber, I went to the bed side and puld of all my Clothes and went in, and thare was this fine lase in the bead. I slipt on my Clothes agayne, and went doune and askt my ost, why she would sarve me so. O, sayd she, thars nobody would hurt you. I tould hur, if I hired a Rome, I would have it to myself; and shoud my self mutch angrey. So she gave me a lite into another Chamber, and thare I lae; but, in the morning, I went to that chamber I used to ly in, for I had left a letell bundell of things on the beds tester. I cam to the dore and gave the dore a shuf, and this fine Mistres Reacht out hur hand out of the bead and opend the dore. So I went in. I doubt mis I am troblsom to you. No, sayd she, you are welcum to me. I tould hur,

I had left a small trifell on the tester of the bead, and I toke it and went my waie. For all theas, and many other of the lyke, I thank God I never yet knew any but thos two wifes that god gave me. But when I conseder my Retched hart, and what I myt with shame and blushing speke that waie, I cannot but sa, O, wonderfull, unspekable, unsarchabl marseys of a god that taketh care of us when we take no Care of ourselvese." (p. 9)

By art or by nature, John Dane thus manages to bungle his pious theme, failing wonderfully to dramatize the role he ascribed to Providence, but qualifying for the praise Benjamin Franklin extended to "Honest John" Bunyan as "the first that I know of who mixed narration and dialogue, a method of writing very engaging to the reader." Dane too mixes narration and dialogue, and he mixes them in discreet proportion. At the instant of the discovery on which the whole passage is centered, his art is silence, the speechless wonder at carnality of a virginal Tom Jones. No verbal reaction intrudes between the discovery and the composed innocence of, "I slipt on my Clothes agayne. . . ." The reader has been asked to avert his gaze from the bed in order to sympathize with the young man's comically indignant protest. The next morning's interview with the usurper of his bed is set forth in dialogue which grants the reader immediate witness to Dane's single-minded recovery of his possessions and the maid's equally resolute sociability.

The whole sequence is finally memorable for its untutored version of negative capability. In the details that Dane sees fit to include—his nakedness when he climbed into bed, the image of the "fine Mistres" welcoming him from bed the next morning—he surrenders his narrative to the sensuality inherent in the experience without any discernible savoring of the memory. There is, perhaps, a super-

131

ficial resemblance between this pattern and the ancient satirical stereotype of the Puritan whose sermons against lust fairly ooze with his own lasciviousness. But Dane not only refuses to take credit for the iron will and delicate tact he dramatizes in his autobiographical self, he concludes by giving thanks to an agency that makes no appearance in the narrative.

I I

In only one sequence does Dane successfully create a unified impression of the role of Providence in his moral experience. The sequence begins when Dane describes his angry reaction to his father's "basting." Carrying two shirts and a Bible, he had awakened his parents early one morning to tell them he was leaving home. With the air of a Dick Whittington, the young man announces that he is going "to seke my fortune." But his mother's words are the more significant in this exchange: "Then said my mother, *goe whare you will, god he will find you out*. This word, the point of it, stuck in my brest, and afterwards god struck it home to the head." The scenes at the inn describe his initiation into the great world, but Dane returns readily to the theme of his pursuit by a relentless Providence as well as to its characterizing metaphor. One Sabbath he had decided to stay away from meeting, "Not being in that trim that i would have bene in"; and as he walked in the fields bordering a meadow, "There was whether fly, wasp or hornet, I cannot tell, but it struck my finger, and watter and blod cam out of it and paind me mutch. I went up to a hous and shoud it, but they knew not what a sting I had at my harte." As the pain and swelling increase, Dane must seek a physician, who plays his part in this drama of Providence not by prescription or surgery—Dane never relates the

132

physical outcome of his affliction—but by replying to Dane's questions in the manner of a Calvinist oracle: "He said it was *the take*. I askt him what he meant. He said it was taken by the provedens of god. This knoct home on my hart what my mother said, *god will find you out*. Now I made great promises that if god would here me this time I would Reforme" (p. 9).

The reform is short-lived, and in time, having moved and changed jobs, young Dane is once again rationalizing his failure to keep the Sabbath: "And so I went in to an orched, and sat doune in an arbore; and, as before, one the same finger and on the same place, I was strucken as before. And as it struck my hand so it struck my harte, for I sudingly Rose up and went into a wood; and thare I cryd bitterly, and now concluded that god, god had found me out. I was now utterly forlorn in my spiret, and knew not what to du, thinking that god had now utterly forsaken me, and that he would here me no more" (p. 10). The sequence eventually concludes with the parents' loving reception of their prodigal son. But Dane must first demonstrate the extent of the care Providence had of him in his "forlorn condition." Jonah-like, he had prepared to escape to the West Indies, until news came that the Spanish had captured the port he wished to reach. In a final moment of bravado the God-fugitive vows to call no port his own but to travel where his journey work takes him. As Dane recalls the trickling away of resistance, though, Providence has already triumphed: "at last, I had sum thouts to goe first home to my father's house."

Understandably, the most impressive sermon Dane recalls from this period (after rejoining his family he procured a job as butler to a "very Religious famely") took as its text, "Ye that ware alents and strangers from the coman-

welth of isrell hath he Reconsild to himself." Like this paraphrase, Dane's narrative transcends its mechanical irregu-
larities to convey a theme with ultimate clarity. He depicts
himself struggling futilely against divine solicitude for his
welfare, and thus achieves agreement between the actions
of this portion of the narrative and their putative moral.
His very helplessness against Providence as autobiographical character makes him less suspect as autobiographical
rhetorician. Who can resist an argument that takes so little
apparent care to wear a presentable face?

Tactful depiction of the actions of Providence will not
rank as the greatest challenge ever to confront literate man,
yet success depends on something more than the aptness of
the incidents themselves. The coincidence of John Dane's
being stung twice when he had foregone worship is less
interesting than his conscious attempt to enlarge the metaphor of the sting of remorse and thus lend another kind of
inevitability to a providential reading of his experience.

III

Occasionally Dane's narrative suggests themes that have
no explicit claim made for them. The notion of life as a
"symbolic pilgrimage through the wilderness of this world"[6]
to the permanent Celestial City tends to emerge from
Dane's grouping of incidents and from the diction to which
he regularly turns in setting them forth. As migrant patriarch of the American Danes who will read his words, he
chooses to begin his narrative by recalling his own father's
removal from Berkhampstead to Stortford and the "wants"
and inconveniences his family suffered as a result. Dane
follows the same thread through his youthful experience

6 Cyclone Covey, *The American Pilgrimage* (New York, 1961), p. 7.

when he describes himself taking leave of his parents in a huff of adolescent self-righteousness. Thereafter his movements from place to place become a staple of the narrative, and the journey-pilgrimage metaphor asserts itself without special encouragement. No forcing of theme dissipates implication when Dane gives his own version of the pilgrim being set back on his path by Providence, despite his preference for wandering into destruction. He and a friend were "going to a dansing on nite, and it began to thunder, and I tould him I doubted we ware not in our waie; and he and I went back againe." Yet in another context, Dane's honorific use of the term "pilgrim" reflects either a past self-deception or the narrator's tribute of sympathy to his younger self. Just before returning to his parents he had despairingly resolved to "goe and work Jurney work thorow all the Counties in ingland, and so walk as a pilgrim up and doune on the earth." The Puritan pilgrim, however, was no aimless wanderer, and conquered his most beguiling temptation by refusing to become a vagabond, as the narrative finally suggests.

For a time Dane's pilgrimage involves nothing more than the duties of a butler, marriage, and successive moves to Wood Roe and Hatfield. No wonder that "a great cuming to nu ingland" should include John Dane, who justifies his decision to his parents by showing them the text he had opened to in the Bible: "Come out from among them. . . ." No wonder, either, that in New England he moves before long from Roxbury to Ipswich, although "thare was no path, but what the ingens had made; sumtimes I was in it, sumtimes out of it, but god directed my waie."

Thus the motifs of the journey, the path, and the pilgrim, provide loose thematic continuity in an episodic narrative that might conceivably have amounted to no more than a miscellaneous grouping of providences.[7] Ageless, always apt, with a potential for cumulative suggestiveness, the journey motif is so satisfactory a form of autobiographical coherence that it tends to divert attention from the narrative's lack of any profound introspection. With Dane's last glance at the path of his journey from deliverance to deliverance it becomes evident that he has described his pilgrimage without establishing its internal equivalent. He excuses himself from returning to difficult terrain: "Manie trobles I past thorow and I found in my hart that I could not sarve god as I should. What thay ware, ware two teadus to menshon." A less informative preface could not be imagined for the narrative that follows:

"But uppon a time walking, with my Gun on my shoulder charged, in the myle brok path, beyond Decon good-hewes, I had severall thouts came flocking into my mynd, that I had beatter make away with myself then to live longer . . . and that it was a greatter evell to live, and to sin against god then to cill myself, with many other satanecall thouts. I cock my Gun, and set it one the ground, and put the musell under my throte, and toke my fote to let it of. And then thare came manie thing into my head; one that I should not doe evell that good myt cum of it. And at that

7 Solomon Mack, an autobiographer who resembles John Dane in his limited literacy, describes numerous calamities by which Providence attempted to bring him to repentance. Mack's recitation is so mechanical, however, and the supply of disasters appears so constant and plentiful that it becomes uncertain whether Providence is the power attempting to instruct Mack or his preserver from the violent means of instruction. See *A Narrative of the Life of Solomon Mack* (Windsor, 1811 [?]). Even Samuel Johnson, philosopher, Anglican, and first president of Columbia (King's College), reveals his Puritan upbringing when he devotes several early paragraphs of his autobiography to "remarkable deliverances." *Samuel Johnson: His Career and Writings,* ed. Herbert and Carol Schneider (New York, 1929), I, 4-5.

time I no more scrupld to cill myself then to goe home to my oune house." (pp. 12-13)

Of the numerous non-sequiturs in Dane's narrative this one is the most startling, for until these concluding sentences it has been possible to guess sympathetically the expository links Dane has not troubled with. His optimism about a new life in New England seems emergent when he ends a description of a hard day's labor in the field by recalling the long draught of water he took from the spring in Roxbury street: "and I never drounk wine in my life that more Refresht me." Also verging on the symbolic is Dane's account of his triumphant encounter with the most feared creatures of the new world. One day on the path to Ipswich he meets "forty or fifty indiens, all of a Roe," but his greeting ("what chere") puts them in good humor and he is allowed to pass on his way. Bold, indignant words are necessary to keep off two surlier types ("one of them a very lusty sannup") farther down the same path, but the idea in both instances is that the path has been made safe by Providence. The reader is then suddenly confronted by a metamorphosis of the autobiographical John Dane from an earnest pilgrim unaware of the comedy in which he occasionally acts to a despairing pilgrim whose pitfalls and quagmires have no names; they are "two teadus to menshon." Dane may have been exercising that species of autobiographical tact which decreed a patriarch's secretiveness when addressing survivors, but more probably he could not have given a name to his despair. The extraordinary experience of consciously choosing between life and death is located, as it must be, on the metaphorical path Dane has traced from the beginning, but a necessary alteration of the definitive term suggests something irrecoverable in his experience, obscure now in time and in its causes and con-

137

ditions: "Though this place is now a Rode, then it was a place that was not mutch walkt in" (p. 13).

The final paragraphs do nothing to discourage the suspicion of depths and darknesses that never reveal themselves on the articulated surface of the narrative. With the end of his written labor in sight, Dane is careful to summarize his apparent theme: "Thus god hath all along presarvd and cept me all my daies." Immediately, he appears to fall back from the superfluous and repetitious evidence of his survival and from the narrow definition of Providence as a charm against mortality. Two succeeding recollections of elevated spiritual experience help correct the imbalance by redefining Providence as God's constraining love, which induces man "to love him that has loved us first" and to contemplate the "Joys of heaven and . . . the vanitys of this world." Dane's memories of encountering Providence in this manner are intense, but briefly stated; one "toke sutch an impreshon of my harte as that I thout I could doe anie thing for god or safer anie thing for god." His last words to "loving Relations" urge them, somewhat enigmatically, to beware of "quenshing sutch motions of gods spiret," lest they incur sorrow and affliction; "and I can speake it to the grefe of my soule, by wofull experans."

Last words tend to be definitive in such a document. Nothing follows these to alter the impression that Dane's thesis and the drift of his narrative are at odds once again. A number of formulas might have helped Dane render experiences he regarded as unspeakable. Instead, he allows this testimony to "Remarkable Providences" to close on the final discordant note of "wofull experans," in effect pleading release from demands of abstract logic that have no more claim on his experience than the demands of formal orthography on its articulation.

138

Thomas Shepard's "My Birth & Life"

One of the best-known Puritan autobiographies, the narrative Thomas Shepard called simply "My Birth & Life," has served well to represent the typical aims of the genre since it was first published in 1832.[8] As might be guessed from the title, Shepard's spiritual narrative is more inclusive of biographical detail than most, studded with names and dates and covering all but the last three years of his life (1605-1649). It recounts such features of his childhood as his mistreatment by a cruel stepmother, after he had grown used to being his own mother's favorite. His education, conversion, and entrance into the ministry, his attempts to preach the Gospel despite episcopal harassment, prepare for and justify the removal to New England, "a land of peace tho a place of tryall." Shepard then turns historian of the colony and gives accounts of the Antinomian controversy, the founding of Harvard College, and the defeat of the Pequods.

Shepard's autobiography is thus a composite of several related kinds of personal writing: sufferings and labors in the ministry, salvation narrative, and a declaration of providences rendered both the author and the colony. Material of the latter sort is partially duplicated in two other autobiographical compositions that survive in the same manuscript; a monitory recital to his son Thomas of "gods great kindness to him" through the perils of a long sea voyage and the threat of several disabling diseases; and a catalogue for his own meditation of numerous debts to the mercy of

[8] Perry Miller and Thomas Johnson chose Shepard's autobiography as the sole representative of its kind for *The Puritans* (New York, 1938), pp. 471-475, and it is the only autobiography treated at length by Kenneth Murdock in *Literature and Theology in Colonial New England* (Cambridge, 1949), pp. 99-117.

divine Providence. A portion of Shepard's diary, which he seems to have begun in England, has also been preserved, with entries dating from November 25, 1640, to March 28, 1644.[9]

I

"My Birth & Life" is more than a capacious repository for the varieties of Shepard's autobiographical writing, although it may seem to lack distinct identity in comparison with their devotion to particular purposes. It would be difficult, for instance, to distinguish the autobiography by its more precise analysis of the evidence for regeneration. Shepard's retelling of the experiences that culminated in his conversion helps structure the total work, since it concludes the period of his youth and, simultaneously, brings to fruition his search for piety and learning at Cambridge. Yet the conversion experience is not elaborately set forth, and it occupies relatively small space in the total autobiography. Shepard describes the process rather mechanically, since he had spoken of it repeatedly from the pulpit and had analyzed it in his own experience at least twice before. With other founders, he had spoken of "the work of grace the Lord had wrought in them" when they met in 1636 to gather a church at Newtown (Cambridge). Subsequently, he committed these oral narratives to writing under the title "The Confessions of diverse propounded to be received & were entertayned as members."[10] Then in

9 A brief description of the diary and other unpublished Shepard manuscripts precedes the modern edition of the autobiography in *Publications of the Colonial Society of Massachusetts*, xxvii (1932), pp. 357-392. The brief narrative Shepard directed to his son has been included (pp. 352-356) under the general title "The Autobiography of Thomas Shepard" assigned by the editor.

10 This is another of the unpublished Shepard manuscripts described in a bibliography preceding the autobiography, *ibid.*, p. 347.

1639, perhaps in preparation for the drafting of the auto-biography, he made a list of fourteen points which enumerated "the good things I have received of the Lord," and again he gave space to the stages of "my conversion."[11] In the autobiography itself, the quest for grace is sealed off from its context and takes the form, once more, of numbered steps. The section is introduced by Shepard's announcement that after three vain and godless years at Cambridge, "the Lord began to call me home to the fellowship of his grace; which was in this manner" (p. 360). The seventh and last numbered item concludes "& so the Lord gave me peace." Outside these limits introspective passages are rare and brief.

Yet in diary entries made ten years or more after the experiences at Cambridge, Shepard exclaims in sentence after sentence at the immense distance separating him from God. David Brainerd, the Indian missionary whose own melancholy diary Jonathan Edwards would introduce, offered a portion of Shepard's diary to eighteenth-century readers as an antidote to enthusiastic delusions, citing the diarist's most prominent characteristics as his great "Self-Emptiness, Self-Loathing . . . and deep unfeigned Self-Abasement."[12] No abstract statement of the classic Puritan conviction of depravity could adequately suggest Shepard's sense of feeble insufficiency in this diary, where he discovers each day as if for the first time, new kinds of "Shame," "Carelessness," "Infirmities," "Weakness,"' and discouragement with "Evils that attend me in my Ministry." In the autobiography one encounters the same figure speaking of his "weake abilities," but the autobiographer has clearly

---

[11] *Ibid.*, pp. 393-395.
[12] Preface to "Meditations and Spiritual Experiences of Mr. Thomas Shepard," *Three Valuable Pieces*, ed. Thomas Prince (Boston, 1747), p. v.

relinquished to the diarist the regular duty of uncovering fresh evidence of the futility of Thomas Shepard.

This division of duties between autobiographer and diarist appears to have been nearly universal in Puritan personal writing. As a device for personal meditation and analysis, the diary would fail of its purpose if the writer could not bring himself to view his most abhorrent self. Implicitly, or by specific direction, the autobiography was public in nature, setting forth an exemplary pattern. Theoretically the purposes complement each other, and modern readers ought not to be scandalized nor cry hypocrite too readily if the Puritan autobiographer simply gives the drift of the worst evidence he has assembled about himself in his diary. Most likely, he intends only to give such evidence its proportionate emphasis in the totality of the spiritual life. In practice, moreover, each writer tends to work out a relation between diary and autobiography that deserves separate comment.[13]

Shepard's distinct concerns in the autobiography emerge more clearly from a comparison of two drafts covering the same sequence of events. The first portion of the autobiographical manuscript, addressed to Shepard's son, Thomas, Jr., displays the divine mercies to which he owed his life and continued good health. If Shepard was writing as late as 1649, the year of his death, the boy would have been thirteen when he read: "see how god hath miraculously preserved thee, that thou art still alive, & thy mother's wombe & the terrible seas have not bin thy grave; woonder at & love this god for ever" (p 352). The incidents recounted in these few pages are duplicated in the longer

---

[13] See, below, pp. 165-167 on Cotton Mather and pp. 191-194 on Jonathan Edwards for the varying degrees of revision to which a diary was subject.

work, which also describes the Shepards' last months in England, where Thomas, Jr., was born, the ocean voyage he survived, and their arrival in New England, where he was baptized.

Understandably the two compositions present these experiences differently. The autobiography tells of a violent storm that nearly robbed Shepard of his family. The mother, holding her newborn son, is thrown against an iron bolt, striking her head; yet the child is "miraculously preserved" and the mother recovers (p. 384). Writing for his son's edification in the earlier composition, Shepard either chose a more impressive instance of the same kind of mercy or recalled the same experience in greater and somewhat variant detail. A storm again tumbles mother and child, this time "against a post," but the mother "being ready to fall shee felt her selfe pluckt back by shee knew not what" (pp. 354-355). Neither Shepard's memory nor his veracity is at question here. The narrative which includes his wife's impression of unseen assistance enables him to tell his son that he may well have been rescued by "angells of god," who, as "ministering spirits for the heirs of life" had marked the child for responsibilities consonant with the great mercy he had enjoyed.

For the same reason, Shepard attempts to forge an indissoluble bond between the son and his memory of his mother by describing other incidents of their mutual deliverance. Finally he directs his son to consider her death, "who did loose her life by being carefull to preserve thine; for in the ship thou wert so feeble & froward both in the day & night, that hereby shee lost her strength & at last her life . . . and therefore know it if thou shalt turne rebell agaynst god . . . the Lord will make all these mercys *woes* & all thy mothers prayers teares & death to be a swift witnesse

143

agaynst thee at the great day" (p. 355). Presumably, young Shepard's burden was rendered more tolerable when he turned to his father's autobiography and read that during one of the many storms that marked this voyage his mother had taken cold, "and got such weaknes as that shee fell into a consumption of which shee afterward dyed." Moreover, in taking autobiographical leave of his wife, Shepard rounds out her life in fulfillment rather than anxiety. Her life ends, not in a frustration which only the son can undo, but in relief at leaving her family among God's people in New England and joy at being received into church fellowship.

The full autobiography is also more detailed concerning the death of the Shepards' first Thomas, "my first borne child very precious to my soul & dearly beloved of me." In the composition intended solely for the second son these feelings have to be assumed. The surviving Thomas needed only to know that he had his name, or his brother's name, from the hands of Providence as it were, because in the second child's deliverance "we thought the Lord gave me the first Son I lost, in this agayne, & hence gave him his brother's name." Thus Thomas Shepard, Jr., spared by a merciful Providence, standing in the place of his brother, and given life by a mother who offered up a holy curse in his name before she died of his "frowardness," had been given much to contemplate in his father's autobiographical directive.

II

Experience which the Puritan autobiographer sets forth as displaying the boundless and tender mercy of God and the sanctifying uses of adversity must also be searched for the pattern of divine wisdom which answers some prayers and ignores others, by which the second Thomas was saved

144

and the first lost when "the Lord would not be intreated for the life of it." At times, Shepard composes a catalogue of thanksgivings which wonder in a near ecstasy of gratitude "that the Lord should fetch me out . . . by such a sweet hand" from the evil and ignorant town of his birth, that the Lord had delivered him from "that Lyon" Bishop Laud, or, when Shepard's personal fortunes become identified with those of the colony, that the Lord should be pleased to deliver his people from the "filthy opinions" of Mrs. Hutchinson and from the "Pekoat furies." But the Lord who had set himself against one's enemies and in whose wrath one had therefore rejoiced could also chastise the saint: "& truly about this time the Lord that had dealt only gently with me before, began to afflict me & to let me tast how good it was to be under his tutoring." As Shepard here indicates, sweet affliction was the pedagogical technique God used on his saints, but no periphrasis could obscure the final knowledge, nor did Shepard attempt to do so, that one's tutoring was at the hands of a most wrathful Jehovah, equally irate against the sinner and those more ostensible children of Satan, the Indians. There is a perfect consistency between Shepard's description of the "divine slaughter" of the Pequods and his own chastisements. Captain Mason had set the Indians' wigwams on fire, but the ultimate cause, in the sentence and in a providential reading of historical events, was divine: "their wigwams . . . being dry and contiguous on to another was most dreadful to the Indians, some burning some bleeding to death by the swoord some resisting till they were cut off some flying were beat down by the men without untill the Lord had utterly consumed the whole company except 4 or 5. girles . . ." (p. 388).

So, too, in the darkest trials of his conversion experience, Shepard recalls, "I did see god like a Consuming fire & an

145

everlasting burning & my selfe like a poore prisoner leading to that fire." In time he would discover further that experiences of "the Lords woonderfull terrour & mercy" were not to be restricted to his adolescence, either physical or spiritual, that God's "dreadfull power" might "cast me into the fire" in more ways than one and at any moment.

Most often, affliction was not physical, or even direct, but reached Shepard through the lives of those he loved—excessively, as the lesson went. His first son died after a fortnight's sickness when "the Lord sent a vomiting upon it wherby it grew faint, & nothing that we could use could stop its vomiting. . . ." Yet the child's death would have to be considered providential, because by it "the Lord now shewd me my weake fayth want of feare pride carnall content immoderate love of creatures, & of my child especially, & begot in me some desires and purposes to feare his name" (p. 381). The "sweet hand" of deliverance had moved freely rather than in response to merit, but this other hand of Providence, it seemed to Shepard, moved in ways more susceptible to pattern. In that darker Arminianism which existed side by side with the idea of free grace, a Puritan held good deeds inefficacious for salvation while believing evil deeds brought forth regular and merited punishment. Thus Shepard takes little credit for his sermons, "the Lord making improvement of my weake abilities as far as they could reach"; yet when he assumed the guilt for the deaths of his children he judged himself fully capable of moving heaven to prompt retribution. It was "hartbreaking to me that I should provoke the Lord to strike at my innocent children for my sake." Capable of bringing down affliction for his sins, Shepard found himself incapable of profiting from its lesson. Thus the first affliction contained the seed of a second and more potent grief. By his immoderate love

146

of a child he had lost it, but failing to remember this lesson, he later loses his "most deare precious meeke & loving wife." Only when it began to appear that the Lord was "rooting out" his family, Shepard concludes, was he brought to realize "that if I had profited by former afflictions of this nature I should not have had this scourge" (p. 392). But was not the consolation for the first child's death thereby removed?

The point here is not to catch Shepard in a theological inconsistency but to indicate that the conditions of autobiographical composition are not those of theological composition or even of the sermon using the device of exemplary model. Shepard may well have hoped that whoever read his manuscript would find it "in effect a sermon on adversity as a stimulus to holiness."[14] The value of a sermon on adversity would surely be increased by the addition of a testimonial such as the one Shepard offers in treating the death of his second wife: "I am the Lords, & he may doe with me what he will, he did teach me to prize a little grace gained by a crosse as a sufficient recompense for all outward losses." But the experience of "My Birth & Life" is not the theoretical and ideal experience of a model created for the sake of a sermon. Shepard's sentence continues past the point of his exemplary acceptance to add, "But this loss was very great," and Shepard then goes on to eulogize his wife for nearly two manuscript pages at the conclusion of his autobiography (p. 392). In effect the eulogy constitutes a faintly subversive argument against formulistic de-

[14] Murdock, *Literature and Theology in Colonial New England*, p. 115. Murdock emphasizes Shepard's intention more than his accomplishment when he describes the autobiography's theme as "God's dealing with errant men . . . it was the record of a good man's life, rich in suggestion as to how a human heart might triumph over doubt, fear, and sin, if properly receptive to God's grace."

scriptions of the way of Providence. The sermon theme
has been repeated again and again—that deep within each
affliction lies buried a sweet kernel of improvement and
consolation—but as Shepard attends dutifully to this theme,
he also advances an autobiographical argument that con-
tends strongly with his exemplary testimony.

I I I

The counter-argument is discernible from the beginning
of the narrative, where Shepard depicts himself thrown on
the mercy of Providence after the death of his mother and
father. He will go on to recall the agents—his brother, and
an "eminent preacher"—through whom Providence reme-
died the neglect of his education and piety. But Providence
was merciful only after it had been indifferent. Shepard first
gives an account of his father's illness, "in which time I do
remember; I did pray very strongly and hartily for the life
of my father & made some covenant if god would do it to
serve him the better as knowing I should be left alone if he
was gone." Human reasons cannot prevail: "the Lord tooke
him away by death" (p. 358).

Another failure twenty years later is described even more
succinctly, with no mention of the arguments God refused,
only that "the Lord would not be intreated for the life" of
his first son, "& after a fortnights sickness at last it gave up
the ghost when its mother had given it up to the Lord"
(p. 381). An element of personal failure is suggested in
Shepard's relinquishing to his wife the posture of exemplary
acceptance, to which, in this passage at least, he cannot
bring himself. His second son, Thomas, however, represented in his very existence a successful appeal to Providence, and in the special autobiographical testament ad-

148

dressed to him, Shepard recalled the "many arguments" he had used "to presse the Lord" for this son's life. In keeping with the announced purpose of the document, Shepard's arguments, as he reproduces them, seem as much addressed to the son as to heaven: "1. The glory the Lord should have by betrusting me with this child, he should be the Lords for ever." Yet even the necessity of giving strong paternal example does not prevent the intrusion of a tone that becomes more pronounced in the autobiography proper. Another argument did not rest on an appeal to the glory of God and it had nothing to do with reason. It was simply the cry of a man with no more arguments to make: ". . . because I thought if the Lord should not heare me now, my soule would be discouraged from seeking to him because I sought for the first & could not prevayle for his life, & this was sore if the Lord should not heare me for this" (p. 354).

The counter-argument of Shepard's autobiography, then, has only emotional content. It does not dispute, except emotionally, the wisdom of divine Providence, or betray a hideous suspicion that the idea of improvement through affliction rationalizes the cruelty or indifference of a non-providential deity. Rather, "My Birth & Life" appears the product of an autobiographer who makes rational use of his experience in filling out the large dimensions of an exemplary figure, and who is then assaulted by emotions too painful to surrender unconditionally to formula.

Especially in the closing passage on the death of his second wife, Joanna, "the eldest daughter of mr Hooker a blessed stock," one discerns Shepard's struggle to affirm that human pain alone is a sufficient argument in appeals directed to heaven. The argument proffered in life, which God "refused to heare," aimed weakly at divine self-interest, as had many of his arguments for the lives of those others

149

he had lost: "I did thinke he would have hearkned & let me see his bewty in the land of the living, in restoring of her to health agayne; also in taking her away in the prime time of her life when she might have lived to have glorifyed the Lord long." There follows a longer and more earnest argument, a eulogy to Joanna, which is not hedged with conditions or baited with rewards. Spoken too late for triumph, yet with a sense that it is not refutable even by God, the eulogy argues that so loving a partner—"she told me soe, that we should love exceedingly together because we should not live long together"—and so ardent a daughter of Christ —"shee knew Jesus Christ & could speake to him, & . . . broke out into a most heavenly hartbreaking prayer after Christ her deare redeemer for the sp: of her life; & so continued praying until the last houre of her death"—could not be lost without desolating her husband and depriving immeasurably God's people, whom she loved "dearly," and was "studious to profit by their fellowship." Shepard not only fails to contract these emotions into an exemplary meditation on immoderate love of creatures or the profitableness of adversity; his summary closing of the narrative admits ultimate failure in applying the formula to his own experience: "thus god hath visited & scourged me for my sins & sought to weane me from this woorld, but I have ever found it a difficult thing to profit ever but a little by the sorest & sharpest afflictions" (p. 392).

While Shepard's autobiography thus proclaims a reconciliation to the way of Providence which it does not fully achieve, the immoderately loving memorial to Joanna constitutes a reconciliation beyond the adequacy of formula. To have been at one with Joanna in life was to experience, and in the autobiographical telling of it to re-experience, her readiness "to dy long before she did dy" and the fullness of Christ in her last reception of the Sacrament, whereby she was "fitted for heaven." To preserve her exemplary last words, Shepard has to speak them himself, ceasing any longer to debate Providence when he recalls her anguished surrender: " 'Lord though I unworthy Lord on woord on woord' &c. & so gave up the ghost."

CHAPTER FIVE

THE MATHERS

Except for the Adamses, who came later, no American
family rivaled the Mathers in an hereditary inclination toward biography and autobiography. The biography of the
first American Mather, Richard (1596-1669), was written
by his son Increase, who told his readers that although he
would remain anonymous he wrote with the authority of
one closely acquainted with his subject and aided by his
subject's manuscripts, including an autobiography to age
thirty-nine.[1] Shortly after he completed the monument to
his father's life, Increase Mather (1639-1723) began the
record of his own. His surviving diaries date from the early
1670's, and in 1685 he concluded the first portion of an
autobiographical manuscript that continued to receive additions until eight years before his death. Cotton Mather
(1663-1728) turned to these documents immediately after
his father's death and in little more than a month had completed the biography published in 1724 as *Parentator:
Memoirs of Remarkables in the Life and Death of the Ever-
Memorable Dr. Increase Mather*. In his turn as biographer
of a revered and learned parent, Samuel Mather (1706-
1785) could consult an abundance of autobiographical

[1] "Preface," *The Life and Death of That Reverend Man of God,
Mr. Richard Mather* (Cambridge, 1670) p. 1r. The autobiography
has not been preserved, but Richard Mather's sea-journal of the
voyage to New England is available in Alexander Young, *Chronicles
of the First Planters* (Boston, 1846).

152

materials beyond his needs or his devices to present them interestingly.[2] His father left more diaries, no doubt, than are preserved in the two substantial volumes of the modern edition, as well as an autobiography, "Paterna," based on the diaries and running to 356 manuscript pages.

The total volume of biographical materials represented in this grouping, and necessary distinctions among the persons who wrote them, stand as mute caution against multiplying generalizations about them. One can say at least that to be a Mather was to produce a eulogistic biography of one's father as well as the documents necessary to one's son for the same task. But it is not clear that the biographies resulting from this tradition may be combined uncritically into the composite biography of an idealized man of God—a Reverend and Learned Dr. Mather of Platonic dimensions —when we see, for example, that Samuel's biography passively accepts direction from the subject's manuscripts, while Cotton dominates the tone and shapes the materials of Increase Mather's *Life*. Simultaneous discussion of the autobiographies of Increase and Cotton Mather would involve even greater difficulties, including psychological speculations beyond the literary study of an autobiographical text. The two Mathers had similar autobiographical habits .in some respects, but the autobiographies themselves require separate consideration

In what we have seen was a well-established tradition, both Mathers addressed their autobiographies to posterity, Increase specifying all his children ("[You] are all of you so many parts of myselfe"), Cotton singling out the first son who gave promise of living to maturity, then directing the manuscript to Samuel when the first son, Increase, was

[2] Samuel Mather, *The Life of the Very Reverend and Learned Cotton Mather* (Boston, 1729).

lost at sea. Both autobiographers make extensive verbatim use of other personal records, beginning with a continuous narrative but filling out their work over a period of several decades with gleanings from diaries or journals. The result, in both cases, is an almost total loss of the retrospective overview that helps distinguish autobiography from diary-keeping. Increase Mather's autobiography is described by its editor as falling into three sections: a narrative to Christmas Eve 1685, an account of Increase's political mission to England from 1688 to 1692, and miscellaneous entries from 1696 to 1715.[3] The middle section is self-justifying but not introspective, and the last section has the characteristics of a diary, with the exception of a long entry for June 2, 1711, which reviews the events and tendency of seventy-two years of completed life in thanksgiving to the Lord "for all his wonderful goodness towards me a most sinfull creature, throughout the whole course of my life."

Cotton Mather's "Paterna" is formally a somewhat more unified document than his father's autobiography. It also begins with a retrospective section on the author's youth and an account of his growth in learning and piety. Ten pages of sustained narrative carry him to age fifteen, but the next fifteen years require forty pages as narrative increasingly gives way to the setting forth of devices for the attainment of piety. After treating his thirty-fifth year, Mather relinquished the procedure of distinguishing his life into "lustres," or periods of five years. The time remaining to forge eternal bonds between his son and righteousness apparently seemed too little to permit leisurely composition. In the remaining half of the manuscript, Mather wills

[3] M. G. Hall, ed., "The Autobiography of Increase Mather," *Proceedings of the American Antiquarian Society*, LXXI (October 1961), pp. 272-274.

to his son the multitude of methods by which he had assaulted heaven's gates. Both autobiographies, then, are intended to instruct offspring, but even a cursory description of contents must note that Cotton pursued his task more single-mindedly and at much greater length.

The *Autobiography* of Increase Mather

In its subject matter alone, Increase Mather's spiritual narrative closely resembles that of Thomas Shepard, who had only recently arrived in New England when Mather was born there. Mather too acknowledges the debt he owed his pious parents, recalling especially his mother's deathbed exhortation that he devote himself to bringing others to righteousness. In Mather's account, also, conversion and university education coincide, and there is much foreshortening of the horrific experiences of conviction of sin which prepared the way for grace: "About which Time the Lord broke in upon my conscience with very terrible convictions and awakenings. . . . I was in extremity of anguish and horror in my soul." A symbolic gesture, writing down "all the sins which I could remember" and burning the paper they were written on "in way of confession," marks a new stage of spiritual development. After a day of secret prayer and fasting, Mather continues, "I gave my selfe up to Jesus Christ," and "had ease and inward peace in my perplexed soul immediately" (pp. 279-280). Unquestionably, Mather counted this as his conversion, although the experience is contained entirely within a paragraph which lacks any detailed description of stages or special workings of the spirit.

Considerably more important in the early passages of the narrative are his recollections of attainment in learning, of

155

his ambitious attempt to enter the ministry in England, and his difficulties as a Non-Conformist at the time of the Restoration. With Shepard he is able to claim the Puritan's badge of honor: "Thus was I persecuted out of two places Glocester and Guernsey, before I was 22 years of age." Unwilling to conform and read the Book of Common Prayer, Mather returned to New England in 1661, where for reasons he deprecates—"being by reason of my 4 years absence become like a stranger, and people are apt to run after strangers though they have little in them of real worth" (p. 286) —a dozen churches invited him to settle with them. In his review of the decade that followed his return, Mather continues to give generous space to vocational decisions, his father's death in 1669 marking their culmination and a new point of departure. His decision to write and publish a biography of his father introduces a group of resolutions that forecast Mather's entrance into the larger arena of the moral and theological life of New England. He had reminded himself that he would have to go about these things "with deep Humiliations and seekings of the face of God," an injunction implicitly obeyed in the narrative's punctuation of its subject's rise in career with grievous "Temptations to Atheisme" and Satanic assaults of melancholy. Mather's vantage point, in 1685, is that of a man who has seen the confirmation of a once troubled hope, "that by these terrible Temptations God would fit me for his service." From this perspective Mather has been able to integrate the materials of his public and spiritual affairs before he attaches the whole of the accomplishment to the theme of reliance on Providence. Mather concludes the first unit of the "Autobiography" by recalling that he had come at last to say, "yea, though I dy for it, I am resolved to Trust in God for his salvation; and let come on me what the Lord will" (p. 294).

Reliance on Providence, as we have seen, had been a thematic staple of Puritan autobiographies, especially those addressed to posterity. Essentially the parent argued that in his deliverance could be seen a Lord whose mercy inspired trust as His will demanded acceptance. Increase Mather's introductory declaration to this effect might be taken for any of a dozen others: "I have thought that the relation of what the Lord has done for your Father, and the wonderfull experience which hee has had of Gods Faithfullness towards him, might be a meanes to cause you to give yourselves entirely to the Lord Jesus and to endeavor to walk with God" (p. 277). Autobiographical arguments supporting this theme sometimes faltered as the writer, beguiled by other attractions in his evidence, spun a different pattern from its finer strands. Frequently, too, the autobiographical argument is logically weak. The experiences used by Anne Bradstreet, Thomas Shepard, or Solomon Mack to demonstrate the clemency and fidelity of Providence are not strongly persuasive, although the ardent fidelity of the autobiographer emerges nevertheless through an argument that cannot contain it.

Against this background, the autobiography of Increase Mather is remarkable for two things at once. It sustains an autobiographical argument for reliance on Providence with impressive evidence, logically employed. And it initiates another argument, carried on simultaneously, and continued at greater length in Cotton Mather's "Paterna," which suggests that Providence is a term an autobiographer may use in retrospect to describe God's recognition of good works.

Increase Mather's autobiographical glorification of Providence cannot be adequately discussed simply by reference to the language of his devotional expressions, if only because the language of many passages has a scriptural precedent. When Mather pauses to sum up the mercies extended to him in his first thirty years of life, "which I have cause forever to bless God for," it is natural that he should express thanksgiving in a scriptural tradition: "Bless the Lord O my soul, and forget not all his benefits, who forgiveth all thine iniquities, who healeth all thi diseases, who Redeems thi life from destruction. . . ."[4] Indeed, Mather speaks of deliberately associating his experience with that of an Old Testament prototype when he reflects on the "sufferings" that ensued from a malicious forgery intended to represent him as treasonous. He had been able to read the Psalms "more feelingly than ever . . . before" because of the "particular application" they had acquired for him. "I could now say, princes have sat and spoken against me. I am filled with the contempt of them that are at ease. The proud have had me greatly in derision. . . . And innumerable other passages in the Psalmes could I then read and pray over so as never before nor since" (p. 310). The consolation of the Psalmist, too, Mather takes as his own in another passage, which he has excerpted from his diary: "If I be the Lords Servant, when I am gone, the Lord will make some of my people sensible of their neglects of me, though unworthy of any respect, in my selfe considered" (p. 298). So complete is the correspondence that at times the autobiographer appears subsumed in the prototype, even as Edward Taylor's "personal" and introspective *Preparatory Meditations* have as their speaker, not Taylor, but a generalized Every-

---

[4] *Ibid.*, p. 300. Psalm 103 sets the theme again when Mather concludes the catalogue of thanksgiving he wrote in 1711, p. 358.

soul, whose imagery comes to him in the broad stream of the history of salvation.

Mather's self-portrait from a scriptural model takes on personal significance only as he adapts the type to the particular events of his life. Experiences involving public service generally are made to conform to the outlines of two figures. Mather is either the Psalmist, reviled by men but remembered by God; or, in a close variation, he is the unheeded prophet, strangely persuaded that some calamity will befall Boston or New England at large. As autobiographer, of course, he can count among his historical materials the events in which God confirmed his warnings—King Philip's War, an epidemic, a fire in Boston. But momentarily setting aside finished fact, he recreates the emotions of the prophet whose warnings will be rejected by the very people he hopes to save: "O Lord God, I have told this people in thi Name that you are about to cut off dwellings, but they will not believe me. Lord who hath beleeved our report. Nevertheless, O Lord God, that you wouldst spare them, if it may stand with thi Holy pleasure" (p. 303). His own losses in the fire were not great, he notes, a mercy in the midst of judgment. The aims of the prophet and of the autobiographer are thus contradictory: the prophet is characterized as pleading to be heard, but the successful filling out of the figure Mather has in mind depends upon his not being heard.

It is not clear from Mather's reporting of this incident whether his congregation had before it an unambiguous statement of options. But in another instance, they are hardhearted beyond a doubt when they ignore a specific prophecy: "During the warr Time, observing the murmurings of the people, and considering I Cor. 10.10. 'Neither murmur ye, as some of them also murmured, and were destroyed of the destroyer.' I was verily perswaded that God would punish that iniquity with some mortal disease, and accordingly I did in publick 3 times declare as much, which some were troubled at me for but the Lord confirmed the work spoken, by sending mortal feavors which were epidemical, and the small pox also whereby many dyed" (p. 302) . The rebukes of the people illustrate how rigorously the man of faith will be tried, but only in theory does it seem possible that God may withdraw his consolations entirely and eternally. The autobiographer adheres undeviatingly to the notion that for the afflicted servant and rejected prophet, withdrawal of mercy is only temporary and apparent. Were it otherwise, autobiography would lose its reason for being and become an instrument of despair. The horror of this prospect leads Mather to say in effect that the autobiographer's alacrity in adjusting his experience to exemplary scripture types must be matched by a similar readiness on the part of God to fulfill His exemplary role by rewarding faithful servants:

"Also, I that day begged of God, that Hee would give me leave to plead with him, (and with Tears and meltings of heart I did plead with him,) that if hee should not answer me graciously, others after my decease, that should see the papers which I had written and kept as remembrances of my walking before God, would be discouraged. For they would see and say, 'Here was one that prayed for bodily and spirituall Healing, yea and believed for it also, and yet hee perished in his affliction without that Healing which hee prayed and believed for; and if but one man should read those papers, Hee would tell others, and then they would conclude that there is not so much in prayer, and that Faith is not such a mighty thing as the word of God sayth it is, so

that prayer, and Faith, and the Name of God will suffer if
I should not be heard crying to him.' " (p. 294)

The passage resembles some of the arguments Shepard
offered for the members of his family, but Mather's plea
is considerably more interesting in its explicit reference to
autobiographical writing, its enlisting God on the side
of successful autobiographical argument. The spiritual narrative of the American Puritans, beginning with the search
for a pattern of experiences which would suggest the presence of saving grace, broadening at times into an edifying
exhibition of all God's gracious and merciful dealings with
the subject, here advances its didactic potential as a rather
threatening argument for the favorable attention of Providence. Mather's prayer was followed, he recalls, by a resolution *"to Trust in God for his salvation: and let come on
me what the Lord will,"* adequate testimony that his intentions were docile. The autobiographical text, on the other
hand, suggests that Providence must be subservient to the
highest aims of autobiography.

A tendency to invert the autobiographical relationship
between man and Providence becomes more pronounced in
Cotton Mather's "Paterna," but his father's narrative indicates just as clearly the meaning of the change. In that sequence of incidents Mather relates concerning his attempts
to forewarn his people of calamitous judgments, one anecdote varies somewhat from those that surround it. After
noting the confirmation of his warnings in Indian attacks
and epidemics, Mather touches briefly on the success of his
efforts to relieve a famine resulting from the war "amongst
the poorer sort of people." More than proximity in time
brings together the events of these two paragraphs. Both
were attempts to perform service (the word is part of the

basic vocabulary of the autobiography) in his calling. By a habitual expression, Mather recognizes that, in such service, Providence is dominant: "it pleased God that some letters of mine to Ireland tooke such effect. . . ." Yet of all the incidents treated in this sequence, only this one closes with an explicit pointing of the moral, a lesson clasped ardently by at least one of Increase Mather's sons: "Let my children in this follow my example. Where they are not able to give and do good themselves let them excite others to do it" (p. 302). Between these two comments on his service, there is no great difficulty in discerning when Mather's voice relaxes in an idiomatic phrase and when its tone becomes strenuous, calling for attention. In the distance between them, the role of Providence diminishes, and autobiography becomes exemplary in its actions rather than its attitudes.

An epidemic of smallpox, especially when it has been forecast as a punishment for sins, preaches its own kind of sermon. As autobiographer, Mather adds that it was also a time when "divine providence put into my hands special advantages for service among his people." The opportunity was seized, he continues, in stirring up the General Court to pass "several wholesome laws for the suppressing of sin" (p. 302). Another turn of the screw—rather, an improvement of the lesson—could bring posterity to see that one need not wait for opportunities dispensed by Providence. With the aims of Providence securely in mind, one could make opportunities, indeed discover them lurking everywhere. When Increase Mather sets down a specimen week illustrating his method for the most "profitable improvement" of his time, he reveals his relation to his predecessors in spiritual autobiography by recording also the prayer by which he entrusted the success of method to the will of God: "Help a poor creatur, I earnestly beseech thee, to improve this Time as shall be most for thi glory. . . ." Yet, it seems equally important to acquaint his children with the pragmatic basis on which his methodism proceeded. They should not think he offered his schedule as an absolute, since he had always been prepared to refer it to circumstances, "or untill I should know a better method" (p. 304). One of the many ways in which Cotton Mather upheld and extended his father's work was by seeking out better methods and by recording a multitude of them in his autobiography. Providence may continue to be an ultimate mover in the autobiographical drama—so Benjamin Franklin will testify—but the stage will be filled with more proximate causes.

The "Paterna" of Cotton Mather

A large measure of disappointment awaits the reader who knows Cotton Mather's *Diary* and who comes to his manuscript autobiography expecting to discover "the True Picture of Cotton Mather." For one thing, Mather has already eluded his pursuer by awarding this title to another composition, wherein "I did, with Black, but yett with too *True* characters, describe my own Vileness at such a rate, that it cannot be Look'd upon, without Horrour of Soul; but I resolved, often to Look upon it."[5] This document has not survived to try the sensibilities of later generations, but there are other reasons why "the True Picture of Cotton Mather" is remote from us in the pages of the "Paterna."

Throughout the work, Mather scrupulously avoids men-

[5] "Paterna" manuscript, p. 172. The manuscript is in the Tracy W. McGregor Library of the University of Virginia. Passages which Mather transcribed from a diary into "Paterna" require a citation of both sources, as here: *The Diary of Cotton Mather*, ed. Worthington Chauncey Ford (New York, 1957), I, 195. Hereafter, references by initials will be given parenthetically within the next.

tioning his name or supplying information "that shall discover unto any one man living *who I am.*" Presumably Mather shares several of his reasons for secrecy with the author he cites (p. 2) as exemplifying a precedent to him. The author of *The Private Christian's Witness For Christianity* gives two reasons for his anonymity: that mockers of experimental religion might not imagine vanity the motive of his work, when he had wished only to display "the vital part of Christianity, experiences therein"; and because, fearing his susceptibility to vanity, he had withdrawn his name from attention "lest it prove Temptation to myself, exciting a corrupt Principle within to puffing up. . . ."[6] Clearly, these intentions are relevant to "Paterna," but they do not explain Mather's so frequently recurring to his desire for secrecy when, at the same time, he leaves a trail that might have been followed by half of Boston.[7] Mather seems to have taken fewer but more subtle precautions against being missed than against being discovered.

Very little of "Paterna" properly belongs to the category of autobiography, if introspection and self-definition are held to be important criteria for the genre. These activities are more readily observed in the diaries, from which Mather took most of the material for "Paterna."[8] In the diaries, the autobiographical self moves about in identifiable circumstances and among persons whose interaction with the subject provides an important basis for self-definition. The absence of names, dates, and places in the near-vacuum of "Paterna" makes for a kind of spectral drama at best—the

[6] *The Private Christian's Witness For Christianity* (London, 1697), pp. 6-7. The work has since been attributed to Sir David Hamilton.

[7] William Manierre has collected the clues to Mather's identity in "A Description of 'Paterna': The Unpublished Autobiography of Cotton Mather, *Studies in Bibliography*, XVIII (1965), pp. 186-187.

[8] See William Manierre's record of sources for most "Paterna" passages, *ibid.*, pp. 201-203.

nameless author rebuking unidentified playmates for their
wickedness or preparing himself in the classical languages
to be examined for entrance by the President and Fellows
of an anonymous college. At worst, when the author is
about other tasks than narration, there is scarcely any experiential substance to the writing.

I

No pattern of drastic and revelatory revision is discernible in passages common to both documents. Usually
Mather copies verbatim from his diary. Here and there one
discovers verbal changes, the deletion of one or two sentences, but rarely any expansion of a passage taken from the
diary. Introductory and transitional remarks are usually
quite brief: "About this Time, I recorded one Special Effect
of my having putt my Soul for Care into the Hands of my
Lord JESUS CHRIST. *My Son,* I charge you to take Notice
of it." The longest continuous piece of original writing in
the "Paterna" is Mather's initial narrative of his youth, education, and entrance into the ministry, covering the years
for which no record is preserved in diaries.[9] As soon as possible he begins to copy out of the diaries, which are extant
from his eighteenth birthday, February 12, 1680/1681.

At first, Mather seems prepared to enlarge diary passages
in order to blend their subject matter and emphasis with
the context of the "Paterna." Thus, copying a meditation
on "cursed PRIDE" from a diary, he adds several sentences
relating it to the stress of the narrative—that God began to

9 This narrative has been examined closely by David Levin, who
points out that aside from a few references in Increase Mather's diary
it is the only source for characterizations of Mather as a youth. See
"The Hazing of Cotton Mather: The Creation of a Biographical Personality," *In Defense of Historical Literature* (New York, 1967), pp.
37-45.

glorify Himself in His servant's earliest years, whose accomplishments were tokens of favor to a chosen instrument. Should his son be similarly chosen, to give eminent service and to speak to multitudes, he would be equally exposed to the temptations of vanity, "Applauding of myself" and "ambitious Affectation of Praeheminencies." So Mather attaches a marginal note to the original meditation: "In my Early Youth, and even at an age wherein [we?] see many [. . . ?] playing their Marbles or Wickers, with one another in the streets, I preached unto very Great Assemblies, and found Strange Respects among the people of God. I *fear'd,* (and thanks be to my Lord Jesus Christ that ever He struck me with such a Fear!) Lest a *Snare,* and a *Pitt* were by Satan prepar'd for such a *Novice!*" (p. 27.) As the work continues, however, Mather's editorial role diminishes. He sometimes addresses his son in a relatively lengthy paragraph, but the work of quoting from himself goes on for the most part without expansion or embellishment.

Deletions and verbal substitutions are slightly more numerous and perhaps more interesting. When Mather quotes a prayer for divine acceptance, but deletes its final sentence, "Lord, Thou art my Aim, and my all, and my *exceeding great Reward"* (D, 1, 22; P, 33), does he fear that his son will find the sentence presumptuous of what the prayer seeks? There seems little profit in such questions, which already betray one's suspicions about Mather. The prayer, as it appears in the *Diary,* is after all a composition based on a previous experience rather than the literal record of an historical speech. It is therefore subject to revision on the same principles that guided its composition. Minus the last sentence, the prayer ends more forcefully (*"O the Power, the Wisdome, the Grace and the Truth of the great*

Jehovah!") and focuses the son's attention on the object of devotion rather than on his father's personal remark.

One is also curious to know why Mather begins copying a paragraph at its second sentence rather than with the first, which read: "Thus the Holy Spirit of God, most mercifully discovered somewhat of the Possession, which Hee had long since taken of mee" (*D*, 1, 37; *P*, 36). The discrepancy might be used to demonstrate that, embarrassed by his son's presence, Mather suppressed a spiritual smugness that he nevertheless felt; yet, the damaging evidence is drawn from the diaries, which were also intended to be viewed by posterity. If Mather had a habit of self-serving revision, it began almost at the point of perception itself, and its motives and methods must also have been concealed in records that precede what we read as the *Diary*. Both phenomena are now inaccessible.

II

The principle that governed Cotton Mather as he selected from his past experience and from its already selective recording in the diaries is explicitly stated and uniformly observed in the "Paterna." He would write no more of his life, he told his son, "than what may just serve as a *Direction* to *yours*. . . . It may be, the *Things*, which the Lord has helped me to *See*, and to *Do*, are some of those *Talents*, which I should Improve unto His glory; and I know not, how to make a better improvement of them, than to leave with you, *my dear son*, such of them as may be your perpetual monitors" (p. 2). In one sense, it seems, Puritan autobiography has only found a new way to be impersonal when a father can leave his son neither possessions nor expressions of feeling, but only *Things*, *Talents*, and with definitive finality, *monitors*. However, when Mather first saw the good he might do his son by making him "a small collection

167

of *Paralipomena*, under the Head of *Methods of pressing after Piety*," he could not yet have established a highly personal relationship with a one-year-old boy.[10] The absence from "Paterna" of details better suited to the popular and sentimental picture of the autobiographical father is understandable on this basis alone. Even after 185 pages of manuscript, about half the total, the son's tender age is evident in Mather's uncertainty "whether I may Live to see you capable of taking in my *Verbal Discourses* on such points as these, or, whether you may be capable of *Reading with understanding* what I have written for you, until I shall be taken from all opportunities of any *Verbal Discourse* with you" (pp. 185-186).

The urgency Mather felt in his autobiographical responsibility to his son cannot be fully sensed in the work itself, but it can be inferred from his beginning to write in the child's infancy, from our knowledge of how keenly Mather felt the necessity of raising up a new godly generation, and from the fact that in July 1700 Increase, or Cressy, was the only surviving son of eight children born to Abigail and Cotton Mather. Later, when Cressy's loss at sea concluded a life Mather had already given up as unpleasing to a sovereign God, though he labored at convincing himself and Cressy otherwise, emotion came to the surface. While the diaries refer frequently to Cressy, the "Paterna," originally meant for him, contains no reflection of his wayward career until Mather's hand is seen writing over a passage he had addressed to Cressy, in which he described his prayers for

10 In July 1700, the date of this *Diary* entry (I, 356), Mather's son Increase was a year old. Recently published, Mather's diary for 1712 contains entries referring specifically to Increase as the son for whom "Paterna" was originally intended. See *The Diary of Cotton Mather, D.D., F.R.S., for the Year 1712*, ed. William R. Manierre II (Charlottesville, 1964), p. 9.

him at the time of his birth. The third person is substituted for direct address ("A Son" rather than "You") ; "my consort" replaces "your mother"; and at the end of a passage recalling the night of Cressy's birth, Mather has lined out the sentence that concludes, "I received a wonderful Advice from Heaven, that this my Son, shall bee a servant of my Lord Jesus Christ throughout eternal Ages" (p. 186).[11] Mather then turns to his remaining son Samuel, just eighteen, whose great promise was evident in the M.A. conferred on him in the year of his older brother's death: "But tho' this were a son of Great *Hopes*, and One whom Thousands and Thousands of *Prayers*, were Employ'd for him; yett, after all, a Sovereign God would not accept of him. He was Buried in the *Atlantick* Ocean. And you my only Son, Surviving, are the person for whom these Memorials are intended and reserved" (p. 187). At this point, too, Mather abandons his laborious attempt to follow his spiritual life chronologically and developmentally through five-year periods. Nothing else in the contents or tone of remaining pages of the manuscript remotely suggests the change in audience. For the purposes of the work, *My Son* remains the same person throughout.

Mather did not always think restrictively of the "Paterna's" usefulness. He could speak of it as intended for all his children: "I would take one of the First Opportunities to record after what manner I have Spent my Sabbath; and from thence transfer it into my *Paterna*, that mine also may go and do Likewise."[12] His diary for 1712 also records an intention to transfer the most notable of his "many Projections, to improve in Piety" from his diary to the "Paterna," "that I may often peruse them, and by the pe-

---

[11] This report stands, however, in the *Diary*, I, 307.
[12] *The Diary of Cotton Mather for the Year 1712*, p. 63.

rusal thereof imprint them on my memory."[13] A year earlier, he had considered leaving the manuscript with his brother-in-law, Nehemiah Walter: "It may sensibly assist him to discharge his Ministry, and improve in experimental Christianity" (*D*, II, 68). It is not clear what dreadful result Mather hoped to avoid in preserving the anonymity of "Paterna"—he resolved to preserve "Modesty and Concealment" in conveying it to Mr. Walter—but by separating his identity from his methods to improve in piety he gained for his work the advantage of broad usefulness and adaptability.

III

Finally, when all questions have been asked regarding Mather's hopes for the work, there remain those questions which must be asked of it as autobiography. Perhaps the idea of a speaker and an audience must now be set aside, since the one is anonymous and the other is isolated much less distinctly than the dedication suggests. It is also possible that speaker and audience are one and the same in Cotton Mather, who begins to speak before his son can hear him and who rarely takes notice of his audience save in exclamation ("Gett good by what I tell you!") and at the time of its loss and replacement. If the terms speaker and audience are irrelevant to the rhetorical situation of "Paterna," however, Mather's own terms are not. In his most explicit comment on the subject, he indicated the relation he wished to establish between his autobiography and his son: "My Son *Increase*, I will now have to set by me especially on the Lords-day Evenings; and Read over to me, first the *Paterna* I have written for him; and Such other things as may be

13 *Ibid.*, p. 6. The same intention was recorded in 1721, *Diary*, II, 603.

most Suitable to him; and make them the Arguments of my most Winning Discourses with him."[14]

It would soon be evident that the argument of "Paterna" was unimpressive to Increase, but Mather's expression of hope for its success supplies additional evidence, if any is needed, of his enormous confidence in the power of the written word to change men's hearts. His son's salvation will depend not so much on those closet interviews of the diary record—in which a boy could be reduced to piety in an overwhelming if temporary victory—but on the winning discourse of a mere manuscript. The self-evident objective of the argument is stated at times in the bluntest terms: "Study and Contrive, as early as you can *To Do Good.*" The argument takes on complication only in its strategy, "that you may not only come to be inspired and inflamed with such Desires, but also be directed, how to *gett* the Desires accomplished" (p. 173). For Cotton Mather it is plain, as it was not to Anne Bradstreet, nor so clearly to Thomas Shepard, that the success of the autobiographical argument depends upon the brilliance of the successes that compose it. As in the *Autobiography* of Increase Mather, evidences of divine favor are intended to stimulate the reader to those acts which God has promised to favor. The difference between father and son in this respect lies in Cotton Mather's great consciousness that his experience can be fashioned to inspirational uses. Whereas in the *Diary* Mather can be seen making pointed requests of heaven and noting the reply in detail, in the "Paterna" he has eliminated details, not only to conceal his identity, but to emphasize the fact of a successful petition over its circumstances. The more "Marvellous and Amazing" the answers to his prayers, and the more inspiring the faith that offered them up, the more

[14] *The Diary of Cotton Mather for the Year 1712*, p. 9.

trustworthy his benefactor. "It is Enough, if I tell you, the Answers have been to Encourage you, *My Son*, unto the Intentions and petitions, as I have thus taught you, to become Serviceable in your Generation" (p. 141).

More frequently accused of vanity than his father, Cotton Mather is also more aware of an inherent vanity in the role of autobiographical exemplar. The "Astonishing Things" done for him in a three-day fast might more discreetly have been buried in his private papers "as I have done many others. I had found conflict in my own Spirit, whether I should have related this or no; Lest there should be some Vanity in the Relation. But the Hope of being useful to you has carried it" (p. 212). It is easy enough to imagine that Mather took pleasure in this duty, but with the labor of his extensive copy work before us, it is no more difficult to take him at his word. He is intent on "winning discourse" and cannot disdain his strongest weapons.

Once, in the opening pages of "Paterna," Mather is forced to reconsider his father's early consignment of him to heaven on the basis, apparently, of intuitive evidence: "Indeed, your Grandfather, tho' he were a wise and a strict parent, would from the observation of some Dispositions in me, comfort himself with an opinion of my being *Sanctified by the Holy Spirit of God, in my very infancy*" (p. 3). The passage blushes momentarily with pleasure before Mather recovers the topic of original sin, protesting that his father had not seen "the instances of my *going astray*, even while I was yet an *Infant*." The protest seems excessive, granting even the most extraordinary opportunities, but it may be the very unlikelihood of his father's characterization that forces him into self-characterization that is equally dubious. Mather's confusion, and his delicate chiding of his father, "usually a wise and strict parent," bespeak a sense of the inappropriateness of beginning his autobiographical argument with an image of himself that was not imitable. He could not tell his son to get himself sanctified in infancy. Even those refinements of the psychology of the elect, which have come to characterize the total contents of Mather's *Diary*, his reports of visitation by angels—"I have my own Angel, who is a better Friend unto me, than any I have upon Earth" (*D*, I, 479; *P*, 211)—and of personal revelations which Mather called "particular faiths"[15] are presented in the "Paterna" as indirectly attainable. With his father,[16] Mather believed that the scriptural role of angels was to deliver men from evil and to convey blessings and benefits —Providence made personal. All those effects which Thomas Shepard would in his ultimate view of things have ascribed to Providence—"Directing my Studies, Assisting my Labours, preventing of Wrong Steps which I have been just ready to take"—as well as the conveyance of particular faiths, Mather sees more immediately as the ministry of angels to one whom Providence has blessed.

If Providence made a closer approach to man in angelic intermediaries, Mather could also tell his son how man could attain the environs of God's providential will: "While you and your opportunities are but Small, Invent as many

15 A marginal note, written "several years" after Mather had described his particular faiths as infallible, records his bafflement at their failure in "one or two considerable Things." (The death of his first wife was one.) Mather cautions his son against delusions and enthusiasms and asks him to be content with *"the ordinary satisfactions of praying and waiting."* Still, the experience yields an exemplary figure, chosen "on purpose" to be humbled as a warning against vain delusions. "Paterna," p. 125.

16 See the passages quoted from Increase Mather's *Disquisition Concerning Angelical Apparitions* (Boston, 1696), in Thomas J. Holmes, *Increase Mather: A Bibliography* (Cleveland, 1931), I, 14. After defining the duties of angels, Mather warns, "Many pretenders to a conversation with Angels, and to a Spirit or Gift of Prophecy, have been great cheats." *Ibid.*, p. 16.

ways to *Do Good,* as ever you can. . . . But Begin Betimes
with your *Little Talents*: It may be; the Lord will Do *Great
Things* for you, and by you, before He hath done." (p. 14)

Notwithstanding the concession of "may be," and
Mather's regular allusions to the "Sovereign Grace of
Heaven," the overwhelming tendency of "Paterna," with so
much of its space occupied by "contrivances," is to make
Providence the handmaiden of a methodically attainable
piety. "Such Things, they may be done: I tell you, they have
been done" (p. 257). A father's autobiographical duties
were exhausted when he had assembled from his experience
the astonishing things done for him by God, things desirable beyond attainment, almost, and when he then made
available from his private reserves the contrivances by which
those desires could be accomplished. The rest, admittedly,
was in the hands of Providence.

I V

Mather's notorious devices for improving any occasion—
when "emptying the *Cistern of Nature*" or in an unlikely
idle interval—are familiar enough from the *Diary*,[17] but
these are only the most vivid examples of a habit that is
equally vigorous in attaining both secular and spiritual
ends. The same flair for economy informs Mather's report
that as a student he "did kill Two Birds with one Stone"
by making articles of natural philosophy the ingredients
of his declamatory exercises (p. 5), and his observation to
his son that if a prayer "did not obtain for my Neighbours,
the Blessings which I thus asked for them, I should obtain
them for *myself*: the prayers would not be Lost" (p. 65). The
logic of both anecdotes, pragmatic in form if not intention,

---

[17] See *Diary,* I, 81-84 and 357. Some of the same material appears
in "Paterna," pp. 55-56.

recommends the particular economy for its desirable result. In his methods, Mather offers his son the promise of gaining a kind of dominance over time and circumstance. The Matherian "contrivance" has this ideal as its motive power, whatever the nature of the object.

Even a lesson on resignation to Providence allows an inference that the determinations of Providence are subject to repeal. Describing his settlement in his father's congregation to a son he no doubt thought would also be called to the ministry, Mather recalls disapprovingly ("I had yett but *Little Grace*") his reluctance to accept, as his father recommended, an invitation to a "Small and mean Congregation." At last, the "terrible Difficulties and Humiliations, of Leaving all my Friends, and Leading an obscure Life among the poor Husbandmen" were overcome by an ardent prayer of submission, proclaiming a readiness to serve the Lord in any place—with the result that "it was not Long before the Lord called me to Serve Him, in as great a place, as any in these parts of the world . . ." (p. 20). In the lesson of resignation, "Therefore, *my son*, become *As a weaned child*, . . ." Mather's "therefore" implies all that has ever been said on the unlikely Puritan marriage of the profit motive and the profitable virtue of deadness to the world. There is no necessary confusion of doctrine in a prayer which begins by characterizing the speaker as a "poor Firebrand of Hell, worthy to be confounded forever," and that concludes by promising, "And when I come to heaven, *whither I am certainly assured, that I shall be, brought,* I will admire thee with Eternal Praises" (p. 16). The prayer testifies stunningly to the freedom and mercy of grace, as blind to depravity as it is beyond desert. Almost as strongly, it suggests a causal relation between promulgating a readiness to accept failure and being delivered from failure. Here, too,

Mather gets two birds with one stone, an economy that extends to the entire autobiography.

Two arguments run through the single work. Addressed to Mather's son, "Paterna" argues the gloriousness of God's favor, the sweetness of his pious service, by reference to an exemplary figure whose experience guarantees the Lord's trustworthiness and the contrivances by which He may be approached. But when the speaker is alone with the sound of his own voice, the same evidence acquires another significance, justifying his fitness for exemplary purposes. In the first argument the exemplar's faith and methods are recommended by their eminent and virtually unvarying success. In the second argument, the success of the exemplar is an open question. Not his standing among the saints, but his very salvation is at issue. The first argument is built upon what most readers of Mather's *Diary* have seen (it is there to be seen): the man's immense confidence in himself as heaven's darling. The second argument is prompted by doubts whose profundity and extent can be only guessed at, but which would have smelled sufficiently of brimstone to horrify a more consistent Arminian than Cotton Mather. Taken together, the *Diary* and "Paterna" seem to exhaust their subject matter many times over; but Mather was well aware that a man's spiritual life is not co-extensive with its written records, though he sometimes wrote as if it were. A wealth of solace awaited him had he been able to convince himself that his lost son's spiritual life and his devotional, perhaps autobiographical, papers were perfectly correspondent: "But, the Soul of the Child! If the Papers which he left in my Hands were sincere and His Heart wrote with his pen, all is well!" The possibility slips away even as Mather attempts to justify his optimism as piety: "Would not my GOD have me to hope so?" (*D*, ii, 753).

The contrariety of these two arguments sends a reader back to Mather's version of the core of Puritan spirituality, the conversion experience. Mather's account takes up only about three manuscript pages, and it is sandwiched between his treatment of two other important matters: a description of the methods of his academic work, and an account of his leadership of a society of young men which gathered to discuss a "Devout Question" each week. The passage begins conventionally. About the time he entered college, Mather recalls, his "diverse miscarriages" convinced him that he never "experienced any more than some *common works* of His Holy Spirit," which meant that he was no more than a "Refined Hypocrite" (pp. 5-6). The nearly fatal disease that attacked so many Puritan adolescents awakens Mather to terrible suspicions of his spiritual estate. As he tells it, Mather not only feared damnation, but also feared being known as damned to those who had thought better of him. "I Trembled, when I thought, that after I had *Hop'd well* of myself, & many Servants of God had *Spoke well* of me, I should be a *Castaway* after all." The question God forced him to consider with "particular urgency" was, " 'How shall I be able to Look my own Father in the Face at the Day of Judgment!' " (p. 6)

Sermons promising mercy to sinners affect him "wonderfully"; but doubts and fears return until he decides to ask his father whether Christ will accept " 'a Vile wretch, that hath been and hath done, as I have!' " His father's lengthy reply, which Mather quotes in full, made the point that while a sinner is abhorrent to a holy man, " 'if the Vile Sinner ever comes to be converted,' " he is clasped to the bosom of the man who had earlier rejected him. " 'This' (he said) 'is an Emblem and Effect of the Spirit of the Lord Jesus Christ.' " Mather felt immediate relief: "I shall never *for-*

get how much those words did *Quicken* me! In my Addresses
to Heaven under the Exercises of my mind, about my *Reconciliation* to God, I now sometimes received Strange,
and Strong, and Sweet Intimations, That I was accepted
of the Lord" (p. 7). There follows next a characteristic report of assurance through application of a scriptural promise to himself and a description of his final deliverance from
melancholy when he had cast the burden of his sins "on the
care of the Lord Jesus Christ." Deliverance began though
with his father's proclamation that veteran saints respond
to the holiness of a gracious man as the Spirit had responded to his repentance. What Mather has proposed as
the source of his greatest potential shame—the high opinion of him, surely excessive, which was held by the servants
of God and corroborated by his father—becomes first a
consoling reflection of God's mercy, then an evidence of
grace.

Mather's self-examination thus finds its most solid evidence outside the self, and lacks both the specialized terminology of stages common in seventeenth-century narratives
and the close psychological scrutiny of the enthusiastic autobiography, largely an eighteenth-century phenomenon in
America. A portion of Mather's testimony may resemble
a passage from Jonathan Edwards' *Personal Narrative*:
"and from that minute I was so much altered by a New
Light, and *Life* and Ease arriving in me, as the Sunrise does
change the world, from the condition of *Midnight*" (p. 8);
but it is not characteristic of the sequence, much less of the
"Paterna" as a whole. Mather's treatment of an experience
of divine revelation asserts the fact of the experience and
lavishes superlatives on that fact; but the content of the
experience usually lies obscured behind Mather's highly
generalized language. He remembers himself "raised with

more than ordinary Delights and Raptures" during a day of secret thanksgiving, yet these emotions have no specific object. Carried to "the very *Suburbs of Heaven*," he has "Glorious Things" revealed to him, but the details of revelation are not forthcoming. Spiritual writers frequently plead the impossibility of conveying directly "the Communications of Heaven." Mather's plea, however, is not accompanied by the search for an appropriate analogy. Attention to such a task would imply an interest in imparting a certain content of spiritual knowledge to his son. Mather does not depict his experience so as to illuminate the manner of the Spirit's dealing with His chosen ones but to demonstrate the Spirit's presence from the evidence of His infallible tokens—in short an argument designed less for the instruction of the son than for the reassurance of the father. Mather's autobiography adopts its own recommendation: "Thus I was (while an ignorant youth) Strangely led on by the *Spirit* of the most High, to go the whole work of conversion often over and over again. And, tho' at the Beginning of a Day Sett apart for such Devotions, I should ever tremble in the Thoughts of the *Travail* that I foresaw I should pass thro' yet I comforted myself, that my frequent Renewing of that Action, would be my Assuring of it." (p. 22)[18]

Having once reduced the ancient tension between theologies of faith and works into the homespun axiom, "A Workless Faith is a Worthless Faith" (*Faith at Work*, 1697), Mather proceeds to demonstrate the worth of his faith by assembling its concrete effects from his diaries. There was sufficient ambiguity, however, in his use of the

---

[18] The same pattern is evident in a later passage: the sign makes present the reality; the effect implies the cause to which it is invisibly linked. "It presently darted into my mind, That if I could be willing to *Dy*, for *Deliverance from Sin*, this was an Infallible Token and Effect of my claim to the Benefits of my *SAVIOURS Death*" (p. 320).

PURITAN SPIRITUAL NARRATIVES

term "worthless" to leave certain problems unsettled for the autobiographer. Did "worthless" mean illusory, non-existent, or did it merely describe a faith that had borne little fruit, implying the possibility and desirability of improvement? Could the writer of spiritual autobiography ever compile enough evidence of a working faith to obviate the necessity of returning to the foundation of it all, "often over and over again," to make certain that it was still there?

Mather's treatise, *Faith at Work*, distinguishes the emphases of Paul on faith and of James on works by pointing out that while Paul speaks of man's justification before God, "*James* treats of that which may manifest our *Justification* unto *men* that See and Hear, our Profession of our Faith; and here Works are significant."[19] Men, then, are more easily impressed than God by good works, but Cotton Mather, studying his own case, is not finally among their number. Unquestionably, he rejoiced at times to see spread before him on the pages of "Paterna" what *Faith at Work* describes as "the proper and Genuine Symptoms of Believers." But the manuscript would have been briefer, notwithstanding his duty to his son, and Mather's interior life more serene, if dealing as he did in good works numbered and dated he could always have thought of salvation quantitatively. Then there could have been an end to his argument.

As an exemplary bequest to posterity, "Paterna" supplies a model of the incessant desire to do good and of constant inventiveness in methods to achieve piety; but Mather is also his own audience, consenting to his own argument, when he exclaims that only gracious piety could account for these phenomena. A heaven-sent conviction, "powerful and *Refreshing*" enough to be entered in both the *Diary* and

19 *Faith at Work* (Boston, 1697), p. 5. The essay was published anonymously, but Samuel Mather attributed it to his father.

180

"Paterna," is premise and conclusion of Mather's torturously circular argument: "Surely, if the Lord intended not forever to glorify mee in Heaven, He would never have putt it into my Heart, that I should seek to glorify Him on Earth" (*D*, 1, 24; *P*, 26-27).

CHAPTER SIX

JONATHAN EDWARDS AND THE

NARRATIVE OF CONVERSION

Probably no Puritan autobiography is better known to students of American literature than the *Personal Narrative* of Jonathan Edwards. It is often the sole representative of its category in anthologies of this period, and readers encountering it for the first time are asked to seek among its outlandishly historical emotions the ancestors of vital elements in later American writing. Edwards' narrative is indeed a useful point of departure for discussing, say, American writers biassed in favor of the heart, but it cannot well represent all Puritan autobiography and may tend to misrepresent earlier spiritual narratives. Comparison of the evangelistic theology of Thomas Shepard and Edwards yields more points of resemblance than would a like consideration of their autobiographies.[1]

Several misconceptions result from an identification of all Puritan autobiography with Edwards' narrative. The communal sense of the earlier autobiographies could not be assumed from a work whose most striking characteristic is its apparent solitariness. It is not addressed to posterity in gen-

[1] Shepard's nineteenth-century editor and biographer, J. A. Albro, pointed out that of "one hundred and thirty-two quotations from all authors" in Edwards' *Treatise Concerning Religious Affections*, "upwards of seventy-five are from Mr. Shepard." Quoted in "Editor's Introduction," *A Treatise Concerning Religious Affections*, ed. John E. Smith (New Haven, 1959), p. 54.

eral or to Jonathan Edwards, Jr., in particular, and it is silent as to its purposes and the occasion of its composition. While there is some mention of persons—"my father," "the Smiths"—and places—New Haven and New York—it seems for the most part a soliloquy begun and concluded abruptly on an empty stage. Edwards' analysis of his spiritual experience finally involves the community by its instructiveness, even to the extent that his public purpose at times seems ascendant over his personal need for the analysis. But the text itself differs in many respects from earlier spiritual narratives.

Most importantly, the *Personal Narrative* is set apart from its predecessors by its exclusive attention to the work of grace in the soul. It is misleading to describe early Puritan autobiographies as narratives of conversion. Most of those we have seen allot only brief space to such an account and tend to see regeneration as a part, central to be sure, of a man's total relation to God, which man also attempts to define by considering the role of Providence in his experience. It may well be that the early requirement of an account of conversion for church membership inculcated a distinction between an institutional autobiography concerned with the mechanics of conversion and a more personal and inclusive examination of one's spiritual estate.

Elizabeth White's *Experiences of God's Gracious Dealing*

In view of the distinction between institutional and personal autobiography, it is interesting that Elizabeth White's *Experiences*, written around 1660,[2] diverge from the usual

2 The subtitle gives 1669 as the year of Mrs. White's death, and she describes herself as unconverted before her marriage in 1657. *The*

seventeenth-century pattern in order to revise testimony originally given for church membership. Having some "notional Knowledge" of what was required, and "indifferently well satisfied" with her condition, Elizabeth White recalls, she had satisfied her examiner without difficulty, "and so unwoorthy I went to the Lord's table" (p. 4). Later, she discovered her great sinfulness: "I thought I had a Heart worse than the Devil, and wondered that I was not consumed in some strange Manner" (p. 6). Good works no longer give consolation, and she begins to doubt her election until she enters a plea for mercy by throwing herself "upon Christ Jesus that sure Foundation." Mrs. White's narrative was not published until 1741. In the time of the Great Awakening it may have been hoped that many would profit from her exemplary discovery of the difference between the notion and the experience of grace. Perhaps the narrative owes its publication to Thomas Prince, the annalist who printed a portion of Shepard's diary (in *Three Valuable Pieces*, 1747) and brought Roger Clap's *Memoirs* to light, and who as "chief intelligencer of revival news,"[3] hoped to extend the work of the Spirit through publicity. In this, Prince followed the recommendation of Jonathan Edwards, who had observed in his *Faithful Narrative* of the 1735 conversions in Northampton: "There is no one thing that I know of which God has made such a means of promoting his work amongst us, as the news of others' conversion." The *Experiences* of Elizabeth White would have made very good news indeed in 1741, but they would also have illustrated, especially to Edwards, the hazards and di-

---

Experiences of God's Gracious Dealings with Mrs. Elizabeth White: As they were written under her own Hand, and found in her Closet after her Decease, December 5, 1669 (Boston, 1741).

[3] C. C. Goen, *Revivalism and Separatism in New England, 1740-1800* (New Haven, 1962), p. 34.

lemmas of the narrative of regeneration—and at about the same time he composed his own.

Amidst the emotional excesses of the Great Awakening, a skilled examiner might have questioned closely a number of Mrs. White's expressions and experiences. Jonathan Edwards suspected evocations of depravity which relied on trite allusions to Satan, though he might have appreciated better Mrs. White's comparison of herself to a spider, "which of all Things is most loathsome to me," or to "a Wolf chained up which keeps its Nature still." As a member of a generation that prided itself on its vigilance against enthusiasm, Mrs. White spoke guardedly of those experiences most subject to criticism. Satan appears in a passage protected by the qualifying phrase, "finding myself much distempered in my Head," and the narrator never claims more than, "I thought Satan stood before me . . . but still thought I saw Satan laughing at me because I had no sleep . . ." (pp. 11-12). Nevertheless, Mrs. White chooses to qualify her memories rather than reject them entirely. Her most affecting experience was admittedly a dream (she climbs a ladder to heaven), yet its residual emotions are indistinguishable from those associated with saving grace: "I was filled with inexpressible Joy, earnestly longing to be Dissolved, and to be with Christ. . . ." She takes the assurance proffered her in the dream as seriously as she takes its prediction of her death in childbed.[4]

Autobiographers recording God's providential mercies faced no similar problem of selection, because for them all events were subsumed under the common or particular providence by which God governed the world. Elizabeth White's purpose is no different from Thomas Shepard's or

[4] The editor notes: "Which accordingly came to pass about twelve years after her Marriage." (p. 13)

Roger Clap's in desiring to "treasure up the Experiences which I have had of God's Goodness to me," but her treasures are exclusively internal and ineffable and potentially ambiguous in their origin. It would be left for Jonathan Edwards to achieve the delicate autobiographical balance between ecstatic praise of God's gracious mercy and the stern exclusion of all that came from mere nature.

Elizabeth White's *Experiences* foreshadow another common dilemma of the conversion narrative—the tendency toward mechanized and obtrusively technical discussions of grace in a narrative that professes to have its source in spontaneous and immediate experience. These autobiographies are distinguished by their greater sensitivity and more exclusive attention to the emotions as the locus of grace. Yet the narrator is aware of his awareness, and makes a point of comparing the rigorous criteria he employs as he writes and the lenient standards of the period when he was ignorant of himself. Mrs. White scorns her "notional Knowledge" as Jonathan Edwards recalls the easy and instinctive piety of his youth. Nathan Cole declares in the first sentence of his "Spiritual Travels" that he was an Arminian until he was thirty: "I intended to be saved by my own works such as prayers & good deeds." In his *Sketches* of his life, Samuel Hopkins, the theological disciple of Edwards, recalls with horror that as a young man he had been led to agree with several "gross Arminians," allowing conversion to consist "chiefly in externals."

Equally common in these autobiographies is the narrator's assertion that he did not identify his conversion when it took place, but only in retrospect. "I had not then the least thought or suspicion that what I had experienced was conversion or anything like it," recalls Samuel Hopkins, for the actual experience had differed much from the idea he had formed of conversion. "And by degrees, I ceased to recollect anything of them, hoping and looking for something greater and better, and of quite a different kind." Nathan Cole quotes himself to the same effect: "What, is this Conversion; I do not know; this is a new way I never thought of being Converted so; I had laid out a way in my mind how I should be converted if ever I was, but this is a way I never thought of before." In both examples, the autobiographer suggests that his previous ignorance was at least corroborative evidence of grace, whose authentic presence would crowd out technical self-awareness, as romantic love displaces clinical reflection on hormonal processes.

The question of what stance the autobiographer will adopt toward his past self or selves confronts all autobiographers, but it is a particularly serious question for the Puritan who narrates his conversion. With his pilgrimage through the deceits of the heart nearly complete, he is expert where the pilgrim was ignorant, composed and steady of view where the pilgrim was inconstant and vacillating in his self-regard. But as the narrator puts on knowledge and becomes more overtly a technician of grace, his work is likely to take on the abstract rigidity of a text on conversion (Mrs. White mentions Shepard's *Sincere Convert*). If, however, the narrator's difficulties approach those of the pilgrim, his autobiography ceases to be exemplary and may even become a dangerous guide. This is the dilemma confronting Jonathan Edwards in the *Personal Narrative*, against which the measure of his autobiographical achievement must be taken.

Jonathan Edwards' *Personal Narrative*

Although the first editor of Jonathan Edwards' *Personal Narrative* described this spiritual autobiography as written for "private Advantage," he also seems to have felt that Edwards had given him implicit permission to make the document serve a public purpose. The sometimes baffling resemblance between authentic and fraudulent spirituality was, said Samuel Hopkins, "a point about which, above many other[s], the protestant world is in the dark, and needs instruction, as Mr. Edwards was more and more convinced, the longer he lived; and which he was wont frequently to observe in conversation."[5] As Hopkins was aware, Edwards' essential act throughout a large body of his published work had been to set nature apart from supernature in the domain of religious experience. The act was no less central to the *Personal Narrative* than it was to other works in which Edwards promoted experimental religion and instructed readers on its glories and pitfalls.

In the controversy between himself and opposers of the Great Awakening, Edwards had put to good use his accounts of the gracious experience of Abigail Hutchinson, Phebe Bartlett, and his own wife, Sarah. But a narrative told in the first person, as Sarah's had been originally,[6] was immensely more valuable to his cause than even the best job of evangelistic reporting. Let the reporter be a "true saint," said Edwards, still he can only judge "outward manifestations and appearances," a method "at best uncertain, and liable to deceit."[7] No such objection could have been

[5] *The Life and Character of the Late Reverend Mr. Jonathan Edwards* (Boston, 1765), p. iii.

[6] *The Works of President Edwards: With a Memoir of his Life*, ed. Sereno E. Dwight (New York, 1829-1830), I, 171-186; hereafter cited as *Works*. Sarah's original relation was drawn up, according to Dwight, at the request of her husband. Edwards then retold her experiences as part of his attempt to vindicate experimental religion in *Some Thoughts Concerning the Present Revival of Religion* (*Works*, IV, 110-118).

[7] *A Treatise Concerning Religious Affections*, ed. John E. Smith (New Haven, 1959), p. 181.

made against his *Account* of the life of David Brainerd, in which Edwards allowed the Indian missionary's diary to speak for itself. A reader's view of "what passed in [Brainerd's] *own heart*" would thus be cleared of such obstacles as an impercipient narrator; yet the reader would be in the hands of a perfectly reliable guide. As a student, Brainerd may have been rash in remarking that one of his Yale tutors had "no more grace than this chair," but Edwards could only praise the discretion he revealed when considering "the various exercises of *his own mind*": "He most accurately distinguished between real, solid piety, and enthusiasm; between those affections that are rational and scriptural—having their foundation in light and judgment—and those that are founded in whimsical conceits, strong impressions on the imagination, and vehement emotions of the animal spirits."[8] In the *Personal Narrative* Edwards had performed exactly those functions for which in 1749 he was praising Brainerd. Both men gave their readers, as Edwards said of Brainerd, an "opportunity to see a confirmation of the truth, efficacy, and amiableness of the religion taught, in the practice of the same persons who have most clearly and forcibly taught it."[9]

Because Edwards could not have introduced his own autobiography in such glowing terms, Samuel Hopkins admiringly supplied the deficit in 1765. But set next to the cautious distinction-making of the narrative itself, his words were superfluous. Since the manuscript of the *Personal Narrative* is lost, we shall never know just how much care Edwards took in composing it. In fact, the text printed by Hopkins gives the appearance of hurried writing.[10] But if

[8] From Edwards' "Preface" to the *Account* of Brainerd's life, "chiefly taken from his own diary and other Private Writings," *Works*, x, 29.
[9] *Works*, x, 27.
[10] Although anthologies of American literature continue to repro-

Edwards spent only a day with his spiritual autobiography, he had spent twenty years or more arriving at the criteria by which he judged his experience. It is possible, of course, that we read precision back into the *Personal Narrative* after watching Edwards at work in, say, the *Treatise Concerning Religious Affections,* but the distinction between autobiography and formal argument, especially for an eighteenth-century New England divine, should not be exaggerated. Edwards' narrative is not identical with his spiritual experience but represents a mature articulation of that experience, its form and language determined in varying degrees by the author's reading of sacred and secular writers, interviews with awakened sinners, and his concerns at the time of composition. The Edwards of the *Personal Narrative* bears more resemblance to the author of the *Religious Affections* than to the young student at Yale who entered the perplexing data of daily spiritual upheavals in his diary.[11]

---

duce the *Personal Narrative* from the Austin (Worcester, 1808) or Dwight editions, the text printed by Hopkins in his 1765 *Life* of Edwards is clearly preferable. As was their habit, the nineteenth-century editors "improved" Edwards' style and also omitted several important passages. All my references are to the Hopkins text, but it is beyond the scope of this study to call attention to all the omissions and revisions of later editions. The indications in the Hopkins text of relatively hasty composition are: (1) the number of sentences lacking a pronominal subject ("On one Saturday Night, in particular, had a particular Discovery . . ."), more than appear in later editions; (2) redundancy of a sort that invites improvement and that Edwards himself might have revised had he taken a second look ("my Concern that I had," or the phrase just quoted). If Edwards intended to make the manuscript more fit for posthumous publication, he apparently never found time to do so.

11 It is very doubtful that the *Personal Narrative* was written after the *Religious Affections* appeared in 1746, but it might conceivably have been written as Edwards prepared a series of sermons given in 1742-1743, on which the *Religious Affections* is based. The only absolute certainty, of course, is that he did not conclude the narrative before January 1739, the date he mentions in its final paragraph.

Edwards set down his spiritual autobiography with more than "private advantage" in mind, then, and he seems in fact to have been governed by the purposes that informed most of his work during the period of the Great Awakening. By narrative example he will teach what is false and what is true in religious experience, giving another form to the argument he carried on elsewhere; and he hopes to affect his readers by both the content and the presentation of his exemplary experience.

I

Something of what Edwards was trying to accomplish in the *Personal Narrative* emerges from a comparison with the *Diary*, which he kept regularly from the last year of his studies at Yale until his settlement in Northampton. The two are profitably read together, but not as if they formed a continuous and coherent piece of writing. A sense of their separate identities is necessary, not only because the *Diary* instructed Edwards alone, while the *Personal Narrative* extends and formalizes its instruction, but also because Edwards was bound to tell his story differently after twenty additional years of introspection and a good deal of pastoral experience. In 1723, for instance, he was greatly troubled by "not having experienced conversion in those particular steps, wherein the people of New England, and anciently the Dissenters of Old England, used to experience it."[12] Subsequent events, however, revealed a great variety in the Spirit's operations, so that in 1741 Edwards allowed that a given work might be from the Spirit even though it represented a "deviation from what has hitherto been usual, let it be never so great."[13] He may even have reached by this

[12] *Works,* I, 93.
[13] *Works,* I, 93.

time the more radical conclusion announced in the *Religious Affections*, that although Satan can only counterfeit the Spirit's saving operations, he has power to imitate exactly the order in which they are supposed to appear (pp. 158-159). In any case, the *Personal Narrative* reveals no more brooding on Edwards' part over the absence of "particular steps."

matches Tracy

The *Diary* exhibits, in general, considerably more doubt, sometimes approaching despair, than could be inferred from an isolated reading of the *Personal Narrative*. Periods of spiritual crisis were marked by such tortured complaints as: "This week I found myself so far gone, that it seemed to me I should never recover more"; and "Crosses of the nature of that, which I met with this week, thrust me quite below all comforts in religion."[14] There are, in addition, all the entries in which, as a kind of running theme, Edwards agonizes over dead, dull, and listless frames of mind. The *Personal Narrative* reflects little of the intensity or number of these entries. Edwards mentions only that at New Haven he "sunk in Religion" as a result of being diverted by affairs; and in a subsequent paragraph he rounds off a similar recollection with the comment that these "various Exercises . . . would be tedious to relate" (pp. 32-33).

The difference between the two versions is striking, yet understandable, if we assume that as Edwards grew in his assurance of grace, these drier seasons lost, in recollection, their original impact. But since Edwards seems to have consulted his diary as he wrote ("And my Refuge and Support was in Contemplations on the heavenly State; as I find in my Diary of *May* 1, 1723") it is more likely that deletions and new emphases were intentional—the choice, for

[14] *Works*, III, 561.

192

example, to minimize emotions arising from dullness and insensibility in a narrative intended to be affecting. The lingering memory of his uncle Hawley's suicide in 1735 would certainly have enforced Edwards' decision: "He had been for a Considerable Time Greatly Concern'd about the Condition of his soul; till, by the ordering of a sovereign Providence he was suffered to fall into deep melancholly, a distemper that the Family are very Prone to; he was much overpowered by it; the devil took the advantage & drove him into despairing thoughts."[15]

Whatever the proximate reason, Edwards felt strongly enough about the dangers of melancholy to edit out any hint of it in the record of his conversion experience, just as in the preface to Brainerd's memoirs he forewarned readers that melancholy was the sole imperfection in an otherwise exemplary man, and just as in his *Thoughts* on the revival of 1740-1742 he excepted melancholy as the "one case, wherein the truth ought to be withheld from sinners in distress of conscience."[16] It was sufficient for readers to know that a Slough of Despond existed, the foul and miry byproduct, as John Bunyan explained, of conviction of sin. Nothing was to be gained, and much would be risked, by bringing on stage the youth who once found himself "overwhelmed with melancholy."[17]

Seen from another point of view, the youth of the *Diary* might by the very miserableness of his seeking illustrate an important lesson. The characteristic of the *Diary* which the author of the *Personal Narrative* apparently found most repugnant was its tendency toward spiritual self-reliance. For even as he reminded himself that effort was ineffectual

[15] *Jonathan Edwards: Representative Selections*, ed. Clarence Faust and Thomas Johnson (Rev. ed.; New York, 1962), p. 83.
[16] *Works*, IV, 163.
[17] Entry for Jan. 17, 1723, *Works*, I, 81.

without grace, the young diarist had also been busy drawing up his "resolutions," seventy of them eventually. In the *Personal Narrative*, Edwards reached back twenty years to untangle these cross-purposes, simplifying his experience somewhat as he fitted it for instruction. Spiritual industry could not be despised; its products were real and of value: "I was brought wholly to break off all former wicked Ways, and all Ways of known outward Sin." What had to be emphasized was that the sum of resolutions and bonds and religious duties was not salvation. Edwards spoke beyond the limits of his own case when he concluded, "But yet it seems to me, I sought after a miserable manner: Which has made me some times since to question, whether ever it issued in that which was saving; being ready to doubt, whether such miserable seeking was ever succeeded."[18]

II

While the pattern that emerges from Edwards' reshaping of some of the materials of his diary helps suggest the more formal, public nature of the autobiography, the later document represents in most ways a fresh beginning on the analysis of his spiritual experience. The first sentence of the *Personal Narrative* reveals Edwards' anxiety to get at major issues, prefacing the entire narrative with a declaration that nearly sums it up: "I Had a variety of Concerns and Exercises about my Soul from my Childhood; but had two more remarkable Seasons of Awakening, before I met with that Change, by which I was brought to those new Dispositions, and that new Sense of Things, that I have since had." A Northampton reader ought not to have

[18] Hopkins, *Life of Edwards*, p. 24. By deleting "was" from the final phrase of this sentence, editors after Hopkins also silenced the passive voice that reminded readers, however awkwardly, whence grace originates.

194

missed the distinctions being made, or the ascending order of importance in the three clauses. Certainly he would have known that in the 1735 awakening more than three hundred persons appeared to have been "savingly brought home to Christ," but that in the minister's *Faithful Narrative* of the work he had dismissed some as "wolves in sheep's clothing," while discovering in those for whom he was more hopeful "a new sense of things, new apprehensions and views of God, of the divine attributes." For the reader of shorter memory, who might have withdrawn from a battle he thought won at an early age, Edwards was ready at the end of the paragraph to deny that a boy who prayed five times a day in secret, who abounded in "religious Duties," and whose affections were "lively and easily moved" had anything of grace in him. He had already explained in "A Divine and Supernatural Light" (1734) that emotions raised by the story of Christ's sufferings or by a description of heaven might be no different in kind from those elicited by a tragedy or a romance.[19] And it was unnecessary to introduce psychology here, since the course of the narrative itself revealed the nature of these early affections. In time, Edwards says, they "wore off," and he "returned like a Dog to his Vomit." It was characteristic of Edwards not to hesitate in applying a text (Proverbs 26:11) to himself, but he may already have conceived an extended application for this simile. In 1746, after his last awakening had ebbed, he used the same expression in charging that persons "who seemed to be mightily raised and swallowed with joy and zeal, for a while, seem to have returned like the dog to his vomit."[20]

When Edwards testifies that a sickness so grave it seemed God "shook me over the Pit of Hell" had only a passing

[19] *Works*, VI, 175-176.
[20] *Religious Affections*, p. 119.

195

effect on resolution, the implication is undoubtedly both personal and general. The emotion aroused by this image could have no other name but terror, but at almost the same time that he preached "Sinners in the Hands of an Angry God" (1741), Edwards was disclosing that terror had been irrelevant in his own experience. Whatever moved him in his New Haven years, "it never seemed to be proper to express my Concern that I had, by the name of Terror" (p. 24). Thus an important distinction was laid down. The experience of terror gave no cause for self-congratulation, since there were persons, like the younger Edwards, "that have frightful apprehensions of hell . . . who at the same time seem to have very little proper enlightenings of conscience, really convincing them of their sinfulness of heart and life."[21]

Edwards' technique through the initial paragraphs of the *Personal Narrative* is to separate the "I" of the narrative from his present self and to characterize the younger "I" as a less reliable judge of spiritual experience than the mature narrator. Thus, Edwards the boy takes much "self-righteous" pleasure in his performance of religious duties, or Edwards the young man seeks salvation as the "main Business" of his life, unaware that his manner of seeking is "miserable." Soon the reader must adjust his attitude even more carefully, for the mature Edwards will begin to describe genuinely gracious experience, while the "I" remains largely ignorant of what has happened. Edwards compiles sufficient evidence for a reader to draw his own conclusions from the passage, but subordinates himself to the mind of a youth who was not yet ready to draw conclusions when he says, "But it never came into my Thought, that there was any thing spiritual, or of a saving Nature in this" (p. 25).

21 *Religious Affections*, p. 156.

One reason for so oblique an approach may be traced, not to the autobiographer's ignorance of his subject, but to the pastor's close acquaintance with the hypocrite, a brash, colloquial figure who appears often in the *Religious Affections,* drawn no doubt from models near at hand. That part of Edwards' purpose which was public and exemplary dictated that he give a wide margin to the "bold, familiar and appropriating language" of those who condemned themselves by announcing, " 'I know I shall go to heaven, as well as if I were there; I know that God is now manifesting himself to my soul, and is now smiling upon me' " (pp. 170-171). At the same time, Edwards remains faithful to personal experience, accurately reflecting the uncertainty and inconclusiveness he could see in his diary; and by preserving intact the uncertain young man, he provided a character with whom readers similarly perplexed could identify.

The evidence that counters and overwhelms the disclaimers attached to these paragraphs emerges from the history Edwards gives of his assent to the doctrine of God's sovereignty. Even after childhood, his mind, which was "full of Objections," and his heart, which found the doctrine "horrible," had struggled against accepting the notion that God in his sovereign pleasure should choose to save some and leave the rest to be "everlastingly tormented in Hell." Suddenly and inexplicably the objections had evaporated, but at the time Edwards found it impossible to describe "how, or by what Means." Only the effects were clear: "I saw further, and my Reason apprehended the Justice and Reasonableness of it" (p. 25). Because the next and most significant stage of his conviction deserved separate treatment, Edwards is content for the moment to imply its essential difference: the doctrine that was now reasonable would later appear "exceedingly pleasant, bright and sweet." In short, common grace had assisted natural principles by removing prejudices and illuminating the truth of the doctrine; saving grace had infused a new spiritual foundation that underlay a wholly different mode of perception through the "new sense" or "sense of the heart" that characterized genuinely spiritual experience.[22]

III

How far Edwards exceeded his Puritan predecessors in the art of uniting instruction with spiritual autobiography, the one reasoned and objective, the other felt and subjective, appears most impressively when he begins to document the experience of the "new man." As he relives the first instance of an "inward, sweet Delight in GOD and divine Things," his prose rises gradually to a high pitch of joyous emotion, sustained by characteristic repetitions and parallelisms and by an aspiring and exultant vocabulary. The paragraph takes its shape so naturally that one nearly overlooks the emergence of relationships that received their fullest elaboration in the *Religious Affections*. Edwards' first ejaculation, "how excellent a Being that was," is a response to the first objective ground of gracious affections, "the transcendently excellent and amiable nature of divine things." When he continues, "and how happy I should be, if I might enjoy that GOD and be wrapt up to GOD in Heaven, and be as it were swallowed up in Him," Edwards proceeds according to the order of true saints, whose apprehension of the excellency of divine things "is the foundation of the joy that they have afterwards, in the considera-

22 The full context for these distinctions may be found in the "Miscellanies" published in *The Philosophy of Jonathan Edwards From His Private Notebooks*, ed. Harvey G. Townsend (Eugene, 1955), pp. 249-251. See especially numbers 397, 408, 628.

tion of their being theirs." The affections of hypocrites, on the other hand, are aroused in a contrary order; they find themselves "made so much of by God" that "he seems in a sort, lovely to them."[23]

To make clear the order of his own affections became crucial for Edwards as he went on to report his visions, "or fix'd Ideas and Imaginations." He ran the risk, after all, of becoming a chief exhibit in the case against enthusiasm should his narrative have fallen into the wrong hands. Nevertheless, when judging experiences similar to his own he was satisfied that lively imaginations could arise from truly gracious affections; and in adding, "through the infirmity of human nature,"[24] he claimed less for his "visions" than some who read him later. Class distinctions and hierarchies in spiritual experience held little interest for Edwards, because all distinctions resolved finally into the ultimate one between the old and the new man. It was less difficult, however, to point out what was not spiritual experience, even in personal narrative, than it was to render the perceptions of the "new sense" with an instrument so imperfect as human language and so indiscriminate in itself as to be the common property of both spiritual and natural men. Moreover, narrative prose was only Edwards' second choice to convey what he felt. Insofar as the medium approached anything like satisfactory expression it was by compromise with another that seemed more natural: "to sing or chant forth my Meditations; to speak my Thoughts in Soliloquies, and speak with a singing Voice." In admitting that the "inward ardor" of his soul "could not freely flame out as it would," Edwards reconciled himself to one kind of defeat, but the attempt, if skillfully managed, might prove affecting to others.

[23] *Religious Affections*, pp. 240-250.
[24] *Religious Affections*, p. 291.

The impossible aim Edwards set for himself in the *Personal Narrative* was to articulate his totally new delight in "things of religion" for readers who could have "no more Notion or idea" of it than he had as a boy, no more "than one born blind has of pleasant and beautiful Colours." He might have taken solace in the consideration that since all expression was in this case equally imperfect, any expression would do. The prose of the *Personal Narrative* deserves respect to the degree that Edwards refused to avail himself of this consolation or to accept language that by this time flowed easily from his pen. Edwards' continual use of the word "sweet," for instance, points up some of the difficulty of judging his art and rhetorical effectiveness in the narrative. If the word seems at one moment to derive from a sensationalist vocabulary, we may regard its use as part of his unique project to make Lockean psychology serve the interests of experimental religion. Simply through repetition the word tends to gather to itself all the sensible difference Edwards was trying to express when he said that the easily moved affections of his youth "did not arise from any Sight of the divine Excellency of the Things of GOD; or any Taste of the Soul-satisfying and Life-giving Good, there is in them." But Edwards' reading of Locke only added new significance to scriptural passages long familiar to him. In the *Religious Affections* he refers the reader to Psalm 119 for a striking representation of "the beauty and sweetness of holiness as the grand object of a spiritual taste" (p. 260), and goes on to paraphrase verse 103 ("How sweet are thy words unto my taste! Yea, sweeter than honey to my mouth"). In this light Edwards appears only to be indulging in the kind of reverent plagiarism common to many spiritual autobiographies, among them that of Sarah Edwards.[25]

Occasionally, too, Edwards declines the full potential of personal narrative by taking over, with little change, passages from his 1737 account of Northampton conversions, making them his own by the mechanical act of altering the pronoun. He could not have avoided reporting that in his own experience, as in that of the converts, "the Appearance of every thing was altered"; but he expands the point by again simply listing natural phenomena over which the "new sense" played, without vitalizing and re-viewing them through personal expression: "God's Excellency, his Wisdom, his Purity and Love, seemed to appear in every Thing; in the Sun, Moon and Stars; in the Grass, Flowers, Trees; in the Water, and all Nature; which used greatly to fix my Mind."[26] However, when Edwards dramatizes a new kind of perception and so involves divine attributes with natural phenomena that abstraction is made vivid and concrete, he begins to communicate something of what it was to confront nature as, in the strictest sense, a new beholder:

"I used to be a Person uncommonly terrified with Thunder: and it used to strike me with Terror, when I saw a Thunder-storm rising. But now, on the contrary, it rejoyced me. I felt GOD at the first Appearance of a Thunder-storm. And used to take the Opportunity, at such Times, to fix myself to view the Clouds, and see the Lightnings play, and

[25] The word "sweet" is used frequently in Sarah's first person narrative.

[26] The comparable passage in the *Faithful Narrative* reads: "The light and comfort which some of them enjoy . . . cause all things about them to appear as it were beautiful, sweet, and pleasant. All things abroad, the sun, moon, and stars; the clouds and sky, the heavens and earth, appear as it were with a cast of divine glory and sweetness upon them." *Works*, IV, 50.

201

hear the majestick & awful Voice of God's Thunder: which often times was exceeding entertaining, leading me to sweet Contemplations of my great and glorious GOD." (p. 27)

Taken together, these successive views of nature in its placid and then terrible beauty would adumbrate the symmetry of the divine attributes. Edwards noted as much in another manuscript not published in his lifetime,[27] but the narrative of his conversion imposed special conditions on viewing "shadows of divine things." When he scrutinized his own spiritual "estate," it was absolutely necessary that he be able to acknowledge a view of God's loveliness and majesty in conjunction, for even "wicked men and devils" were sensible of His "mighty power and awful majesty." Against the background of the recent awakening Edwards was moved to observe in the *Religious Affections* that "too much weight has been laid, by many persons of late, on discoveries of God's greatness, awful majesty, and natural perfection . . . without any real view of the holy, lovely majesty of God" (p. 265). To express the ideal vision in the *Personal Narrative*, Edwards chose the language of theological paradox over that of sensationalism, although we do hear symmetry and can observe the proportion Edwards maintains through a dexterous manipulation of his terms. The passage also reveals an infiltration into prose of the "singing voice," whose rhythms were still alive in the memory, inseparable from the experience that originally provoked them:

"And as I was walking there, and looked up on the Sky

[27] "As thunder and thunder clouds, as they are vulgarly called, have a shadow of the majesty of God, so the blue skie, the green fields, and trees, and pleasant flowers have a shadow of the mild attributes of God, viz., grace and love of God, as well as the beauteous rainbow." *Images and Shadows of Divine Things*, ed. Perry Miller (New Haven, 1948), p. 49.

and Clouds; there came into my Mind, a sweet Sense glorious Majesty and Grace of GOD, that I know not how to express. I seemed to see them both in a sweet Conjunction: Majesty and Meekness join'd together: it was a sweet and gentle, and holy Majesty; and also a majestic Meekness; an awful Sweetness; a high, and great, and holy Gentleness." (p. 26)

Through heightened paradox the unawakened reader might be brought to see dimly and to seek the same sense of God's natural and moral perfections balanced and intermingled with each other. Edwards strove to make the path more clear and more inviting as well when he singled out for relatively extensive treatment that which constituted "in a peculiar manner the beauty of the divine nature." At its center the *Personal Narrative* focuses on the experiential realization that holiness is the divine attribute which primarily elicits the love of the true saint. God's underived holiness could not, of course, be encompassed by words; it could only be loved. But the holiness of creatures, deriving from the divine object of their love, yielded to definition in the *Religious Affections* as "the moral image of God in them, which is their beauty" (p. 258).

In the *Personal Narrative*, Edwards had already embodied the relationship between the holiness of God and the holiness of man in two successive and integrally related "moral images." The first describes the soul as "a Field or Garden of GOD," its multitude of flowers representative of individual moral excellencies. Since holiness comprehends all these excellencies, as its beauty sums up their individual loveliness, Edwards closes in immediately on a single, consummate flower: ". . . such a little white Flower, as we see in the Spring of the Year; low and humble on the Ground, opening its Bosom, to receive the pleasant Beams of the Sun's Glory; rejoycing as it were, in a calm Rapture; diffusing around a sweet Fragrancy; standing peacefully and lovingly, in the midst of other Flowers round about; all in like Manner opening their Bosoms, to drink in the Light of the Sun" (pp. 29-30). Each felt quality that Edwards noted in his perception of holiness—"Purity, Brightness, Peacefulness & Ravishment to the Soul"—finds its correspondent physical detail in the image. The life of the flower, as it drinks in light and sustenance from the sun and returns its own fragrance, is the life of grace, continuous in God and the regenerate man; and the second image is finally enlarged to the scope of the first to include a fellowship of saints. Edwards' tendency toward pathetic fallacy, the flower's "rejoycing as it were, in a calm rapture," only reminds the reader that this is personal narrative and not an exercise in typology.

I V

Not every sight to which the "new sense" gave access evoked an ecstasy of joy. Acuteness of spiritual perception could also compel disgust and nausea when eyes seeing for the first time began to search the depths of one's depravity. So hideous a view as Edwards reported would have taxed any vocabulary, but his own had so far been richest and most novel when he expressed the affection of love. For this other task he might have been forced to depend entirely upon the communal vocabulary of the Calvinists vis-à-vis man's corruption had his sensitivity to language not intervened. Edwards' awareness of the problems involved in verbal self-chastisement compares with that of his fictional fellow minister, Arthur Dimmesdale, who found that he could excoriate himself as the "vilest of sinners," not only with impunity, but with the ironic dividend of being revered the more for his sanctity. Regardless of their denotative content, formulary expressions, given wide currency, were quickly emptied of meaning—as Edwards well knew from his experience with hypocrites, men fluent in "very bad expressions which they use about themselves . . . and we must believe that they are thus humble, and see themselves so vile, upon the credit of their say so."[28]

When Edwards is most likely to suggest to modern readers an inverse pride in his corruption rather than the "evangelical humility" (the sixth sign of gracious affections) he hoped he had, we discover that a question of language is at the root of the difficulty. It is not the rank of "chief of sinners" that he covets, nor is Edwards vying with his fellow townsmen for a place in the last ring of hell when he rejects their expression, "as bad as the Devil himself," because it seemed "exceeding faint and feeble, to represent my Wickedness." The full text of this passage, as printed by Hopkins, makes clear that Edwards is in fact rejecting language he thought inadequately proportioned to its object: "I thought I should wonder, that they should content themselves with such Expressions as these, if I had any Reason to imagine, that their Sin bore any Proportion to mine. It seemed to me, I should wonder at my self, if I should express *my* Wickedness in such feeble Terms as they did." (p. 37)

The rationale that lies behind Edwards' greater dissatisfaction with attempts to convey a sense of his wickedness than with parallel attempts to express his delight in divine things is given fully in the *Religious Affections*. There Edwards explained that to the saint the deformity of the least sin must outweigh the greatest beauty in his holiness,

---

[28] *Religious Affections*, pp. 316-317.

because sin against an infinite God is infinitely corrupt, while holiness cannot be infinite in a creature (p. 326). No expression, then, could take the measure of infinite corruption, and before accepting a simile that only traded on the reputation of Satan, Edwards preferred to draw on the resources of his own rhetoric. He begins by bringing together two images that suggest physical immensity, and then associates them with the key word "infinite," which is extracted at last from its concrete associations and made to reproduce itself rhythmically:

"My Wickedness, as I am in my self, has long appear'd to me perfectly ineffable, and infinitely swallowing up all Thought and Imagination; like an infinite Deluge, or infinite Mountains over my Head. I know not how to express better, what my Sins appear to me to be, than by heaping Infinite upon Infinite, and multiplying Infinite by Infinite. I go about very often, for this many Years, with these Expressions in my Mind, and in my Mouth, 'Infinite upon Infinite. Infinite upon Infinite!'" (p. 37)

Even if he had improved on pallid representations of wickedness, Edwards only pushed the question one step further. Did the improvement arise from a greater conviction of sin or from a natural ability in prose expression? Just how rigorously Edwards dealt with himself in answering such questions appears in a subsequent reflection that immediately dissipated any complacency in mere verbal skill: "And yet, I ben't in the least inclined to think, that I have a greater Conviction of Sin than ordinary. It seems to me, my Conviction of Sin is exceeding small, and faint." Typically enough, Edwards' ruthlessness here is a double-edged sword that also cuts away from himself. As a public document, the *Personal Narrative* might only provide hypocrites with a new model for their deceptions, a thesaurus of expressions (such as "infinite upon infinite") that proclaimed conviction or other classic signs of grace. Edwards could not prevent a prostitution of his narrative, but he knew that the hypocrite found it difficult to claim anything in small amounts, and he would explain in the *Religious Affections* how mimicry eventually confounded itself: "But no man that is truly under great convictions, thinks his conviction great in proportion to his sin. For if he does, 'tis a certain sign that he inwardly thinks his sins small. And if that be the case, that is a certain evidence that his conviction is small. And this, by the way, is the main reason, that persons when under a work of humiliation, are not sensible of it, in the time of it."[29]

Simultaneously, then, Edwards convinces the reader that his self-scrutiny has been unremittingly honest, while he offers instruction that is meticulous in its distinctions, and affecting in its language. The *Personal Narrative* is relatively brief, set against Mather's "Paterna" or Shepard's "My Birth & Life"; but it is not incomplete. Like all autobiographers, secular or spiritual, Edwards fashioned a coherent narrative by using his total experience selectively; we judge it incomplete only by our curiosity about the interior life of his last harrowing years. He could scarcely

[29] *Religious Affections*, p. 334. The relationship between Edwards' personal experience and his public pronouncements on experience often presents interesting problems. In the passage quoted above, Edwards almost seems to be settling for himself the question of why he could record no more conviction of sin than we find described in the *Personal Narrative*. But another cross-reference, a sentence from the narrative, printed only by Hopkins, contains the essential logical distinction he employed to discuss conviction in the *Religious Affections* (pp. 323-336): "That my Sins appear to me so great, don't seem to me to be, because I have so much more Conviction of Sin than other Christians, but because I am so much worse, and have so much more Wickedness to be convinced of" (p. 37).

have added a word to the felt distillation of all he ever thought on all that finally mattered.

Nathan Cole's "Spiritual Travels"

Completed by 1765 and still available only in manuscript,[30] Nathan Cole's "Spiritual Travels" has received recent attention in a study of the Separatist movement in New England. As an illustration of "the response of the common people to the religious issues of the day,"[31] Cole's narrative is particularly useful for the social and religious historian of the period. It indicates vividly the kind of impact a preacher like George Whitefield had on rural New England, it presents a classic awakening and conversion as results of Whitefield's preaching, and it suggests the relation between the Pentecostal conversions of the Great Awakening and the neo-Puritan movement to erect churches whose membership would again be limited to the saints. Cole's narrative is also a marvel of Puritan autobiography, with real if limited virtues as literature, an enthusiastic complement to Edwards' *Personal Narrative*, and a revealing contrast to Samuel Hopkins' *Sketches*.

A farmer rather than a professional student of grace, Nathan Cole could scarcely be expected to produce a narrative so cunningly theological as Edwards'. At the same time, he makes no effort to maintain a guise of innocence when he assesses the significance of his experience. Cole always provides the reader with adequate orientation to the

30 The manuscript of the "Spiritual Travels" is in the possession of the Connecticut Historical Society. From page seven to page twenty-six the running title is "Spiritual Tryals." My references are to the page numbers given in the manuscript even though pagination goes awry in several places.

31 C. C. Goen, *Revivalism and Separatism in New England, 1740-1800* (New Haven, 1962), p. 136.

nature of the work he describes. With his help, one recognizes the familiar pattern of awakening: conviction of sin, severe depression, joyful conversion, and subsequent assurance, punctuated by periods of spiritual deadness. Yet the narrative is not formally schematic. Progressing chronologically, it is never especially coherent and becomes less so when Cole attempts to depart from his experience to point a lesson. His concern for a pure "Gospel Church" appears in the account of his conversion as a mechanical imposition, although the theme has its place later in the narrative. Transitions are obscure, as when Cole leaps from a meditation on the letter and the spirit to an account of his difficulties with "hireling Ministers" without specifying the connection (p. 33). At several places in the manuscript Cole asks the reader to skip ahead several pages, implying his own dissatisfaction with the work's organization in a late attempt to mend it.

Explicitly didactic passages are nearly as rare in this autobiography as in Edwards', but writing, or dictating,[32] in more leisurely fashion and at greater length, Cole finds time at one point to reproduce an allegorical lay sermon he once addressed to an unbeliever. In the allegory Cole makes himself captain of a band of soldiers (his sins) pitted against "a great Good General" who is able to gain the advantage when the soldiers bind up their captain and desert him. Although the captain has clearly demonstrated his contempt for his enemy, the General no sooner gains the victory, his sword at the prisoner's breast, than he "immediately cuts off all my bonds and sets me at liberty" (p. 47). Whether or not the martial allegory is original with Cole, it is an effec-

[32] The manuscript is in the hand of a copyist with insertions and corrections by Cole. A description by Leonard W. Labaree of the total contents (twenty-two items) of the Nathan Cole manuscript volume is on file with the Connecticut Historical Society.

tive piece of instruction brightened by Cole's characteristic verve: "So coming up he looks me right in the face, I scringe and expect nothing but death in a moment." As a simplified paradigm, however, it bears only general resemblance to the narrative of his own experience, which in its actual unfolding grants precedence to the specific, the experiential, and the dramatic.

Like *Grace Abounding*, Cole's "Spiritual Travels" can be described schematically, although it is actually carried forward through emotional peaks and depths rather than by the extension of logical relationships.[33] Cole allows an initial sentence for the information that he was an Arminian until he was thirty, then plunges immediately into the frequently quoted description of his twelve-mile race to hear Whitefield preach in Middletown and of the "heart wound" he received there.[34] No less intense is the crisis of prolonged depression that follows or the elated vaulting into freedom that signals his conversion. An indication of the importance Cole attached to joining with a true Gospel church is that this event, too, makes an emotional peak in the narrative when Cole describes the transporting vision that accompanied it.

I

The power of immediacy is Cole's chief virtue as a writer, an effect he achieves through the suggestiveness of his de-

[33] In this quality, as in the enthusiasm of the spiritual experience it reports, the "Spiritual Travels" resembles Bunyan's autobiography. See Roger Sharrock's "Analysis of Contents" in his introduction to *Grace Abounding* (London, 1962), p. xxxii. Sharrock finds Bunyan's narrative unique "in its psychological penetration and freedom from rationalization into stock Calvinist formulae."

[34] Most recently this passage has been given attention in *The Great Awakening: Documents Illustrating the Crisis and Its Consequences*, ed. Alan Heimert and Perry Miller (New York, 1967), pp. 182-186.

tails, in the cumulative and emphatic rhythms of key passages, and as a result of his habitual inclination to render his experience dramatically. Even in the allegory, Cole becomes the captain and suffers his terrors. These qualities are most noticeable in the four sequences of greatest intensity, but they are distributed liberally enough throughout the narrative to justify studying it as more than an historical document. Whatever Cole's purpose in writing, he rarely satisfied himself simply by recording information. He need not have given more than the personal sum of Whitefield's visit to Middletown—his own awakening. The furious ride to town no doubt earned inclusion to demonstrate the seriousness of his concern. In addition, though, Cole has the kind of double vision which is a major gift of the skillful autobiographer: he retrieves his own experiences in plentiful and pungent detail, but he also sees them against a background which enlarges the significance of the central action without sapping it of its authenticity.

One such background was of course scripture. Cole first hears of Whitefield preaching at Philadelphia "like one of the Old apostles, and many thousands flocking to hear him preach the Gospel" (p. 2). When Whitefield reaches Middletown the context changes from primitive Gospel times to an eschatological future. The day of the great preacher's coming is not only a day of awakening, but the day of doom, when Cole describes himself running to get his horse from the pasture and "fearing that I should be too late," a phrase he soon repeats. It is as if there were a moment of reprieve for one of the giddy heads in Michael Wigglesworth's poem. The last day appears imminent also through the wide angle of Cole's seeing, his inclusion of so much awakened humanity in his view:

"... and when we came within about half a mile or a

211

mile of the Road that comes down from Hartford Weathers-field and Stepney to Middletown; on high land I saw be-fore me a Cloud or fogg rising; I first thought it came from the great River, but as I came nearer the Road, I heard a noise, something like a low rumbling thunder and pres-ently found it was the noise of Horses feet coming down the Road and this Cloud was a Cloud of dust made by the Horses feet; it arose some Rods into the air over the tops of Hills and trees and when I came within about 20 rods of the Road, I could see men and horses Sliping along in the Cloud like shadows and as I drew nearer it seemed like a steady Stream of horses and their riders, scarcely a horse more than his length behind another; all of a Lather and foam with sweat, their breath rolling out of their nostrils every Jump; every horse seemed to go with all his might to carry his rider to hear news from heaven for the saving of Souls, it made me tremble to see the Sight, how the world was in a Struggle." (pp. 3-5)

The ministers are arriving at the meeting house just as the Coles dismount, but there is time for a final glance at the multitude, a view so fascinating even in recollection that Cole must break in between the copyist's lines to add another image: "I turned and looked towards the Great River and saw the ferry boats running swift backward and forward bringing over loads of people and the Oars rowed nimble and quick; everything men horses and boats seemed to be struggling for life; *The land and banks over the river looked black with people and horses.*"[35]

The evocation of furious motion in this sequence depends on more than the report that many persons were in fact "pressing forward in great haste." Cole moves back and

[35] "Spiritual Travels," p. 5. Italics indicate the sentence added by Cole.

forth between massive group images and startlingly singular details—the horses' breath, the "nimble" oars of the ferry boat—while his short periods accumulate their own kind of momentum in breathless procession. His syntax is generally simple and linear, so that memories clamoring for articulation seem played out at an accelerated pace through the narrow channel of their entrance into prose. In other contexts, too, as when a litany of desolation renders Cole's achievement of a full view of his sins, his prose is ignorant of the luxury of relaxation. The passage concludes appropriately: "my nature was just wore out—" (p. 9).

When Cole moves abruptly from the despair of his humiliation for sin to subsequent joy, the absence of transition accords with his claim that he did not realize at the time what had happened to him. An obsessive image of fire, which for obvious reasons assumes prominence in his period of humiliation, provides the only element of continuity and thematic relation between the two sequences. In the narrative, as in his experience, Cole pursues fire: "Hell fire was most always in my mind; and I have hundreds of times put my fingers into my pipe when I have been smoking to feel how fire felt. And to see how my Body could bear to lye in Hell fire for ever and ever" (pp. 6-7). Moaning his desire to be "a Dog or a toad or any Creature but Man," he had known all the same that he could not rid himself of his damned soul: "I was as it were in the very mouth of hell. The very flashes of hell fire were in my Mind. . . . Hell fire hell fire ran Swift in my mind and my distemper grew harder and harder upon me, and my nature was just wore out—" (pp. 8-9). Cole's mother comes to speak with him, hoping to relieve his despair, but he sends her away. For the rest of the night he lies awake with his "pining thoughts" until the next day when someone enters his room and replenishes the fire: ". . . and it burnt up very briskly as I lay on my Bed with my face toward the fire looking on, with these thoughts in my mind, Oh that I might creep into that fire and lye there and burn to death and die for ever Soul and Body; . . . And while these thoughts were in my mind God appeared unto me and made me Skringe: before whose face the heavens and the earth fled away; and I was Shrinked unto nothing; I know not whether I was in the body or not, I seemed to hang in open air before God, and he seemed to Speak to me in an angry and Sovereign way." (p. 11)

Although the speech is a stern reminder of the divine prerogative of election, it is followed by an immediate sense of freedom and by prolonged ecstasy. Cole describes some of the same effects from his experience as Jonathan Edwards: his theological scruples disappear, and his sorrow for sin is greatly increased. But the autobiographical drama emphasizes physical joy and replaces the torturous image of fire with the light of the presence of God: ". . . I believe I felt just as the Apostles felt the truth of the word when they writ it, every leaf line and letter smiled in my face; I got the bible up under my Chin and hugged it; . . . now my heart talked with God; now every thing praised God; the trees, the stone, the walls of the house and everything I could set my eyes on, they all praised God; . . . And all the air was love, now I saw that every thing that was sin fled from the presence of God: As far as darkness is gone from light or beams of the Sun for where ever the Sun can be seen clear there is no darkness." (pp. 12-13)

The several conversations which have already appeared in Cole's narrative are some indication of the extent to which he is willing to use dialogue in recreating his experience. A conversation with Satan, who found Cole whittling and urged him to turn his knife on himself, is not easily forgotten; but Cole's imagination seems inherently dramatic, compelled to return from the past with its speeches intact. Of course the author tells a great deal more than he shows, but his dramatizing skills are considerable, as the most recurrent of his editorial comments indicates. Cole's frequent interjection of "Poor me" is less a directive statement than the comment of an audience, an exclamation from the more complacent Nathan Cole of the present at meeting his former agonized self in vividly faithful reproduction.

Let one conversation—between Cole and his wife—illustrate his taste for the dramatic. The process leading to conversion apparently began later in Mrs. Cole and never went beyond the stage of extreme depression. Cole's reaction was to set aside all his rigorous criteria and venture aloud the opinion that she had experienced "a very Clear gospel Conversion, for I thought it my duty to lift up the hands that hung down," a decision justified dramatically by the scene that precedes it:

". . . and one day as she was so far borne down with it that she was at her wits end while she was talking about it, so that she screamed out three or four times as loud as she could which surpriz'd me, and she said it will fall on me, I said what will fall, she said a great Cloud, I said it won't, She screamed out and said it will, it will, it is close to my head now, a great black Cloud; I said it was not, She said where be I. I told her she was here in the house; she said oh I am raving distracted what shall I do, I told her *i hope not*; She said I never shall have my reason again; I told her she wou'd *i hope*, She said Oh I shall faint away, I said no you won't *i hope* but I helped her unto the bed as fast as I cou'd and gave her some water."[36]

[36] "Spiritual Travels," p. 25. The italicized words were inserted by Cole. His first reply to his wife's declaration of madness originally read, "I told her she was not." It is of course impossible to say

The gist of this conversation, eighteen years distant when Cole fetched it back, could easily have been established by summary narrative, yet he appears generally unwilling to resort to generalized description. Like the apostles of experimental religion, his narrative preaches heart knowledge over head knowledge, although it seems unlikely that Cole has taken pains to adjust the tone of his autobiography to this conviction. We simply have an autobiography that is often successful in achieving consonance between its ideas and the quality of the experience it renders, as when Cole describes the "sealing evidence" of his election.

Three months after his apparent conversion an illuminating vision revealed simultaneously to Cole his own salvation and the items of his doctrinal faith. The latter kind of knowledge he states in conventional, credal terms: "I saw what free Grace was; I saw how stubborn and willfull man was; I saw it was nothing but accepting of Christ's Righteousness and the match was made." Taking doctrine as its object, the verb "saw" would have failed to suggest by itself the kind of heart knowledge that revivalist divines preached was beyond the natural man's intellect, if Cole had not located doctrine in an experience that seemed literally visual: "I fell into a prayer and continued so untill I came to the place of my work and then I had a glorious Sight. It seemed as if I really saw the gate of heaven by an Eye of faith, and the way for Sinners to Get to heaven by Jesus Christ; as plain as ever I saw any thing with my bodily eyes in my life, I looked round to see if I could almost point and shew them the strait way to heaven by Jesus Christ: I saw what free Grace was. . . ." (p. 17)

whether Cole wished to revise his memory or the sense of the dialogue, but the speaker of the revised lines knows what pity will not let him say.

216

II

Natural and supernatural experience seem continuous in the two-dimensional sight Cole portrays in himself, and the continuity is more impressive for Cole's willingness elsewhere to make a stern Edwardsean distinction between the flesh and spirit—as when he reports that in his conversion his soul "was viewing God" while his "fleshly part" was "working imaginations" (p. 11). Presumably Cole had been instructed on the dangers of imagination—although the lesson did not extend to his dialogues with Satan—but the habit of anchoring his transporting visions to natural experience, as an autobiographical act, owes no perceptible debt to ministerial caution. Cole reduces this act to a simile that implies at once the gravities of heaven and earth: "I have often thought of the springs of a trap that will keep down no longer than they are held down—so were my heart and thoughts for almost a year, I was forced as it were to pull down my thoughts some times to see what was my Duty to do here in this world for the support of my family and then they would fly right up again to God" (pp. 17-18).

Again, relating a dream in which he has attended a meeting of the Saints and been ravished by their melodious singing, Cole must describe what he carried from his dream into his waking experience; and in the length of another sentence he brings their company entirely into "this world." In the dream, he had been trying to learn their song, so that as he awoke he could speak the last words, "which were these—And in the name of Jesus Christ Jerusalem shall stand for ever, Stand for ever, stand for ever.—My heart and soul was in a sweet frame, and I seemed to hear their sound of praise for many days and when I was with them I seemed to feel perfectly their feeling, they felt all as one as

217

if they had been made up all into one man, all drinked into one Spirit and oneness, and whatever trouble or affliction they went through in this world they had borne it patiently as Coming from the hand of God." (pp. 37-38)

Like Edwards, Cole is far from an inarticulate surrender to the ineffable, but his simile of the trap implies that he has not overcome euphoria without effort. As he portrays the struggle to bring his visions into the world, finally identifying it with his effort to gain dominance for the pure Gospel church, Cole argues that while the soul will always "fly right up again to God," the body cannot "keep the world of[f] at arms end." This was admittedly a borrowed argument, and Cole gives prompt credit to the "Old Christian" from whom he had it shortly after his conversion. ". . . he told me he knew the Spot of ground I stood upon; says he you stand upon the top of mount pisgah, and you see the promised land and you think you shall presently be there" (p. 20).

In the course of the narrative, "the world" becomes a metaphor of double significance, referring to the sufferings Cole accepted, as the Saints of his dream had, from the hand of God, and also to the arena in which he felt himself called to bear witness "for the cause of God," that is, for the cause of a purified church. Chronology emphasizes the relation between the two meanings. Sufferings were God's method, Cole indicates, for teaching him to live by faith as well as by sight. Having attained assurance he could relax and make peace with the world, "and I became almost like a man of this World; almost a Sleep in Security." Then God attacked him in his body. "He gave a wound on my legg . . . and I began to think I must die with it" (p. 39). His wife's sanity proves to be irretrievable from the depression she

218

has fallen into. Cole recalls her "all this time . . . Crying out in her distress Oh dreadfull Oh dreadfull Oh dreadfull, dreadfull, dreadfull, and I was sitting three months or thereabouts in the furnace of purification and the sound of dreadfull from my wife continually in my ears night and day almost" (p. 51). Both trials grow more intense. Mrs. Cole loses her reason utterly, and "the dropsy and Scurvy humours fell down again into my leggs." The image by which Cole interprets his sufferings resembles closely but has transcended the obsession of his earlier humiliation: "Now all this was the Lords doings; and proved a great blessing to me, he brought me into a fiery furnace" (p. 50).

Through divine correction, Cole was learning a lesson that had eluded him at the time of his conversion. Within five years of that experience he had separated from the standing Church that had claimed him as a member for fifteen years. By 1747 it had become clear to him that both church and communicant told a solemn lie in allowing the unconverted to come to the Lord's Supper. Separation cost him "what the world calls a fine reputation" and earned him "Scoffs, reproaches, and mockerys," but Cole described himself as entirely ready to give up the world and its estimate of him so long as "the light of Gods countenance sweetened all." Only when affliction descended on him did he realize that "the principal thing he corrected me for" was giving up the world so entirely that Satan and the unscriptural practices of the standing churches would soon predominate in it, unless he advanced himself "as a witness for the cause of God." His separatism was never intended to be absolute and self-sufficient, the Lord was saying. The way to heaven began in transcendent vision but it passed through Mr. Frothingham's church, just as a metaphor issuing from heaven took on tangible reality in the world:

"Now the Lord bid me arise and go forward after the flock; and make speed to go forth by the footsteps of the flock; now my heart said Dear Lord blessed be thy name I will obey; now my mind looked away into Gods word to find the foot steps of the flock, and as my mind was following the foot steps of the flock in the Bible; I came right upon Mr. Frothingham's Congregational Church in Middletown; they stood right in the way; with their faces heaven ward I purposed full if the Lord would give me a measure of healing I would endeavor to Joyn myself with them the first opportunity." (pp. 55-56)

Joining with this congregation in turn brought other obligations. Though he had hoped to be excused from public testimony because he could "only give a few blundering hints; and Jump from one thing to another," he saw that he was obligated to put his meanest talents "to usery." Thus the autobiography of Nathan Cole is the fruit of his divinely prompted attention to the world, another "blundering way of uttering my gift," at the same time that its most impressive passages argue, in their large vision and elevated colloquialism, the reconciliation of earth to heaven and heaven to earth.

At most points in this narrative, the distance from Cole as autobiographer back to Winthrop or Shepard seems very great. Nevertheless the term Puritan still applies to the essential thrust of his work: he finds the source of all his values in the experience of a divine reality, impelling him to actions that incur the abuse of unenlightened men. Cole is also the autobiographical Puritan in his view of those who fall outside this frame of experience. Once an outsider himself, he was awed by the charismatic Whitefield, "for he looked as if he was Cloathed with Authority from the Great

God." As Cole traces the process by which "the Cause of God" finally stood clear for him, he speaks more and more evidently as an insider. The shift in point of view is complete when Cole, describing his triumph over a "hireling minister," puts on Whitefield's robes: "and as I came round in the [Alley?] to come at the door, the faces and eyes of the assembly turned as I went round, with a sober amaze in their Countenance; as if I had been some strange Creature, from some other nation or World" (p. 62). In the last pages of the manuscript the lessons of adversity and the fire of purification, which comprise the argument of Cole's "Spiritual Travels," seem lost on the polemicist who closes it, speaking no longer to the world that had been "in a struggle" to save itself but to that shrunken portion of it which could consent to the destruction of all the rest: "Now we have nothing to do in the Cause, but stand and look on, and the men of the World tear one another to peices, Just as they did us; . . . for the Lord seems to have taken us into the Secret Chambers of his promises; and hide us untill the indignation be over past &c." (p. 67).

Sketches of the Life of Samuel Hopkins

Had he not suffered a paralytic stroke in January of 1799, Samuel Hopkins might have been able to bring his autobiography to a fit conclusion in the eighteenth century. Instead, although he resumed writing again in December, the *Sketches* of his life close with an anachronistic passage dated January 10, 1800, which examines once again the evidence for and against his salvation. Early in the autobiography Hopkins had indicated the direction in which he looked as he wrote, while also professing his doctrinal and temperamental loyalties: "I conclude I and my ancestors descended from those called *Puritans* in the days of Queen Elizabeth, above two hundred years ago, and have continued to bear that denomination, since, and were the first settlers of New England."[37] This ready subscription to the title of Puritan suggests the fullness of the transformation by which a term of opprobrium, having been accepted by its designates, began to acquire for some of their descendants honorific and reverently nostalgic connotations.

Hopkins' claim was valid enough, even though for him the relevant past was not the days of Elizabeth but the time of the great revivals in New England when his awakening had come through the agency of David Brainerd and when he had learned his New Divinity directly from Jonathan Edwards. He could easily demonstrate himself the physical Puritan by noting his habit, worthy of a Richard Mather, of spending eighteen hours a day in his study, "generally rising at 4 o'clock in the morning." More essentially, Hopkins qualifies for membership in the tradition when he characterizes himself and those who believe with him as "the most sound, consistent and thorough calvinists," who are for that reason "the most hated, opposed and spoken against, by arminians, deists, and persons who appear to have no religion" (p. 98). Doctrines change; a system which one generation calls Edwardsean the next will refer to, after it has undergone "some improvement," as Hopkintonian, or Hopkinsian. But the conviction that these "sentiments," which most men curse, contain a terrible yet serene and saving truth, marks the Puritan in any generation.

The *Sketches* of Samuel Hopkins' life do not treat directly those ideas which, embodied in his immense *System*

[37] *Sketches of the Life of the Late Reverend Samuel Hopkins*, with an Introduction by Stephen West (Hartford, 1805), p. 23.

of Doctrines (1793), made "the transition from Calvinism to moralism" for New England theology.[38] The autobiography only records Hopkins' humble conviction that he had passed the torch faithfully, even with "some improvement." It also displays the troubled recognition that while his close study of the manuscripts of Jonathan Edwards guaranteed that the master's ideas would be extended into the next generation, there was no rewriting the *Personal Narrative*, autobiography disdaining the laws of inheritance. Better prepared than most of his contemporaries to argue the subtle pattern of experience that proclaimed grace, Hopkins struggles at length to assemble it from his past, unaware that his autobiography would not consist in the bare frame he was able to put up but in the struggle itself.

I

The final year Samuel Hopkins spent at Yale was also the year in which New England experienced the most widespread and convulsive religious revival of its history. Already a church member in good standing, the "sober, serious" student saw or spoke that year with the most prominent figures of the Great Awakening. In October of 1740 he was among the large crowd that heard George Whitefield's public sermon at Yale and was also with the smaller group of students who heard him in private. Hopkins notes as a sign of his deadness to grace that he only "approved of him" and was "somewhat impressed by what he said" (p. 30). Other students appeared to grow more attentive to religion, however, and when Gilbert Tennent came in March thousands were overcome by the "remarkable and mighty power" that attended his preaching. The work was

[38] Joseph Haroutunian, *Piety Versus Moralism* (New York, 1932), p. 92.

carried into each room in the college by several students whose earlier conversions prompted them to exhort others. Samuel Buell, who had startling success preaching from Edwards' pulpit in 1742, was one of these students. It was David Brainerd who visited Hopkins and said enough to convince him that he was no Christian. Then just before commencement, Jonathan Edwards came to New Haven. After hearing Gilbert Tennent, Hopkins had thought him "the greatest and best man, and the best preacher that I had ever seen or heard." But Edwards' preaching evoked "such an esteem" that Hopkins "concluded to go and live with Mr. Edwards, as soon as I should have opportunity" (p. 38).

In all, Hopkins evokes a revivalist's golden age, when preachers were eloquent, conversions plentiful, and a great teacher could be consulted in his study. Against this background he assesses his own performance in the century that dragged on and finds "little or no success." The time of "great revivals" seems beyond recall, except autobiographically. "No such thing has happened under my preaching," Hopkins admits, "though some individuals have appeared to be in some degree awakened" (p. 124). Unquestionably, he grants, the fault was his, the result in part of too great a concern for "knowledge of the truth" and too little attention to "good language and a proper delivery." Yet even admitting that his pulpit manner was "very bad and disagreeable," a description concurred in by his contemporaries,[39] Hopkins could not fully account for his failure

[39] The entry on Hopkins in the *Dictionary of American Biography* quotes William Ellery Channing: "he was the very ideal of bad delivery." The dullness of Hopkins' sermons may have contributed to his dismissal from his first pastorate in Great Barrington, Massachusetts, but there were more solid grounds: his stern theology and conservative views on church membership, combined with Whiggish political sentiments.

224

unless he groped beneath the externals of declamatory technique. As an eighteenth-century memoirist, he might have been free to discuss a lifelong attempt to master the art of public speaking, but as a Puritan autobiographer he was inclined to seek answers in the soul. The failure to be another Whitefield or Tennent or Edwards in the pulpit had to be regarded as the possible sign of another and more awful failure. Perhaps he had not been able to preach grace, because he had no experiential knowledge of it, his pulpit labors only making him more conscious of a "want of a proper sense of the things of which I have been speaking" (p. 121).

As a young minister, Hopkins had witnessed Jonathan Edwards' efforts to lay bare the root of spiritual experience in what he had called "a sense of the heart." A half-century later he was attempting to show that he had not forgotten the lesson of the priority of affective experience: "And the exercises and experiences of my own heart were the ground of my preaching, in general, and led to those passages of scripture and subjects which I chose for my public discourses" (pp. 59-60). The argument should readily have convinced the "particular friends, and relatives" to whom he addressed his *Sketches*. His claim that he had delivered those truths of "practical and experimental religion, which were the dictates of my heart" was adequately supported by testimony in various sections of the autobiography that he had experienced "high religious enjoyments in the exercise of those affections which appeared to be truly gracious" (p. 59). Hopkins had made the trial himself. Standing, he imagined, in the place of an external observer, viewing the exercises reported by the autobiographer, "I should think them an evidence that he was a real Christian" (p. 111).

And in this conclusion, he added, the observer was quite possibly deceived.

As autobiographer, Hopkins could avail himself of the forms and vocabulary of nearly two hundred years of spiritual narrative in New England. As a professor of experimental religion, he could refer the ambiguities of the heart to Edwards' exhaustive treatise on religious affections. Yet he could not finally account for what seemed missing in his narrative and ineffectual in his preaching. He knew only that in both cases it was more than a matter of delivery.

Anxiety to detect the presence of grace is of course the most predictable feature of a spiritual narrative, and there is no establishing whether, autobiographically, Hopkins worried more or less than Cotton Mather or Nathan Cole. But Hopkins' manner of stating his doubts strikes even the widely exposed reader of spiritual narratives as an unusually negative variation on the formula. Whereas Jonathan Edwards declines to claim the grace that his evidence claims for him, Hopkins says, "I have never in the course of my life . . . come to a settled conclusion that I had no grace; but my doubts have frequently rose very high" (p. 85). Here and in other introspective passages, the tone of the autobiographer's commentary on himself reveals more than a count of hopeful or dubious passages.

II

As Hopkins' title suggests,[40] his narrative does not make sustained progress toward a coherently foreseen conclusion. Diffusion and repetition become most pronounced after Hopkins returns to the work following his stroke. The three-fourths of the total which had already been written

[40] The title is taken from Hopkins' own description of the work, "Some brief sketches of my past life" (p. 23).

comprises a unit treating the most important stages of his spiritual life as well as his career as pastor and theologian. Hopkins' autobiographical pattern first departs from this thoroughly familiar outline in its report of a rather decent childhood. Lacking the kind of youth that bristled with the outcroppings of depravity, Hopkins refuses to exaggerate his youthful "neglect of a future world" or his "foolish" but quite normal "imaginations of what I should be and do in this world" into anything more impressive. Far from being "volatile and wild," he was "of a sober and steady make . . . disposed to be diligent and faithful in whatever business I was employed. . . ." In college there were "openly vicious" companions to be had, but Hopkins recalls avoiding company of all kinds, "being attentive to my studies." No wonder the young man made his profession and was accepted in church membership before he was twenty. Only when Hopkins adds a final touch to the portrait of his unblemished youth does the rhetorical drift become clear. He makes at last the damaging admission that in his unregenerate state, he had been as innocent of a capacity for self-deception as he appeared to be of sin: "When I thought of confessing the sins I had been guilty of that day and asking pardon, I could not recollect that I had committed one sin that day. Thus ignorant was I of my own heart, and of the spirituality, strictness and extent of the divine law."

As instruction, the condemnation of a sober undergraduate who threatens to be exemplary even without grace might have attracted readers who could no longer be impressed by the wicked and wanton adolescents of many spiritual narratives. But if Hopkins does not record a past so stunningly wicked as usual, neither is his regeneration presented with anything like the energy that often appeared equally in passages of self-condemnation and ecstatic trans-

227

port. Neither literal nor metaphoric lightning strikes in the conversion experience of the *Sketches*. For the very reason that Hopkins "had not the least thought or suspicion" of anything extraordinary, the experience must be taken as his conversion, although as in Edwards' narrative there were positive indications also: "I had a sense of the being and presence of God, as I never had before. And the character of Jesus Christ the mediator came into view, and appeared such a reality and so glorious; and the way of salvation by him so wise, important and desirable, that I was astonished at myself that I had never seen these things before, which were so plain, pleasing, and wonderful." (p. 35)

Hopkins' announcement shares the metaphor of physical sight with comparable passages in Edwards and Cole, but there are important differences too. Whatever the original experience consisted in, Hopkins' metaphor is incomplete, lacking an object for sight. When Edwards views the serene and awesome in nature, he manages to suggest the doctrine in which his vision is subsumed. Cole is blatantly explicit about his commitment to a purified Church, yet he immerses his doctrines in the stuff of experience and makes a consistency of the whole. Hopkins renders a vision that is almost purely doctrinal. The "character" of Jesus Christ does not in fact come "into view" but remains a doctrinal abstraction. Terms that imply a movement of the affections, "desirable," "pleasing and wonderful," are also abstract (as "sweet" is not) while the remaining adjectives derive from a notional vocabulary. The way of salvation by Christ is "wise" and "important," its truth and efficacy "plain," that is, logically evident. The "real Christian" as Hopkins defines him in his *System of Doctrines* could easily be exchanged for his autobiographical Christian, although sur-

228

prisingly the theological passage is more adjectivally fulsome and energetic:

". . . the truths revealed in the Scriptures relating to the
being and perfections of God, his law, and moral government, the state and character of man, the character and
works of the mediator, the way of salvation by him, the nature of duty and true holiness, etc., are seen in their true
light as realities, beautiful, divine, important, excellent,
harmonious, glorious, and above all things else interesting
and affecting, and the mind is filled with this spiritual,
marvelous, glorious light."[41]

The key sentences in which Hopkins treats his conversion
amount to what had become a set piece of spiritual autobiography. No doubt his long career of controversy and
apologetics and a habit of deference to the language of
Jonathan Edwards tended to stultify Hopkins' articulation
of his own experience, particularly in his seventy-fifth year.
Advanced age makes comprehensible his apparent lack of
self-consciousness in allowing his narrative to run into the
most conventional forms and phrases. But as he speaks in
the final portion of the *Sketches,* Hopkins displays a kind
of fatigue not wholly attributable to age and illness. Having
taken up his autobiography once again, he seizes the opportunity to review his review of his life and in doing so
reveals inordinate self-consciousness as the source of his
weariness. Starting from Edwards' definition of true virtue
as the soul's benevolent consent to being in general, Hopkins
proposes a simplified and more personal version of the idea
as an interest which draws his attention away from selfish
concern with his own estate. When the grand interest, that

---

[41] Quoted in Frank Hugh Foster, *A Genetic History of the New England Theology* (Reissued; New York, 1963) , p. 183.

is "the glory of God, and the best interest of his kingdom," appears secure, Hopkins says, he rejoices and is satisfied. "And this so engrosses my thoughts and reflections, that I do not attend to the interest of any individual person, my own or anyone else, . . . as not worthy of any regard, in comparison with the general interest of the whole" (p. 108). Adhered to without variance or relief, this proposition would annihilate both the impulse and the subject matter of autobiography. In his humanness, Hopkins suffers the wandering of his attention from the grand design. His very strictures against self-consciousness indicate that he observes the operations of his mind with alert interest, while his failure to be properly indifferent adds to his discontent with himself.

Wherever he turns, Hopkins encounters contradictory demands to consider the whole or to attend only to a part of it. Numerous as are the passages in which he doubts he has been "a real Christian," he confronts a situation essentially different from that of the early Puritan autobiographer who could not be certain that the manuscript before him contained certain evidence of divine favor. Hopkins' dilemma is more excruciating because he is aware of the manner in which his mind creates the dilemma:

"But as my mind cannot have a view of all objects with equal clearness and attention, at one and the same time, but different objects are more attended to, and make greater impression at some time than at others, so when I . . . reflect upon the views and affections and enjoyments I have experienced in attending to the person, character, and works of Christ, . . . the inference seems to be plain that I am a friend to these objects: . . . When . . . I attend more to my own character; and my depravity, stupidity, unbelief, and the evil and deceitfulness of my heart rise into

230

view, I am disposed to call in question my own good estate, and to suspect that my exercises fall short of real christianity." (p. 108)

The moral and theological terms Hopkins uses do not disguise the psychological character of the entire passage, or of others like it. The Puritan autobiographer here moves outside the question of his graciousness to consider the very apparatus with which he had hoped to judge his standing, and finds that he is constituted to confirm his most exalted hopes and darkest suspicions. "It is very unhappy, but too late to be helped," said Emerson, plumbing the depths of subjectivity in *Experience*, "the discovery we have made that we exist. That discovery is called the Fall of Man. Ever afterwards we suspect our instruments."

III

Conscious of his doubts, but even more conscious of the mind doubting, Hopkins leads his autobiography into familiar channels of expression or lapses into impersonal professions of doctrine as almost the only alternatives to endless vacillation. The controlled uncertainty of Edwards' *Personal Narrative* needs to be compared with a passage from Hopkins in which the autobiographer qualifies, refines, hesitates, and reverses himself to attain no more than the certainty of the place from which he originally set out:

"Had I reflected judiciously on my own exercises, I might have rationally judged them to be agreeable to the truth, and an evidence that I was a friend to Christ; but I did not so reflect as to make this conclusion. This view and sense of things still abides with me, but at different times in a higher and lower degree; but not so that I can infer from it, without hesitation, that I am a real christian and shall be saved. My views and exercises appear to me, so much below the truth, and so inconstant that, sometimes, I doubt of their reality, or of their being real christian exercises: and I have such a deceitful heart, that I fear delusion: though at times all doubts subside." (pp. 107-108)

The maze-like quality of the passage was perfectly evident to its writer. "Thus my mind fluctuates, and passes from one object to another," Hopkins concluded, with nearly all he would write before him.

But the pattern does not predominate, could not be imagined to do so, for most of the length of these *Sketches.* Tangible accomplishments represent for Hopkins, as they do for Cotton Mather, an autobiographical haven from chartless wanderings in search of grace. Hopkins records not just the fact of his theological labors, but the full weight and substance of their results. There is greater value for the autobiographer than for his audience in the notation that the *System of Doctrines* appeared in two large octavo volumes, running to 1,244 pages, for which more than twelve thousand subscribers paid three dollars a set. In this "laborious work," which he regarded as his "greatest public service," and in all those works "detecting error and displaying and vindicating the truth," Hopkins found persuasive evidence that he had been a means of "promoting the true interest of the church, or kingdom of Christ" (p. 92). The improvements he had made in the tenets of the New Divinity encouraged him to project a rapid increase in the number of "Hopkinsians": "these sentiments appear to be coming more and more into credit" (p. 103). The small portion of optimism which self-scrutiny seemed to justify was thus given over entirely to a theology whose future course would diverge considerably from Hopkins' estimate. Yet his autobiography left him little choice, pushing off the past into irrecoverable distance, arguing an identification between the remoteness of the days of a Great Awakening and the elusiveness of gracious affections, which "soon abate and subside, and I am left as stupid and senseless as ever: and what I thought I had experienced seems like a dream, and as if, it was not a reality" (p. 120). Suspicious, even contemptuous of delusion, the Puritan autobiographer has now learned more than he needs to know of man's tendency to argue his salvation from extraordinarily weak evidence.

Franklin and Spiritual
Autobiography

Benjamin Franklin effectively settled the question whether his personal narrative might be thought of as spiritual autobiography when he referred to the manuscript as, simply, "Memoirs of my life." Nevertheless, there are persuasive reasons for considering Franklin's "Memoirs" against the background of early spiritual autobiography. Questions of sequence and development in American autobiography inevitably focus on Franklin. Is his the last Puritan autobiography, a translation of the narrative of salvation into secular terms? Or is Franklin the first authentic American autobiographer, displaying in his rise to success a mythic embodiment of the New World's possibilities? Should Franklin also be credited with a leap into modern autobiography, in his objectivity about himself and his implicit knowledge of the uses of a persona as narrator? To trace forward the lines leading from early spiritual autobiography to later representatives of the autobiographical mode in American literature is to encounter the many-sided Franklin, about whom all these things may be true at once. My own view is that in nineteenth-century America, Franklin was imitated more by deed than by autobiographical word, whereas the form and ingredients of early spiritual autobiography proved viable in a number of major

234

contributions to American literature, among them *Walden, Song of Myself,* much of Emily Dickinson's poetry, and *The Education of Henry Adams.*

I

The significance of Franklin's autobiography for American culture has been recognized from the beginning. Benjamin Vaughan, who had already edited some of Franklin's non-scientific writing in 1779, needed only Franklin's outline of his projected memoirs as a basis for observing: "All that has happened to you is also connected with the detail of the manners and situation of *a rising* people."[1] Vaughan's remark, made somewhat "at hazard" since he had not read the manuscript, has been echoed many times since 1783, frequently enough suggesting that other observers have written at a similar distance from the autobiographical text. Franklin's rise to affluence, his involvement in the struggle for independence, and his habit of inventing things may be generalized about in terms applicable to American cultural history and without recourse to the *Autobiography.* But like most American literature before 1830, Franklin's *Autobiography* derives major ingredients from England. Its Americanness cannot be discussed without noting that Ben Franklin, the archetypal apprentice studying hard to make good, is at least as much a product of English literature and society as of the American Dream. The Young Tradesman whom Franklin addressed in 1748 with the advice that "The Sound of your Hammer at Five in the Morning, or Nine at Night, heard by a Creditor

[1] Franklin apparently wished Vaughan's letter included in his manuscript. See *The Autobiography of Benjamin Franklin,* ed. Leonard W. Labaree, Ralph L. Ketcham, Helen C. Boatfield, and Helene H. Fineman (New Haven, 1964), p. 135.

235

makes him easy Six Months longer,"[2] could also learn from George Lillo's domestic tragedy, *The London Merchant*,[3] what befalls the apprentice who allows himself to be diverted from his task. The Young Tradesman who appears in the *Autobiography*, easing the minds of creditors as he wheels home his own supplies of paper, is a stock character following conventional advice. And although Lillo's George Barnwell is a very sentimental bad example, he has his equivalent in Franklin's characterization of his ne'er-do-well companions, Collins and Ralph, the one too drunk to join Franklin on a visit to the Governor of New York, the other a dissolute, would-be poet, likeable, but a burden and temptation to the earnest young printer. The affable "strumpets" Franklin is warned against by a grave, sensible Quakeress resemble more the "gallant dainty dame" who tempts Barnwell to destruction in the popular ballad[4] than the more complicated Mistress Millwood of Lillo's drama, but the family resemblance is close enough.

The two earliest reactions to the *Autobiography* on record refer Franklin's work to established traditions. Without specifying the body of writing he had in mind, Benja-

[2] "Advice to a Young Tradesman, Written by an Old One," *The Papers of Benjamin Franklin*, ed. Leonard W. Labaree and Whitfield J. Bell, Jr. (New Haven, 1961), III, 307.

[3] Lillo's drama was so successful that it went through eight editions from its first production in 1731 to 1740. There were also five pirated editions in the same period of time. See the editor's Introduction, *The London Merchant*, ed. William H. McBurney (Lincoln, 1965), pp. ix-xi. Staged ninety-six times in England between 1731 and 1747, the play was given to American audiences by at least two acting companies in the 1750's. See Arthur Hobson Quinn, *A History of the American Drama* (New York, 1923), pp. 8-9.

[4] Lillo took his plot from an old ballad, first printed in 1650: McBurney, *The London Merchant*, p. xv. The ballad is printed as an appendix to this edition, pp. 86-89, and may have been known to Franklin, who composed several "wretched" pieces himself "in the Grubstreet Ballad Stile."

min Vaughan remarked, "This style of writing seems a little gone out of vogue, and yet it is a very useful one."[5] Franklin's Quaker acquaintance, Abel James, compared the same portion of the narrative to the journals of public Friends, noting the great influence on youth of "Writings under that Class."[6] More recently, the first section of the *Autobiography*, which has the largest proportion of narrative, has been compared to a picaresque novel.[7] *Joseph Andrews* (1742), in particular, serves up two passages that indicate the transatlantic currency of certain types and ideas in the exemplary literature of the period and the immersion of the *Autobiography* in those influences. One of Franklin's earliest lessons in self-reliance comes with the discovery that an offer by Sir William Keith to "set him up" will never be fulfilled, that in fact it was Keith's "known Character to be liberal of Promises which he never meant to keep" (p. 87). In telling this story, Franklin does away with the element of suspense from the outset in order to emphasize the youth's innocence and the vulnerability of a hope for future success which is based on gratuity rather than industry: "I believed him one of the best Men in the World." The revelation of his folly in voyaging to London on a promise is shocking to "a poor ignorant Boy," but the narrator speaks from larger experience in commenting, "It was

5 Letter to Franklin, *Autobiography*, p. 138.

6 Letter to Franklin, *Autobiography*, p. 134. James might well have been thinking of a journal like Thomas Chalkley's, which exhorts youth to sound mercantile virtues in language more familiar to us through Franklin's writing. Franklin printed Chalkley's *Works* in 1749. The anecdote Franklin uses in the *Autobiography* to rationalize his lapse from vegetarianism is mindful of Chalkley's observation: "Sailing in the great Deeps we saw the Wonders of the Lord, particularly in divers Kinds of Fish, they living upon one another in the Sea, the great Fishes on the small Ones; and Mankind too much resembles them in that Respect" (*Journal*, pp. 98-99).

7 Robert Sayre, *The Examined Self: Benjamin Franklin, Henry Adams, Henry James* (Princeton, 1964), p. 18.

237

a Habit he had acquired. He wished to please every body; and having little to give, he gave Expectation." The boy would have done well to read in *Joseph Andrews* the chapter in which Parson Adams has been promised a handsome living, lodging for the night, and horses for the next day by a gentleman who subsequently leaves word that he has gone on a long journey. In this case, an inn-keeper, rather than Franklin's Quaker merchant, confirms the gentleman's known character. The event justifies the suspicions of Joseph Andrews, who cites it as "a maxim" among the serving class in London "that those masters who promise the most perform the least."[8]

An even more exemplary portion of Fielding's work is Wilson's memoir of his life as a London dandy.[9] In the midst of debaucheries from which he was later reclaimed, Wilson had associated himself with a group who agreed to be guided by infallible human reason and by "a certain rule of right," propositions that seemed attractive until he saw one member steal another's wife and two others renege on their debts. Young Franklin is both leader and victim of such a group in the *Autobiography*, first convincing Collins and Ralph of the truth of his Deistic arguments, then, having been wronged by both men, "and recollecting Keith's conduct towards me, (who was another Freethinker) and my own towards Vernon and Miss Read which at times gave me great Trouble, I began to suspect that this Doctrine, tho it might be true, was not very useful" (p. 114).

Demonstrations of literary influence are, of course, notoriously untrustworthy, especially in the case of the autobiographer, to whom literary models may be entirely

[8] Henry Fielding, *The History of the Adventures of Joseph Andrews*, The Modern Library (New York, 1939), p. 205.
[9] *Ibid.*, pp. 235-263.

238

irrelevant. Presumably, Franklin mentions his "Inclinations for the Sea" and his father's apprehension that "I should break away and get to sea," because these details help along the narrative of his attempt to discover an appropriate vocation, not because Robinson Crusoe obeyed a similar inclination over similar paternal objections. However, when Franklin gave literary form to his narrative about a Young Tradesman he could scarcely escape from the presence of such characters as George Barnwell, Joseph Andrews, Robinson Crusoe, and John Bunyan's allegorical pilgrim, Christian, to whom the autobiographical Franklin has frequently been compared in his progress through the obstacles and temptations of a deceitful world. Whether, in any case, the figure of Benjamin Franklin embodies characteristics diffused through the society from which he emerged or was shaped out of the plentiful didactic literature of his time, he answers to a number of conventional expectations about young apprentices.

I I

In England and in America, the Puritan background contributed to these expectations. Franklin's *Autobiography* may be taken as a type of all the secular covenants made between Americans and a Puritanism trimmed of its forbidding theology. As John Cotton told Franklin's Boston ancestors, the true Christian will not rest until he finds some "warrantable calling," by which, he explained, "we not only aim at our own, but at the public good." In the *Autobiography*, Franklin acknowledges this debt indirectly when he cites the influence of Cotton Mather's *Essays to Do Good* "on some of the principal future Events of my Life." Yet Franklin will never be mistaken for a Puritan spiritual autobiographer. He follows a Puritan custom in addressing his "Memoirs" to his son; like Cotton Mather he shares with his reader the methods which experience had proved most useful for attaining his ends; and like Thomas Shepard he desires to thank Providence for favorable dispensations toward him. But *The Autobiography of Benjamin Franklin* carries on no inquisition of the soul. The narrative records, but is not itself a quest, an act of potential discovery.

The work of John Bunyan which most attracted Franklin and which is most often associated with the *Autobiography* is *Pilgrim's Progress*, rather than the spiritual narrative, *Grace Abounding*. In the former, the perils of the journey must be adequately characterized for the work to serve its purpose; but to show how Christian arrived finally at the Celestial City, these perils must be endurable and Christian's temptations conquerable. *Pilgrim's Progress* is a journey of discovery for Christian more than for Bunyan. One may wish to distinguish the speaker of *Grace Abounding* from the autobiographical character, but through most of the work the distinction is only technically valid. In a real sense, both may succumb to despair, both discover grace. *Pilgrim's Progress* (1678) not only follows *Grace Abounding* (1666) in time; its journey allegory is predicated upon the real quest undertaken in the autobiographical act.

This essential distinction is sometimes obscured by monolithic versions of Puritan autobiography: "For the Augustinian Christian, and the Puritan, personal history had order because God's ways were orderly and life was a period in which God revealed his order to his servants. For Franklin the possibilities of such revelation were exceedingly remote, and everything depended on each man's imposing some rational order on his daily life . . . or on his discover-

240

ing order by his own investigations."[10] All Puritan autobiographers, we have assumed, found the same order in
their lives, the indisputable order of the system that described the theology and mechanics of salvation. But in
Puritan autobiography, attempted and realized arguments
diverge so frequently for the evident reason that autobiographers were forced to seek answers to the question of grace,
not in the system, but in the heart.

Anne Bradstreet and Thomas Shepard encourage posterity to holiness through all the means afforded by autobiography—with one exception; to stress emulation of the
parent risked distracting one's children from their own
quest for grace. Edwards' *Personal Narrative* argues the
necessity of stringent criteria in judging spiritual experience, but it does not set forth an exemplar who would be
usefully imitated by spending "much time in viewing the
clouds and sky, to behold the sweet glory of God in these
things." Because the experience is carefully defined as an
effect rather than a cause of grace, its imitation would be
pointless. The pilgrim who moves through the first two sections of Franklin's *Autobiography* is himself exemplary in
both a positive and negative sense, in his virtues and errata
alike, and the Puritan autobiographer he resembles most in
this respect was also, interestingly enough, the most prolific
biographer of Puritan saints.

Cotton Mather works consistently to enlarge the exemplary features of his subjects both in "Paterna" and in the
gallery of lives he drew up for the *Magnalia Christi Ameri-
cana*, though he must counter vanity in writing about himself by making the character anonymous and by reducing
him to his methods. Franklin too reveals more of his methods than of himself, and in recommending devices genially

[10] Sayre, *The Examined Self*, pp. 34-35.

allows his name to be associated with the author of *Essays to Do Good*. The two men shared a common Enlightenment passion for projects in benevolence and membership in the Royal Society. In their respective styles—Mather's science would always support scripture—each had demonstrated an intention "to describe the *phenomena* of nature, to explain their causes. . . ."[11] Similarly, both men preferred instruction which emphasized, as Franklin said, the "Means and Manner of obtaining Virtue," not the "mere Exhortation to be good."[12] In the age of Newton it was common knowledge that an effect, goodness, could not be expected from men who remained ignorant of its proper cause. The doctrine of free grace was preached as soundly by Cotton Mather as by his predecessors, but the *Essays to Do Good*, and their autobiographical equivalent, "Paterna," share with Franklin the elation of the New Science at being able to describe and participate in the great cause and effect system of Nature for the benefit of man and the greater glory of God.[13]

[11] Colin Maclaurin, *An Account of Sir Isaac Newton's Philosophical Discoveries* (1775), quoted in Carl Becker, *The Heavenly City of the Eighteenth-Century Philosophers* (New Haven, 1932), p. 62.

[12] Concentration on the means of effecting good was also appropriate for Mather as a pastor to Christians not subject to hierarchical authority and immersed in rapid social change. See David Levin's Introduction to his modern edition of *Bonifacius: An Essay upon the Good* (Cambridge, 1966), p. xv. Franklin, incidentally, would have read the portion of *Bonifacius* in which Mather, concealing his authorship of some advice on making pastoral visits, quoted from "the memorials of one who long since did so, and then left his PATERNA to his *son* upon it . . ." (p. 75). The running title, *Essays to Do Good*, identified this work, even in Franklin's time, rather than the more descriptive subtitle, "An Essay Upon the Good, that is to be Devised and Designed, By Those Who Desire to Answer the Great End of Life, and to Do Good While they Live."

[13] Mather exudes this feeling as he begins his work: "The *essay*, which I am now upon, is only to dig open the several *springs* of *usefulness*; which having once begun to run, will spread into *streams*, which no *human foresight* can comprehend. *Spring up, O well!* . . . Perhaps almost every proposal to be now mentioned, may be like a

It is true that the amount of substantial empirical science in Franklin's *Autobiography* comes to very little. First readers must always be disappointed that the kite experiment receives only passing mention. But the utilitarian habit of mind flourishes everywhere as Franklin describes his probing for the agent of control, the cause whose effect is certain, and expresses his admiration for the success of men like George Whitefield, whose power is observable in his effects. "It was wonderful to see the Change soon made in the Manners of our Inhabitants," observes Franklin, before citing another and scarcely believable result of the preacher's power: "he finish'd so admirably, that I empty'd my Pocket wholly into the Collector's Dish, Gold and all" (pp. 175-177). Curious about the engine of his undoing, Franklin brushes aside questions of religious, social, or psychological causation to measure immediately the radius of Whitefield's voice and to compute the number of his auditors.

For Franklin the equivalent engine had been his prose, which he valued as a "principal means of my Advancement." As the narrative makes clear, control attained through the means of exercise and imitation leads eventually to significant results in one's personal fortune and in the affairs of others. A piece of his own writing, Franklin points out, created a clamor for paper money which the legislature could not neglect and brought the printing contract to his own house.[14] Whether or not it was true that

---

stone falling on a *pool*; *reader*, keep thy mind *calm*, and see, whether the effect prove not so! That one *circle* (and *service*) will produce another, until they extend, who can tell, how far? and they cannot be reckoned up." *Bonifacius*, p. 33.

[14] However, Franklin's memory shortened the distance between cause and effect. The editors of the *Autobiography* show that he received the contract to print currency, not immediately, but two years later, in 1731 (p. 124n).

"Verse-makers were generally Beggars," as Josiah Franklin remarked on observing his son's interest in poetry, the experience of the *Autobiography* argues at least that poetry does not appear to be a cause of anything good, except perhaps better prose: "I approv'd the amusing one's self with Poetry now and then, so far as to improve one's Language, but no farther," observes Franklin (p. 90), echoing Mather's qualified approval of writing poetry "to sharpen your sense and polish your style for more important performances" in his *Manuductio ad Ministerium* (1726).

The Puritan aesthetic is at work here, of course, refusing to grant poetry the status of a "warrantable calling," but Franklin is less concerned with the sensualism of the imagination than its inefficacy. The temperance of the young apprentice dining on bread, raisins, and water makes no sermon on starving the body to save the soul, but it does make clear the sequence of good effects proceeding from control of appetite: money is saved, books are bought, which may be read, with a clearer mind, in the period otherwise spent taking a meal. Incident after incident recounts similar discoveries of power over nature as the protagonist extends his control over an increasingly large network of causation. The project for achieving moral perfection, which would have seemed a staggering implausibility in the context of Edwards' *Personal Narrative*, becomes an understandable and perhaps inevitable ambition for the protagonist of Franklin's *Autobiography*. To gain control of the causes of virtue in himself seems no vain hope in view of his past successes. At just this point, however, Franklin has propounded his autobiographical argument in its most extreme form. Having exhausted all his devices, the protagonist must finally accept the speckled ax of human fallibility. The experiment has been disappointing,

244

but Franklin proffers his methods rather than his achievement as exemplary. A speckled ax cuts as well; method tends, however gradually, toward improvement. Sin may be an operable disease, even though the patient will always lack Adam's health.

III

The anecdote of the speckled ax belongs of course to the narrator, a witty, veteran traveler who stands apart from the developments of the narrative, measuring the protagonist against later experience. Understandably, modern readers have been especially alert to the recurring note of irony in the narrator's voice, but it is obviously overstating the case to suggest that Franklin never meant all he said about industry and frugality. His amusement at an innocent youth's estimate of human perfectibility does not hinder him from carefully reproducing his thirteen commandments, a sample chart of moral health, and the daily "Scheme of Employment." The passage informing the reader that "a little black Spot" imaged Ben Franklin's offenses invites a large measure of irony, and the narrator uses none. Instead, a pattern of unconscious symbolism suggests that both protagonist and narrator have forgotten what Puritans knew about human depravity. Franklin tells how the paper on which he recorded his faults "became full of Holes" with frequent erasure, making it necessary to transfer his chart to ivory leaves, "on which the Lines were drawn with red Ink that made a durable Stain, and on those Lines I mark'd my Faults with a black Lead Pencil, which Marks I could easily wipe out with a wet Sponge" (p. 155). There is no certainty in sin, which passes away, but the indelible red lines of method remain forever.

When irony appears, it signifies, to be sure, that the autobiographer is not wholly within his autobiography. Yet a reader has no direct sight of the wider life thus implied. Franklin draws a larger circle than the Puritan in delimiting experience fit for autobiography, but he defends his borders as carefully. Anecdotes that threaten to assert an independent reason for being are at last fashioned for display as exemplary versions of method and control. In successive paragraphs Franklin describes his relation with the widow from whom he rented in London and a visit to another of her boarders, the Roman Catholic anchoress who lived in the garret. The cameos in which Franklin recalls his conversation with these ladies impress the reader again with his ability to work effectively in miniature, scenically as well as in the pithy saying and the bagatelle. The brief sketches of the young American apprentice sharing an anchovy and a pint of beer with his landlady, charmed by her stories of the times of Charles II; later, inspecting the room of the seventy-year-old recluse who confessed her vain thoughts daily, taking in her solemn explanation of a picture of Veronica's handkerchief—these reminiscences finally justify their existence in Franklin's summary remarks, which call attention to the two shillings rent his landlady abated him for his companionship and to the illustration provided by the lady in the garret "on how small an Income Life and Health may be supported." With the sense of a duty to be performed, the didactic impulse edges aside others, nostalgic, curious, ironic, in order to carry on its argument.

It seems evident, then, that Franklin had no intention of allowing irony's counterpoint to become a counter-argument which would reduce the earnest apprentice to ludicrous sobriety and self-esteem. Irony forms part of a rhetoric sufficiently flexible to mediate between the demands of two very different audiences, the urbane readership that would set down copies of Voltaire in order to take up the memoirs of Franklin, and plain-minded readers like Abel James and Benjamin Vaughan. The harmony between Franklin's didacticism and his irony is well demonstrated in the characterization of Keimer, his first employer, whose failure as a printer coincides with Franklin's success. With obvious relish, Franklin relates the story of how Keimer, an enthusiast and dogmatist, agrees to practice vegetarianism with his apprentice. Eventually, flesh craves its kind, and Keimer invites Franklin and two ladies to share a roast pig with him, "but it being brought too soon upon the table, he could not resist the Temptation, and ate it all up before we came." Franklin treats Keimer's surrender as no more a vice in itself than his vegetarianism was a virtue. What Franklin enjoys is the vanquished dogmatist. He turns equal scorn on the Croaker, a local prophet of doom who maintains that Philadelphia is "a decaying Place . . . going to Destruction," and who must later buy property at five times its original worth. Yet the *Autobiography* offers no better example of delusion and the fixed idea than in its chief character, who goes penniless to England believing his own high opinion of himself is shared by the former governor, who prefers to rationalize vegetarianism when it is as easy to rationalize a taste for cod, and who conceives ambitious projects for moral perfection. Irony becomes at last the only device against an enthusiastic purveyor of devices and through its liberal use Franklin enforces his ban on "every Word or Expression in the Language that imparted a fix'd Opinion."

The history of "ambivalence toward Franklin and his

247

legend" pointed out by the Yale editors of the *Autobiography* is in part the history of attention to one pole or the other of Franklin's autobiographical argument. D. H. Lawrence, gifted with nearly infallible intuition in his *Studies of Classic American Writers,* lays bare the Franklinian code in the mechanistic non-soul of American materialism; but as a kind of dogmatist himself, Lawrence lacks patience to appreciate the Franklin who, failing to achieve moral perfection, reflected that after all "a perfect Character might be attended with the Inconvenience of being envied and hated" (p. 156). Exclusive emphasis on Franklin the ironist and shape-shifter, on the other hand, tends to neglect the powerful appeal of Franklin's *Autobiography* to the same desire that energizes the quest for grace, the hope of triumph over nature and limitation. Such a hope is universal and must account in the deepest sense for the popularity of Franklin's *Autobiography* abroad, though its proper setting has been the physical and economic wilderness of America. Neither a spiritual autobiography in the tradition of the Puritans and Quakers nor an American achievement in its formal characteristics, Franklin's *Autobiography* yet achieves a distinctly American mixture of naive perfectionism and skeptical empiricism, assuring its reader through autobiographical example that the world has yielded repeatedly to the onslaught of method, while reserving irony as a defense against hoping too much. Whatever we now find shallow or derivative in the *Autobiography* proved serviceable in its own time at least. If Franklin's example continues to survive its period of material service, it will do so on the strength of his argument that a man can make tolerable progress casting ahead of himself with reason, retaining only a settled bias against self-deceit.

The Quaker and Puritan
Autobiographical Modes:
Thoreau, Whitman, Dickinson, and Adams

I

In a broad view Quaker journals and Puritan spiritual narratives look nearly alike. They share a staple subject matter in the experience of conversion, recall providential events gratefully, and together obey the didactic, evangelizing impulse that makes a communal responsibility of autobiography. The spiritual autobiographies of both groups derive energy from a principle of quest. The Puritan, having decided to reopen the question of grace for definitive autobiographical treatment, and observing formerly persuasive evidence disintegrate, might within the context of his narrative find himself a pilgrim once again. God's mercy to sinners, and the ultimate wisdom of Providence, would never be subject to persistent doubt; but whether these were truths for other men or for oneself might be an open question. For the Quaker, for John Woolman especially, autobiography was a place of vision as well as a means of conveying it. The endless journeying of the public Friend can be seen as the physical counterpart of his search for illumination and of the moral effort to conform his will to the divine.

The din of sectarian controversy in the seventeenth century frequently makes it difficult to detect slight variations in a single refrain. By giving special attention to the doctrine of the Holy Spirit, Geoffrey Nuttall has demonstrated both continuity and gradual differentiation from conservative Presbyterianism through more radical Puritanism to the Quakers.[15] To conservative reformers, the divine life of grace, formerly in the custody of Popes and holy bones, was communicated by the Spirit through two principal means, scripture and the ordinances. Yet this greater economy of forms permitted no relaxation of vigilance against Roman idolatry. Christ was not got by a wet finger, omnivorous scripture readers were warned. Puritan theologians described baptism and the Lord's Supper as seals of the covenant, not curatives for the unregenerate. Quaker doctrine obviated such warnings by eliminating the sources of idolatry. No fear of deifying scripture need afflict the cautious and well-disposed Friend to whom Truth was revealed by an inward motion of the Spirit. No need to depend on church or ministers as custodians, expositors, or judges of grace when the seed of divine life might be brought to bear fruit in any man. Thus the materials and the dimension of the autobiographical quest differ from Puritans to Quakers. The more tangible stuff of Puritan autobiography was drawn from identifiable emotions appearing in discernible order and from events and experiences, whether beneficial or chastizing, that bore the clear stamp of Providence. A new spiritual sight suggests the graciousness of the autobiographical character in Jonathan Edwards' *Personal Narrative*, but Edwards, finally uncomfortable amidst visionaries, strategically tempers his emphasis on "imaginations." David Ferris had to leave his Presbyterianism behind in order to follow the Light and, as a Quaker autobiographer, have freedom to describe the full range of his illuminations.

Puritans sermonized against mere legalism, but they abhorred and exiled Antinomians. When, precisely two hundred years after the trial of Anne Hutchinson, Emerson

[15] *The Holy Spirit in Puritan Faith and Experience* (Oxford, 1947).

renewed the case against an idolatry of forms before the Harvard Divinity School, he was exiled for his heresy, escaping of course the punishments formerly dealt out to Quakers, though he too had spoken against historical Christianity and denounced an ennervated priest class. With the Quakers, Emerson affirmed that any rationalizing of the Spirit's operations tended toward the systematic confinement and eventually the dissipation of vital piety. The purer Puritanism opts always for infinity.

II

Autobiography in the illuminist-antinomian tradition, then, whether written by Quakers or Transcendentalists, cannot exhaust the dimension it explores. Because, in its relation to spirit the self is finally unsourced and unspeakable, autobiography cannot be content to describe a finished history in rationalized pattern. Rather, autobiography is present at the act by which the spirit realizes itself and must conclude arbitrarily, since the well of Truth, like Walden Pond, has no bottom and the appetite for infinity no satisfaction. For the Quaker autobiographer this act, whose analogue is the speaker's rising to share his inspiration in meeting, takes place in the midst of others whom in some sense it includes. The Quaker writes, as he speaks in meeting, with a sense that what he says is not entirely his own either in its origin or its application. Yet as Woolman's manuscript revisions make clear, it may paradoxically be necessary for the autobiographer to make deliberate adjustments in order to clarify the object of vision. There was a moral imperative to remove obstructions between the audience and Truth. Strategies toward union of the autobiographer and his reader might legitimately be employed without dishonor to the Spirit—though Woolman's strategies

251

are so integrally a part of his character as to make terms of art irrelevant. The unity thus established between the journalist and his reader could serve as a type of perfection in the more difficult encounters, the collisions between selves that took place outside the medium of autobiography.

A Puritan autobiographer often addresses the more exclusive community of his own posterity, but the difference between his autobiographical rhetoric and the Quaker's has nothing to do with the numbers or consanguinity of the audience. The divergence of autobiographical arguments in Thomas Shepard's narrative indicates that while the speaker may overtly address the composition to a son, he is also submitting his experiential arguments to a judging God who dwells both in eternity and in that part of the autobiographer which habitually doubts all evidence of grace. The fuller revelation of the latter God, prophesied in Samuel Hopkins' autobiography, comes in the poetry of Emily Dickinson and *The Education of Henry Adams*. In Edwards' *Personal Narrative*, Puritan autobiography attains an equilibrium between a principle of isolation, which risks calling evidence of grace into question, and a principle of instruction, which extends the benefit of the narrator's inquiry to the community. Other spiritual autobiographers writing at about the same time and in the same general tradition elevate one principle or another. Cole's *Spiritual Travels* and Samuel Hopkins' *Sketches* isolate themselves about equally, though for different reasons, from their social context. Cole treasures up a private vision, and, following his failure to save his wife, finds himself unwilling or unable to extend it to others. Even while writing as the solicitous pastor, Samuel Hopkins seems equally isolated, not in the hot mystical core of experimental religion but outside the rational system that describes it, at times even outside the mind that describes the system. Like Henry Adams, he thus preserves himself from a rash faith, but cannot be saved from the critical force of his own mind.

Increase and Cotton Mather, and Benjamin Franklin after them, find ways of being more serviceable, but at the expense of diminishing the principle of risk that gave previous instructions their force and vitality. The magnetism by which Increase Mather's "I" affixes itself to exemplary type figures, while not a new technique in Puritan didactic writing, becomes symptomatic of a more mechanical principle of autobiographical self-definition. As autobiographers, both Mathers work toward and occasionally achieve unprecedented control over their evidence, no longer deriving conclusions by the process of timorous induction in which Thomas Shepard is still suspended at the close of his narrative. Somewhat tentatively in the autobiography of Increase Mather and triumphantly in the "Paterna," conclusions are wrought out of a closed system of deduction. God must so conduct himself in His dealings with His servants that an account of their lives will be a source of hope not dismay. Good works cannot win grace, but God must be exonerated from so conspicuous an irrationality as a servant who, though he had no grace, was abundant in its usual effects.

In Franklin's *Autobiography*, the tendency toward deductive self-characterization seems anomalous in a man who attempted to clear his mind of presuppositions and whose habit of induction was demonstrated most successfully in his scientific experiments. The *Autobiography*, however, records a finished experiment. From the narrator's eminence in the present, straight lines lead back directly to causes in the early experience, even the heredity of young Ben Franklin. When great-great-grandfather Franklin is

253

shown contriving a device for reading the family Bible without being detected by Queen Mary's soldiers, and when we learn that grandfather Folger wrote a verse "in favour of Liberty of Conscience . . . with a good deal of Decent Plainness and manly Freedom," and that grandfather Franklin was "a chief mover of all publick Spirited Undertakings," we are on our way to deducing with the author the autobiographical character of Benjamin Franklin. Even with its harmless irony, the anecdote of the young projector who led his playmates in constructing a stone wharf partakes of what Henry James called "that economy of observation after the fact"[16] which is the luxury and special temptation of autobiographical argument.

Autobiographical writing gains in drama, intensity, and achievement as it struggles against the closed system of which James speaks and which was latent in Puritan rationalism. Jonathan Edwards' antagonist in the *Personal Narrative* is not the threat of damnation, but the superstructure of logic he had built to protect and enshrine heart religion. The great danger was that he should only be deducing his salvation from his own texts on the "Distinguishing Marks" of grace; yet Edwards gives no such impression. Readers still find him uncertain of his conversion[17] even though he speaks unambiguously of times "before I had it [grace]," "before my conversion." Edwards' scrupulous testing of ordinary pious language and his straining to transcend boundaries of expression make real the possibility of failure as surely as if the narrator were a fledgling in grace. Emily Dickinson and Henry Adams are two descendants of the Puritans whose writing about self

[16] *Henry James, Autobiography,* ed. Frederick W. Dupee (New York, 1956) , p. 126.
[17] See Perry Miller, *Jonathan Edwards* (New York, 1959) , p. 208; and Sayre, *The Examined Self,* p. 38.

254

frequently attains a similar kind of tension as the mind attempts to achieve release from its own rational constructs. For them, the quest of consciousness does not take place within the expanding limits of Thoreau's and Whitman's universe of Light, but within self-constructed labyrinths of mind. No sooner does the protagonist-consciousness of a Dickinson poem or of the *Education* repose faith in such a construct than it proves incapable of bearing the trust. The Puritan self which was willing to surrender to a perfected structure asserts its identity against structure and breaks free, only to be tempted again and failed again by rational equivalents of the ideal purified church.

To stress these continuities of autobiographical pattern is to go beyond purely informational glosses on Calvinist terms in Emily Dickinson or on the Quakerish primitivism Whitman achieves by rejecting the world's names for months and days. One may note the possible echo of Woolman's first autobiographical sentence in the opening of *Song of Myself* ("I now thirty-seven years old in perfect health begin . . .") or compare the social testimony of Woolman's *Journal* and *Walden*, yet fail to isolate the dynamic of continuity in these first person works or the results in form of their common preoccupations. The definitive first-person utterances of Thoreau and Whitman owe no individual debts, of course, to John Churchman or David Ferris or even to Woolman, but they have participated in the transformation of the theology and piety of reforming Protestantism into central romantic doctrines, a process which can be observed almost in its entirety in Emerson.[18]

18 Hoxie Neale Fairchild gives a deprecating but substantially valid history of Emerson's spiritual descent: "Puritanism sloughs down into Unitarianism; Unitarianism sloughs down into a romantic transcendentalism partly indigenous and partly fabricated from English, German, and Oriental materials": *Religious Trends in English Poetry.*

Thoreau and Whitman continue to explore the dimensions of illuminist autobiography with the hope of introducing Light into the gathering darkness of American society. Emily Dickinson and Henry Adams refused the Puritan Christianity of their inheritance, yet their first-person writing engages in something like a quest for grace precisely for this reason, and they find themselves in rhetorical situations comparable to those of their Puritan predecessors. Emily Dickinson speaks of writing a "letter to the World"; but her most carefully constructed poems are arguments addressed to herself or hurled at God, and the deadly earnestness of her pursuit frequently leaves all audiences behind. Henry Adams speaks ostensibly to students desiring education, but his argument too is reflexive and within its solipsistic limits employs an "economy of observation after the fact" as consistently as any Puritan's reading of Providence. These works deserve the name of autobiography as little or as much as Edwards' *Personal Narrative* or Woolman's *Journal* and for many of the same reasons. In brief space, I would like to suggest some of the possibilities for further study in relating major features of Puritan and Quaker autobiography to their most prominent descendants.

III

The chief benefit of setting *Walden* and *Song of Myself* against the background of Quaker autobiographical writing

---

Vol. III: 1780-1830, Romantic Faith (New York, 1949), p. 12. Fairchild's genealogy provides no estimate of the relative importance of these elements, but Perry Miller's essay, "From Edwards to Emerson" is enormously suggestive about the native strain, not simply in Emerson's thought, but in his conception of his mission. See *Errand into the Wilderness* (Cambridge, 1956), pp. 184-203. Frederick Tolles makes judicious use of Emerson's affiliations with Quakers and his reading in Quaker books in "Emerson and Quakerism," *American Literature*, x (March 1938), pp. 142-165.

is, I think, to heighten awareness of the rhetorical aspects of both works and to establish a vocabulary that helps describe their functioning. To call them spiritual autobiographies of a sort provides only a general orientation to their content, but in relation to the Quaker journal the term has quite specific implications for form. The speaker in Woolman's *Journal*, or *Walden*, or *Song of Myself* is never merely retrospective about a life in the past; he strives to isolate the principle of life itself and to share it with, proffer it to, the reader. Admittedly, terms of art have increasing appeal as one moves from one-dimensional autobiography to more distanced forms of writing about self, but it is appropriate to recall Whitman's caution against belletristic appropriation of documents in the first person: "No one will get at my verses who insists upon viewing them as a literary performance, or attempt at such performance, or as aiming mainly toward art or aestheticism." Whitman's words apply equally well to *Walden* and the *Journal* of John Woolman. Both works willingly violate the intuitional theology that informs them by attending frequently to strategies of planned illumination. Woolman's revisions from manuscript to manuscript seem the merest tinkerings in comparison with Thoreau's shaping of *Walden* over a period of eight years, through seven manuscript versions, by repeated plunderings and redisposition of his journal materials.[19] There appears a considerable distance to be covered between Whitman—a quite carnal Quaker even when he agrees with Woolman that "a kelson of the creation is love"—and a peerless didact like John Churchman,

[19] See J. Lyndon Shanley, *The Making of Walden* (Chicago, 1957). Perry Miller has shown that the journals themselves are "anything but spontaneous. They are extracted out of a previous manuscript, have already been gone over, been rigidified." *Consciousness in Concord* (Boston, 1958), p. 23.

257

whose intention in writing autobiography was "to encourage the humbled, carefull traveler in the way of his duty." Yet the distance seems less when Whitman's bolder version of the traveling Friend, the Camerado, announces, "I tramp a perpetual journey (come follow all)." Thoreau, too, while denying his audience the pleasures of exotic travel narrative among the Chinese and Sandwich islanders, offers to share with them the benefit of his having traveled a good deal in Concord.

Priorities must be kept clear. Autobiography was not the preeminent genre for Whitman and Thoreau because it could be put to moral uses; but as the inevitable and all-subsuming genre, autobiography was also, like Nature itself, moral and instructive. Calling for the poet that Whitman eventually became, Emerson had praised Dante for daring "to write his autobiography in colossal cipher, or into universality." Thoreau reminds readers in the first few sentences of *Walden* "that it is, after all, always the first person that is speaking." Reviewing his career, Whitman could confess without embarassment to mediocre talents for description and dramatic situation because the time had come, he felt, to render all themes subjectively, "through the utterance of one, . . . the born child of the New World." A conviction of the primacy of the self's version of things helped indicate how the conviction might be extended, and excluded automatically the didactic methodism of autobiographers like Cotton Mather or Franklin. In his remarks on philanthropy, Thoreau puts the Mather-Franklin exemplar on trial and finds it wanting: "As for Doing-good, that is one of the professions which are full." Rejecting a religion of devices for a more primitive theology, Thoreau asserts the priority of Spirit to law, grace to works, being to act: "If I were to preach at all in this strain, I should say rather, Set about being good." Even among Quakers, John Woolman was unusual in recognizing that the autobiographer parted with his second best when he urged his methods rather than his vision on an audience. To deserve the name, the authentic traveling Friend of spiritual autobiography must promise, in the first person, the Open Road's endless potential for discovery:

> I give you myself before preaching or law;
> Will you give me yourself?
>   will you come travel with me?
> Shall we stick by each other as long as we live?

As spiritual autobiographers, then, Thoreau and Whitman offer no finished and imitable patterns but autobiographies of the present through the medium of whose "I," the one who sees, the reader's capacity for sight may be radically altered. Didacticism is not an element added on to the self's articulation. The autobiographer accomplishes his didactic ends—for Thoreau, "to front only the essential facts of life"; for Whitman, "to fill man with vigorous and clean manliness, religiousness, and give him *good heart* as a radical possession and habit"—as Woolman did, by rendering his vision available to his readers. The actions of the autobiographer are not what he has done but what he is presently seeing: "Walden was dead and is alive again"; "I am afoot with my vision."

The literary forms which accomplish unity between the reader and the vision of the autobiographer will vary with the rhetorical ingenuity of each writer. Thoreau exploits Yankee thrift and Yankee curiosity about his doings at the pond, in order to initiate a discussion of economy which employs a materialistic and commercial vocabulary while working subtly to demolish it. The reader for whom such

words have made up reality sees them overturned by paradox and at times nearly carried out of sight by Thoreau's
extravagant punning. His guide has lost him, intentionally,
in order to help him find himself again.[20] Increasingly
docile to Truth, the reader can begin to assimilate the
organic vocabulary of Nature requisite to the saving vision
of the chapter on spring. Thoreau's final achievement as
spiritual autobiographer very much resembles Woolman's.
He does not appear so much to be purveying the words of
life as articulating the life shared in Nature by autobiographer and reader. The generally chronological structure
of *Walden* is never more important in itself than the rhetorical structure designed to restore Nature by making possible a new sight of its most profound reality.[21]

Bound to chronology even less than Thoreau, Whitman
also explores more varieties of autobiographical argument
in *Song of Myself*, coaxing the reader out of systematic
thought and into a passive waiting on Light, drawing him
into a confessional identification with the repressed life of
the twenty-ninth bather, exemplifying in his barbaric yawp
the self's pleasure at its own creation. As autobiographical
song rather than narrative the poem has always presented
the problem of describing its most comprehensive pattern;
yet the problem is not a new one: "But these words are so
strangely jumbled together that every line has good sens in

[20] The speaker in Robert Frost's "Directive" thus describes his own
strategy. In its argument, the poem is a faithful précis of *Walden*,
and brings the reader at last to life-giving waters. Frost's imagery of
transience, "the house that is no more a house, / But only a belilaced
cellar hole, / Now slowly closing like a dent in dough," apparently
has its original in Thoreau's chapter, "Former Inhabitants; and Winter
Visitors."

[21] The scheme of *Walden* answered directly Emerson's challenge in
Nature: "The problem of restoring to the world original and eternal
beauty is solved by the redemption of the soul. The ruin or the blank
that we see when we look at nature, is in our own eye."

it, but all together none . . . handsom words, som dreaming conceits interlarded with undeniable truths, . . . endless tautologies, and no connexion. . . ."[22]

So ran a seventeenth-century description of "a good *Quakers* book," accurately but imperceptively describing what Jackson Cope has termed the "incantatory style" of the early Quakers. Characterized by incredible repetition, this style is not intended for the examination and display of given ideas. Instead, it is "an epistemological tool," a process-style through which the speaker, self-hypnotized, arrives at a time-conquering vision of the Word within the words of Scripture.[23] In doing so, the speaker extended his own vision to others. It is not surprising, therefore, that Whitman, who chanted his songs believing as the Quaker did, in an Inner Light, should also wish to distinguish his autobiographical strategy from that of the conventional didact: "I seek less to state or display any theme or thought, and more to bring you, reader, into the atmosphere of the theme or thought—there to pursue your own flight." This medium, surely, is the primal atmosphere of breath, echoes, ripples, whispers, into which the reader is introduced at the beginning of *Song of Myself,* thereafter to be joined to the

[22] John Vincent Canes, *Fiat Lux* (1662), quoted by Jackson I. Cope in "Seventeenth-Century Quaker Style," *PMLA,* LXXI (September 1956), p. 738.
[23] Edwin Cady speculates that although Quaker censors finally suppressed the incantatory style, its oral survival may well have influenced Woolman's rhetoric. *John Woolman* (New York, 1965), p. 136. Cady quotes a European visitor who, when he visited a Quaker meeting in Philadelphia in 1749, was fascinated by the group's "peculiar mode of expression, which is half singing, with a strange cadence, as it were, with a half or occasionally a full sob" (p. 60). For Whitman's response to Quaker preaching, see his essay on Elias Hicks in *November Boughs.* Whitman urges the reader to acquire Hick's *Journal,* describes his preaching as a "magnetic stream of natural eloquence," and credits Hicks with "an unnameable something behind oratory, a fund within or atmosphere without, deeper than art, deeper even than proof."

protagonist, "crotch and vine," in all his life processes, triumphs, and ebbings of vision, in all of his "changes of garments." For all their differences, Woolman's *Journal* and Whitman's *Song of Myself* closely resemble one another in effecting this kind of unity between speaker and reader. By contrast, Thoreau's more calculating rhetoric is sometimes contemptuous of those who are incapable of being persuaded by it. A hierarchy which places the French-Canadian woodchopper at a level of happy animality and gives poor John Field webbed feet does not tolerate sinners as easily as Whitman's loving and structurally democratic catalogues.

I V

If the writing about self of Emily Dickinson and Henry Adams is tragic, it is tragic according to the patterns of Puritan spiritual autobiography. The cornerstone doctrine of Puritan theology—God's absolute and irreproachable sovereignty—implied always the necessary defeat of man. Even in his mercy, God was not to be denied. In Edward Taylor's poem, *God's Determinations*, sinners are pursued by grace until they surrender. Emily Dickinson has been described as turning the experience of defeat into gains for consciousness; pain and perception are intimately associated in the tragic economy of loss.[24] The theme is indeed a familiar one in her poetry and the very existence of the poetry is evidence of the theme's validity. Yet there is no definitive Emily Dickinson poem, no structural point in her gathered writing at which one can say that here, climactically, vision outruns suffering. Her nearly 1,800 poems exhibit something more like the unresolved conflict of the

[24] Richard Wilbur, "Sumptuous Destitution," *Emily Dickinson: Three Views* (Amherst, 1960).

spiritual autobiographies of Shepard and Hopkins or the diaries of Michael Wigglesworth and Cotton Mather.

As students of the mind of Emily Dickinson have noted, one of the earliest and most important crises of her life was her decision not to be included among the awakened Christians gathered in during her year at the Mount Holyoke Seminary. She could not then lie in response to the question of grace, but neither could she escape from it thereafter. In the poem "I should have been too glad, I see—,"[25] the experiential referent is the speaker's sudden and devastating loss of a possible human ecstasy. But the poem consists in the speaker's challenge to the arguments for defeat, as if a Puritan like Thomas Shepard were disputing the hard way of Providence with him. The challenge operates through an irony of apparent acquiescence ("I should have been too saved—I see—"), and the adoption of a religious vocabulary as the proper vehicle for rejection ("So Savior—Crucify") conforms to this irony. The point remains, however, that the poem's originating experience is almost wholly submerged in this vocabulary and that, as a result, the poem comes to be about its arguments with God rather than the experiential referent. Its most important action is not the past defeat to which it alludes, but its movement toward the final line, " 'Faith' bleats—to understand!" For rhetorical daring the choice of "bleats" is worthy of Shepard or Increase Mather in their disputations with God. The speaker rests her case on a claim of "faith," redefined to mean, not certitude, but what an earlier Puritan would have called humiliation.

Like the Puritan confronting a cruel Providence, Emily Dickinson frequently took pain and its ultimate referent,

[25] No. 313 in *The Complete Poems of Emily Dickinson*, ed. Thomas H. Johnson (Boston, 1960) .

death, as a personal attack. Her adherence to the doctrine of divine sovereignty ("imperial affliction"), then, is not credal, but a form of respect for a worthy antagonist. The doctrine is further enforced by the plight of consciousness, which is driven to attempt an enlargement of its circumference, but must always fail to bring infinity within its limits. Yet consciousness has no other worthy objects: "The Riddle we can guess / We speedily despise—." As Puritan autobiography has its origin, not in graciousness but in the lack of it, a portion of Emily Dickinson's poetry—referred to alternatively in one poem (564) as "Prayer" or "Art" or "Tactics"—depends for its existence on the "Infinitude" it characteristically attempts to transcend. Poems in which the speaker's quest of mind succeeds in moving beyond its limits are either about death ("Because I could not stop for death") or result in the death of poetry: "awed beyond my errand— / I worshipped—did not 'pray.' " The soul does not enjoy its "Superior instants" without a "Mortal Abolition" (306), an ambivalent expression suggesting death as much as mystic withdrawal. Emily Dickinson is, then, most like the Puritan spiritual autobiographer when she is an anti-mystical poet, excessively aware of the sophistries and frauds that almost induce belief, longing for the Sacrament from which she has had to exclude herself.

The multiple discriminations of a mind scrutinizing its own perceptions make Emily Dickinson's poetry immensely more difficult in the individual instance than in its patterns, and this is no less true for *The Education of Henry Adams*. Respectful attention to the substance of Adams' intellectual odyssey calls for acquaintance with diverse kinds of knowledge, and in some detail. Yet one may say a great deal about the Adams family and nineteenth-century geology and fail to describe the autobiography's basic lines of force. Adams is arguing his defeat, his damnation, and the eventual defeat of the universe itself through an ever-increasing dissipation of its energies. In addition, moreover, to the failures of self and cosmos which the *Education* delineates and from which it takes its tone, it wills the failure of its most explicit argument, for, according to the book's deterministic themes, the Henry Adams whose education is being described could have viewed experience only in dual terms. The objective validity of Adams' description of history as a procession from unity in the thirteenth century to multiplicity in the twentieth is undermined from the beginning by the narrator's demonstration that, given his circumstances, the boy "could not but develop a double nature," could not but feel "that, for him, life was double." Emerson described the phenomenon in *Experience*, his own descent into the hell of subjectivism: "Given such an embryo, such a history must follow." From experience Emerson had caught sight of a pattern within this sense of life: "one lives in a sty of sensualism, and would soon come to suicide." In the final paragraphs of the *Education*, "strolling down to dine under the trees at Armenonville," Henry Adams learns that his friend John Hay is dead. The narrator, observing that education has now ended, and speaking of it from outside time, finds that his remaining actor has no motive to continue longer and notes his "assent to dismissal. It was time to go." He has extended autobiography to its furthest limit, taking his responsibility more seriously than men who write only about their lives; but the death of "Henry Adams" at the hands of Henry Adams is also the work's inevitable thematic conclusion.

The chapters in which Adams develops his theory of history may well seem a tiresome appendage to the story of an education which had "done its worst" by 1871, the year before his marriage, and provoke readers to ask for an inside narrative of the years that followed. Familiarity with the strict delimitations of Puritan autobiography would discourage such an expectation at the outset. The narrative of a search for grace, or for education, tyrannizes over all others and renders them insignificant by exclusion. But unlike Edwards' *Personal Narrative*, which excludes uniformly and unvaryingly, the *Education* narrows to its final solipsistic rationalism through stages. The most evident of these is the break between the chapters "Failure" and "Twenty Years After," covering the years of Adams' marriage and his wife's suicide in 1885. Another break, much earlier in the narrative, occurs in the chapter "Berlin," which at one point places the young American in a music hall, drinking beer. The climactic incident of the chapter bears detailed comparison with Edwards' *Personal Narrative* as Henry Adams, having declared "that he loathed Beethoven," appears to undergo an aesthetic conversion:

"Sitting thus at his beer-table, mentally impassive, he was one day surprised to notice that his mind followed the movement of a Sinfonie. He could not have been more astonished had he suddenly read a new language. Among the marvels of education this was the most marvelous. A prison-wall that barred his senses on one great side of life, suddenly fell, of its own accord, without so much as his knowing when it happened. Amid the fumes of coarse tobacco and poor beer, surrounded by the commonest of German Haus-frauen, a new sense burst out like a flower in his life, so superior to the old senses, so bewildering, so astonished at its own existence, that he could not credit it, and watched it as something apart, accidental, and not to be trusted."[26]

[26] *The Education of Henry Adams*, The Modern Library (New York, 1931), pp. 80-81.

In language Jonathan Edwards would have found familiar, an experience of conversion has just been set forth in its distinguishing marks: suddenness, awe, inexplicability, a rapturous "new sense," and a consequent alteration of mind, as accidental almost as Edwards' happening on the text from which he marked the beginning of his delight in a doctrine no less abhorrent than Beethoven. But like previous appeals in the *Education* to a non-utilitarian sense of the heart, many of which have clustered as associations around the memory of summer in Quincy, this one must be rejected. Education which is both accidental and aesthetic is no education at all for the twentieth century. From this mock-conversion experience, the autobiography takes a decisive direction. Up to this point the dualities of Henry Adams' life have been held in balance. Law, the utilitarian and commercial force of Boston, has been balanced by the affective and antinomian force of Quincy. The material advantages, as the narrator says, "seemed to lie wholly in State Street"; but Boston's standards are judged inferior from the perspective of Quincy. The Bible given to each child at birth by the President comments on the silver mugs supplied by grandfather Brooks, and Adams can still say that "on the whole" the boy "learned most" in the summer, reading Scott "and raiding the garden at intervals for peaches and pears." A doctrine of grace has contended equally with a doctrine of works, but the scene in the beer-garden defines the autobiography's subsequent recital of defeat.

The willful pattern of failure in the *Education* is nowhere clearer than when Henry Adams is damned by utilitarian values which the narrator has never accepted, and which he has in fact opposed by a counter-argument drawing upon the subversive, affective values of summer and art

267

and sex. Strongest at the beginning—the chapter "Quincy" gives way to "Boston"—the counter-argument becomes increasingly futile and distasteful to the narrator. After turning on sensual nature, which has betrayed him in the death of his sister, Adams is able to carry on his counter-argument only through the distanced form of the Virgin, "believed in" as Eliot said in *Gerontion*, "In memory only, reconsidered passion." In the final chapters of the *Education*, the mind has cast off all ties to sense. In a definitively Puritan obeisance to sovereignty, Henry Adams has decided as the twentieth century begins that "the mind could gain nothing by flight or by fight; it must merge in its supersensual multi-verse, or succumb to it." The autobiographical act, while an act of identity, must persist for the Puritan even into the sole absolute, extinction.

V

A recent study of Puritan piety and intellect based to a large extent on an inspection of the diaries of Samuel Sewall and Cotton Mather concludes that "puritans, at some level of their being, transmuted raw feeling into feeling sanctioned by their code."[27] Any inquiry into autobiographical writing makes clear that, allowing for a large variety of codes, one might so describe the rationalization of any group, including twentieth-century Americans. The difficulty is, of course, that no reader of autobiography has available for study the entity "raw feeling," any more than an historian is immediately in touch with a substance, "history." Samuel Sewall's terse, moralizing reflections on the deaths of his children may be cited as an example of the way Puritan ideas patterned responses "in the approved

[27] Robert Middlekauf, "Piety and Intellect in Puritanism," *William and Mary Quarterly*, Ser. 3, XXII (July 1965), p. 470.

way." Yet these are not responses encountered in the instant of their appearance, nor in any record of their approval by a synod on emotional orthodoxy, but in a diary, where reflection and didactic motive, operating in their acknowledged functions, did indeed relate the experience of death to the idea that sin and death were inseparable companions and that death "led ultimately to conformity with Christ." But this is only to discover that Puritans were Christians, as it would be possible to discover from Franklin's *Autobiography* that the writer was a Deist, or that the poetry of Emily Dickinson comprises an autobiography of definitive instants which is neither Christian nor Deist.

The question is not whether men attempt to order their experience, but how. The prevalence of the autobiographical mode in American literature provides a fascinating range of replies to this question. Literal-minded travel narratives like *The Oregon Trail* and *Two Years Before the Mast* occupy an important place next to the symbolic explorations of the protagonist-consciousness in *Moby Dick*. The autobiographies of Theodore Dreiser and Henry James deserve, I think, to be moved forward in the canon of each man's art. The problem of design and truth is crucial in contemporary Negro autobiography, for men like Malcolm X and Claude Brown are constrained to modify their rhetoric for an audience which is also the source of their grievance. The first to speak in this extensive autobiographical colloquy were Quakers and Puritans, whose contributions were, as they hoped, instructive.

BIBLIOGRAPHICAL ESSAY

I · PRIMARY SOURCES

THE supply of spiritual autobiographies written in the seventeenth and eighteenth centuries continues to exceed present demand, although American literary and cultural historians have come increasingly to recognize the uses of autobiographical documents. A number of sources lead one to the published works available for primary study, and the task could be enlarged by systematic investigation of the manuscript holdings of the major historical societies.

To begin, one may consult the biography section of the separate volume indexes to Charles Evans' *American Bibliography*, 14 vols. (Chicago and Worcester, 1903-1959), then read the autobiographical titles in the microprint series, *Early American Imprints, 1639–1800*, ed. Clifford K. Shipton, American Antiquarian Society. Use of the *Bibliography of American Autobiography* (Madison, 1961), compiled by Louis Kaplan, will help detect autobiographies written before 1800 but published perhaps many years later. The *Bibliography* index distinguishes both conversion narratives, a relatively small category, and autobiographies by clergymen, a large category, but, needless to say, not one interchangeable with the category of spiritual autobiography. If only as a listing, the *Bibliography* has filled a major need, but the entry on Jonathan Edwards' *Personal Narrative* suggests some of its limitations; assisting compilers appear to have cited whatever edition of an autobiography came to hand, in this case an 1830 edition of the *Works*, and the annotation, necessarily brief, is sometimes erroneous or misleadingly superficial: "A spiritual account, closing with 1723." Nevertheless, I am surprised that the

271

sources revealed by Kaplan have not been used more extensively, particularly by those in American Studies.

Working in a period before autobiography had acquired clear generic distinction, one is likely to discover personal narrative in a variety of places, such as wills and genealogies, or as a portion of a diary or journal. John Woolman's *Journal*, for instance, is not mentioned in Kaplan, but appears in both Harriette Forbes, *New England Diaries, 1602–1800* (Topsfield, 1923) and William Matthews, *American Diaries: An Annotated Bibliography of American Diaries Written Prior to the Year 1861* (Berkeley, 1945). The Quaker journal, as a mixed genre, and as the product of a transatlantic community, must be investigated through more inclusive bibliographies, the fullest of which continues to be Joseph Smith's *Descriptive Catalogue of Friends' Books*, 2 vols. (London, 1867). A few items of interest turn up in the *Friends' Miscellany*, edited by John and Isaac Comly through 12 volumes, beginning in 1831.

II · THE HISTORICAL BACKGROUND

Because the basic pattern of early American spiritual autobiography originated in England, it is useful to acquire a rudimentary knowledge of what William Haller called "The Rhetoric of the Spirit," either from his own *The Rise of Puritanism* (New York, 1938) or from Roger Sharrock's description of the standard contents of mid-seventeenth-century spiritual autobiography in his Introduction to *Grace Abounding* (London, 1962). Haller's specific treatment of Puritan autobiographies and diaries is quite brief, however (pp. 93-99). Many more examples come into view in William York Tindall's chapter on *Grace Abounding* in *John Bunyan: Mechanick Preacher* (New York, 1934). Tindall's exclusive emphasis on "works produced for the guidance of others and for the advertisement of their own conversion, call and gift by enthusiastic preachers" has been criticized by G. A. Starr, who offers evidence in *Defoe and Spiritual Autobiography* (Princeton, 1965) that "spiritual autobiography was the common property of English Protestantism, not the private domain of enthusiasts." Starr's initial chapter provides a concise survey of this property, but it is intent on describing the structures, typical of spiritual autobiography, which also organize experience in Defoe's fiction, and gives less attention to the inner dynamics of belief that make for differences of form. A larger range of doctrine is covered in an unpublished dissertation, *Seventeenth-Century British Autobiography: The Impact of Religious Commitment* (Stanford, 1965). The writer, Ivan Dean Ebner, concludes that "theological issues, especially those relating to epistemology," were a primary determinant of autobiographical form and content.

Less literary in approach than its title suggests, Luella Wright's *The Literary Life of the Early Quakers, 1650–1725* (New York, 1932) provides much useful information on the development of the Quaker journal out of the variety of forms by which the Society articulated its experience. Owen Watkins surveys the "pioneer writings" of English Quakers, mostly narratives published during the 1650's, and relates the aims of the Quaker evangelist to his use of biblical language and incident in "Some Early Quaker Autobiographies," *Journal of the Friends Historical Society*, XLV (1953), pp. 65-74. While its suggestions are broad and not specifically related to the journal, Howard Hintz's *The Quaker Influence in American Literature* (New York, 1940) helps bridge the gap between the tenets of historical Quakerism and the themes of such writers as Emerson and Whitman.

Commentary on the autobiographical writings of individual American Puritans has been scattered and brief. Josephine K. Piercy devotes only a few pages of her *Studies in Literary Types in Seventeenth-Century America, 1607–1710* (New Haven, 1939) to journals, diaries, and autobiographies, but I have profited from her selection of examples. In a sense, Perry Miller spoke everywhere on the personal writings of the Puritans. His essay on "The Augustinian Frame of Piety" attempts to locate the thrust behind doctrine and together with "The Practice of Piety," also from *The New England Mind: The Seventeenth Century* (New York, 1939), places a reader in the center of the Puritan drama of soul. For Miller, who approached even theological discourse as drama, the Puritan could not escape writing personal narrative. Miller and Thomas Johnson exhibited only Thomas Shepard's spiritual autobiography, however, in their major collection *The Puritans* (New York, 1938), and it is much abbreviated. Kenneth Murdock pursues the relation between Puritan doctrine and personal literature in his *Literature and Theology in Colonial New England* (Cambridge, 1949), and works toward establishing the shape of a "typical Puritan autobiography" through attention to the example, again, of Thomas Shepard.

III · CRITICISM OF AUTOBIOGRAPHY

Only very recently has autobiography been read with the degree of critical awareness attained by the most conventional criticism of fiction and poetry. Often approached simply as vicarious experience, even while its form is governing the manner of one's participation, the genre of autobiography has long required such a work as Roy Pascal's *Design and Truth in Autobiography* (Cambridge, 1960). I am very much in debt to Pascal's book for its treatment of

274

the problem of autobiographical truth and its depiction of the "double character" of the autobiographer as both object and subject, heir to an historical life and prisoner of his present self.

Two other works, concerned with English spiritual autobiography, deserve mention as criticism. Margaret Bottrall's *Every Man a Phoenix* (London, 1958), while offering chapters on Bunyan and Baxter, moves outside the parochial self-analysis of the Puritans into other seventeenth-century examples of introspective writing. Though I came to it only lately, the most penetrating work I have read in the area of my own project is John Morris's *Versions of the Self: Studies in English Autobiography from John Bunyan to John Stuart Mill* (New York, 1966), which devotes a major section to Puritan, Quaker, and Methodist autobiographers as the "largely unacknowledged pioneers of the modern sensibility." Morris writes with discriminating sympathy of the religious autobiographer's struggle to achieve wholeness in a "second birth," and extends his inquiry into the "normal vision" of autobiographers like Roger North and Edward Gibbon and the special case of Boswell's *Journals*.

The autobiographical mode in American literature has already received attention, frequently but not always stressing the characteristic stamp it acquired from its origins in early spiritual autobiography. Edwin Cady places Woolman's *Journal* among a "major group of American classics, often thought unclassifiable, but clearly 'confession forms' in [Northrop] Frye's sense" in *John Woolman* (New York, 1965). My final chapter is an attempt to deal with some of the works Cady cites, but not out of an equal interest in their cultural significance. An example of this critical interest is an essay co-authored by William Spengemann and

L. R. Lundquist, "Autobiography and the American Myth," *American Quarterly*, xvii (fall 1965), pp. 501-519. I have difficulty, however, with the size of this essay's controlling abstraction and with its willingness to minimize the importance of formal context in using fragments of personal statement by, for example, Christopher Columbus and Mae West.

Robert Sayre's *The Examined Self: Benjamin Franklin, Henry Adams, Henry James* (Princeton, 1964) demonstrates well the benefits of thorough acquaintance with the life and mind of the autobiographer as a preparation for autobiographical criticism. If anything, there is some sacrifice of attention to the autobiographical texts of James and Adams, but Sayre's opening chapter, centered on Franklin, states suggestively the problem of autobiographical form in America. Franklin's *Autobiography*, I suppose, has been commented upon more extensively than all the spiritual autobiographies written in early America. Charles Sanford's characterization, "An American Pilgrim's Progress," *American Quarterly*, vi (winter 1954), pp. 297-310, still makes sense despite qualifications of its thesis that have since appeared. The problem of irony and identity in the *Autobiography* is deftly handled by John William Ward, "Who Was Benjamin Franklin?" *The American Scholar*, xxxii (autumn 1963), pp. 541-553. David Levin, emphasizing Franklin's Puritan and Enlightenment background, challenges the stereotyped figure which has dominated so much reading of the *Autobiography*. See his chapter on Franklin as "The Puritan Experimenter in Life and Art," in *In Defense of Historical Literature* (New York, 1967).

In a number of critical works, separately concerned with varieties of self-writing in American literature, one can discern the thematic interests and analytic techniques of a broadly coherent approach to this genre. Chief among these are Perry Miller, *Consciousness in Concord* (Boston, 1958), whose long Introduction traces the "strategems of consciousness" in Thoreau's *Journals*; Sherman Paul, "Resolution at Walden," *Accent*, XIII (1953), pp. 101-113; Jonathan Bishop, *Emerson on the Soul* (Cambridge, 1964); Paul Brodtkorb, *Ishmael's White World: A Phenomenological Reading of* Moby Dick (New Haven, 1965); Albert Gelpi, *Emily Dickinson: The Mind of the Poet* (Cambridge, 1965); and Howard Waskow's chapter on monodrama in *Whitman: Explorations in Form* (Chicago, 1966). Taken together, these critical efforts argue the worth of a versatile definition of spiritual autobiography.

I · PRIMARY WORKS

The following titles are either new, authoritative editions of autobiographical works treated in my text, or are in a few cases works that have come to light since 1968.

Anthony, Susanna. *The Life and Character of Miss Susanna Anthony*. . . . *Consisting Chiefly in Extracts from Her Writings, with Some Brief Observations on Them*. Ed. Samuel Hopkins. Worcester: Leonard Worcester, 1796. [See pp. 14–50, "Containing an account of the first part of her life, written by herself, in the 28th year of her age." The diary extracts presented by Hopkins are, he says, "but a small part of her writings, the whole of which take up above a thousand pages."]

Bradstreet, Anne. "To My Dear Children." In *The Works of Anne Bradstreet*. Ed. Jeannine Hensley. Foreword by Adrienne Rich. Cambridge: Harvard University Press, 1967.

Brainerd, David. "From His Birth . . . " [autobiographical narrative]. In Jonathan Edwards, *The Life of David Brainerd*. Ed. Norman Pettit. New Haven: Yale University Press, 1985. 100–153. [The *Life* consists of lengthy extracts from Brainerd's Diary, heavily edited by Edwards.]

Cole, Nathan. "The Spiritual Travels of Nathan Cole." Ed. Michael J. Crawford. *William and Mary Quarterly* 3d ser. 33 (January 1976): 89–126.

Edwards, Jonathan. "An Account of His Conversion, Experiences, and Religious Exercises, Given by Himself"

[*Personal Narrative*]. In *Jonathan Edwards: A Profile*. Ed. David Levin. New York: Hill and Wang, 1969.

Fiske, John. *The Notebook of the Reverend John Fiske, 1644–1675*. Ed. Robert G. Pope. *Collections of the Colonial Society of Massachusetts*. Vol. 47. Boston: The Society, 1974.

Franklin, Benjamin. *The Autobiography of Benjamin Franklin: A Genetic Text*. Eds. J. A. Leo Lemay and P. M. Zall. Knoxville: University of Tennessee Press, 1981.

Franklin, Benjamin. *Benjamin Franklin's Autobiography: An Authoritative Text*. [A clear-text reader's edition of the above.] Norton Critical Edition. Eds. J. A. Leo Lemay and P. M. Zall. New York: W. W. Norton and Co., 1986.

Hoskens, Jane. *The Life and Spiritual Sufferings of that Faithful Servant of Christ, Jane Hoskens, A Public Preacher Among the People Called Quakers*. Philadelphia: William Evitt, 1771.

Mather, Cotton. *Paterna: The Autobiography of Cotton Mather*. Ed. Ronald A. Bosco. Delmar, N.Y.: Scholars' Facsimiles and Reprints, 1976.

Mixer, Elizabeth. "The Relation of Mrs. Elizabeth Mixer, As desiring to Join to the Church in full Communion. . . ." In *An Account of Some Spiritual Experiences and Raptures and Pious Expressions of Elizabeth Mixer*. With a Preface by the Rvd. Mr. James Hale. New London [Conn.]: T. Green, 1736. 15–24.

Shepard, Thomas. *Thomas Shepard's "Confessions."* Eds. George Selement and Bruce C. Woolley. *Collections of the Colonial Society of Massachusetts*. Vol. 58. Boston: The Society, 1981.

Shepard, Thomas. *God's Plot: The Paradoxes of Puritan Piety: Being the Autobiography and Journal of Thomas Shepard*. Ed. Michael McGiffert. Amherst: University of Massachusetts Press, 1972.

Taylor, Edward. *Edward Taylor's "Church Records" and Related Sermons,* Eds. Thomas M. and Virginia L. Davis, Vol. 1. *The Unpublished Writings of Edward Taylor.* Boston: Twayne Publishers, 1981. [Taylor's Relation appears on pp. 97–104; see also the Relations of other Westfield Church Founders, pp. 104–17.]

II · SECONDARY WORKS: AUTOBIOGRAPHY, GENERAL

The following bibliographies, and the bibliographical essays by Olney and Spengemann, will provide the student with a wide and discriminating view of criticism in the field of autobiography.

"A Selected Bibliography of Full-length Studies in Autobiography and Biography, 1980 to 1985"; "Full-length Studies before 1980"; "Articles 1980 to 1985," *A/B: Auto/Biography Studies,* Vol. 1, no. 4 (Dec. 1985): pp. 12–26.

Olney, James. "Autobiography and the Cultural Moment: A Thematic, Historical, and Bibliographical Introduction"; "Bibliography." In *Autobiography: Essays Theoretical and Critical.* Ed. James Olney. Princeton: Princeton University Press, 1980.

Spengemann, William C. "The Study of Autobiography: A Bibliographical Essay." In *The Forms of Autobiography: Episodes in the History of a Literary Genre.* New Haven: Yale University Press, 1980.

III · SPIRITUAL AUTOBIOGRAPHY IN EARLY AMERICA

The following selection of scholarship and criticism includes some broadly relevant studies of autobiographical writing in America as well as more specialized studies of autobiographical writers in the early period. Diary writing and Indian captivity narratives, which have received increasing attention, are represented here, and selected historical works appear as the necessary accompaniment of serious literary study in the field. The number and quality of these works suggest that there has been no abatement of interest in mapping the endlessly covert inner spaces inhabited by the godly-minded in early America. A bibliography of writings on Franklin's *Autobiography* would be redundant in view of the fully annotated listing available in the Lemay and Zall reader's edition noted above.

Andrews, William L. *To Tell a Free Story: The First Century of Afro-American Autobiography, 1760–1865.* Champaign-Urbana: University of Illinois Press, 1986.

Arksey, Laura, Nancy Pries, and Marcia Reed, eds. *American Diaries: An Annotated Bibliography of Published American Diaries and Journals.* Vol. 1: *Diaries Written from 1492 to 1844.* Detroit: Gale, 1983.

Banes, Ruth. "The Exemplary Self: Autobiography in Eighteenth-Century America." *Biography* 5 (Summer 1982): 226–39.

Bell, Robert. "Metamorphoses of Spiritual Autobiography." *ELH* 44 (1977): 108–26.

Bercovitch, Sacvan. "The Ritual of American Autobiography: Edwards, Franklin, Thoreau." *Revue Française d'Etudes Américaines* 7 (May 1982): 139–50.

Brauer, Jerald. "Conversion: From Puritanism to Revivalism." *Journal of Religion* 58 (1978): 227–43.

Breitwieser, Mitchell Robert. *Cotton Mather and Benjamin Franklin.* Cambridge: Cambridge University Press, 1984.

Bushman, Richard. "Jonathan Edwards and Puritan Consciousness." *Journal for the Scientific Study of Religion* 5 (1966): 383–96.

Cady, Edwin. *John Woolman*. (Great American Thinkers.) New York: Washington Square Press, 1965.

Caldwell, Patricia. *The Puritan Conversion Narrative: The Beginnings of American Expression*. Cambridge: Cambridge University Press, 1983.

Cohen, Charles. *God's Caress: The Psychology of Puritan Religious Experience*. New York: Oxford University Press, 1986.

Couser, G. Thomas. *American Autobiography: The Prophetic Mode*. Amherst: University of Massachusetts Press, 1979.

Delaney, Paul. *British Autobiography in the Seventeenth Century*. New York: Columbia University Press, 1969.

Delbanco, Andrew. "Thomas Shepard's America: The Biography of an Idea." In *Studies in Biography*. Ed. Daniel Aaron. Cambridge: Harvard University Press, 1978.

De Prospo, R. C. "The 'New Simple Idea' of Edwards' Personal Narrative." *Early American Literature* 14 (Fall 1979): 193–204.

De Prospo, R. C. *Theism in the Discourse of Jonathan Edwards*. Newark: University of Delaware Press, 1985.

Ebner, Dean. *Autobiography in Seventeenth-Century England: Theology and the Self*. The Hague: Mouton, 1971.

Edkins, Carol. "Quest For Community: Spiritual Autobiographies of Eighteenth-Century Quaker and Puritan Women in America." In *Women's Autobiography: Essays in Criticism*. Ed. with an Introduction by Estelle C. Jelinek. Bloomington: Indiana University Press, 1980.

Ellison, Julie. "The Sociology of 'Holy Indifference': Sarah Edwards' Narrative." *American Literature* 56 (1984): 479–95.

Fendelman, Earl. "Toward Walden Pond: The American

Voice in Autobiography." *Canadian Review of American Studies* 8 (1977): 11–25.

Grabo, Norman S. "Jonathan Edwards' *Personal Narrative: Dynamic Statis.*" *Literatur in Wissenschaft und Unterricht* 2 (1969): 141–48.

Griffith, John. "Jonathan Edwards as a Literary Artist." *Criticism* 15 (1973): 156–73.

Grimes, Mary Cochran. "Saving Grace Among Puritans and Quakers: A Study of 17th and 18th Century Conversion Experiences." *Quaker History* 72 (1983): 3–26.

Hall, David D. "The Mental World of Samuel Sewall." In *Saints and Revolutionaries: Essays on Early American History.* Eds. David D. Hall, John M. Murrin, and Thad Tate. New York: W. W. Norton and Co., 1984.

Hambrick-Stowe, Charles E. *The Practice of Piety: Puritan Devotional Disciplines in Seventeenth-Century New England.* Published for the Institute of Early American History and Culture. Chapel Hill: University of North Carolina Press, 1982.

Jelinek, Estelle C. *The Tradition of Women's Autobiography: From Antiquity to the Present.* Boston: Twayne Publishers, 1986.

Johnson, Paul David. "Jonathan Edwards's 'Sweet Conjunction.'" *Early American Literature* 16 (Winter 1981/82): 270–81.

Kagle, Steven. *American Diary Literature: 1620–1799.* Boston: Twayne Publishers, 1979.

King, John O., III. *The Iron of Melancholy: Structures of Spiritual Conversion in America from the Puritan Conscience to Victorian Neurosis.* Middletown, Conn.: Wesleyan University Press, 1983.

Lesser, Wayne. "Jonathan Edwards: Textuality and the Language of Man," in *Critical Essays on Jonathan Edwards.*

Ed. William J. Scheick. Boston: G. K. Hall, 1980.

Leverenz, David. *The Language of Puritan Feeling: An Exploration in Literature, Psychology, and Social History.* New Brunswick: Rutgers University Press, 1980.

Minter, David. *The Interpreted Design as a Structural Principle in American Prose.* New Haven: Yale University Press, 1969. [See pp. 69–85 on Edwards and Franklin.]

Rosenblatt, Paul. *John Woolman.* New York: Twayne Publishers, 1969.

Rosenwald, Lawrence Alan. "Cotton Mather as Diarist." *Prospects* 8 (1983): 129–61.

Saltman, Helen. "'Contemplations': Anne Bradstreet's Spiritual Autobiography." In *Critical Essays on Anne Bradstreet.* Eds. Pattie Cowell and Ann Stanford. Boston: G. K. Hall, 1983.

Sasson, Diane. *The Shaker Spiritual Narrative.* Knoxville: University of Tennessee Press, 1983.

Scheick, William J. *The Writings of Jonathan Edwards: Theme, Motif, and Style.* College Station: Texas A & M University Press, 1975. [See pp. 58–66 on Edwards' *Personal Narrative.*]

Selement, George. "The Meeting of Elite and Popular Minds at Cambridge, New England, 1638–1645." *William and Mary Quarterly* 3d. ser. 41 (1984): 32–48.

Tipson, Baird. "The Routinized Piety of Thomas Shepard's Diary." *Early American Literature* 13 (Spring 1978): 64–80.

Tucker, Bruce. "Joseph Sewall's Diary and the Rhythm of Puritan Spirituality." *Early American Literature* 22 (Spring 1987): 3–18.

Van Der Beets, Richard, comp. *Held Captive by Indians: Selected Narratives, 1642–1836.* Knoxville: University of Tennessee Press, 1973.

Van Der Beets, Richard. *The Indian Captivity Narrative: An*

American Genre. Lanham, Md.: University Press of America, 1984.

Vaughan, Alden T., and Edward W. Clark, eds. *Puritans Among the Indians: Accounts of Captivity and Redemption, 1676–1724.* Cambridge: The Belknap Press of Harvard University Press, 1981.

Watkins, Owen C. *The Puritan Experience: Studies in Spiritual Autobiography.* New York: Schocken Books, 1972.

Weddle, David L. "The Image of the Self in Jonathan Edwards: A Study of Autobiography and Theology." *Journal of the American Academy of Religion* 43 (March 1975): 70–83.

Willauer, George J., Jr. "Editorial Practices in Eighteenth-Century Philadelphia: The Journal of Thomas Chalkley in Manuscript and Print." *Pennsylvania Magazine of History and Biography* 107 (1983): 217–34.

INDEX

Ames, William, 100
Antinomian controversy, 104-106, 109
Ashbridge, Aaron, 25n, 38, 39
Ashbridge, Elizabeth, 10; life of, 30; *Account of the Life*: 30-39; as moral action, 31, 34ff; editions of, 31n

Bartlett, Phebe, 188
Baxter, Richard, *Reliquiae Baxterianae*, 89
Boorstin, Daniel, 7
Bradford, William, 121
Bradstreet, Anne; "Religious Experiences": 113-18, 241; didactic intent, 113-14
Brainerd, David, 141, 222, 224; diary of, 189
Brown, Claude, 269
Buell, Samuel, 224
Bunyan, John, 90, 96, 193, 239; *Grace Abounding*, 25, 87-89, 90n, 210, 240; *Pilgrim's Progress*, 90, 240

Chalkley, Thomas, 10, 41, 42; life of, 16; *Journal*: 16-22; defense of life as merchant, 17-20; exemplar of business virtues, 20-22; *Journal* printed by Franklin, 237n
Chappel, William, 90
Chauncy, Charles, 24
Churchman, John, life of, 11n; *Journal*: 10-15; didacticism of, 11-12; tension between didactic and personal, 13-14
Clap, Roger, 112; career, 119-20; *Memoirs*: 118-26; relates personal and group history, 119-22
Cole, Nathan, "Spiritual Travels": 186-87, 208-21, 252; emotional structuring, 210; dramatic qualities, 211, 215; prose of, 213

Collins, Elizabeth, *Memoirs*, 46, 47
confessions of faith, 91, 140; as institutional autobiography, 183
confessions of injured females, 30
conversion, experiences of Quakers and Puritans compared, 25, 48, 250; in autobiographies: of Ferris, 25; of Elizabeth Ashbridge, 32-33; Taylor's diagram, 100-101; of Winthrop, 101, 107-10; of Clap, 123-24; of Shepard, 140-41; of Increase Mather, 155; of Cotton Mather, 177-78; of Edwards, 197-98; of Cole, 213-14; of Hopkins, 228; New England Puritans as technicians, 90-91
conversion narrative, as stimulus to awakening, 184; dilemma of, 186-87; dilemma in Hopkins, 230-32
Cope, Jackson, 261
Cotton, John, 105, 113
Culverwell, Ezekiel, 100, 101, 107

Dane, John, *Declaration of Remarkable Providences*, 126-38; manuscript of, 127n
Dickinson, Emily, 235, 252, 255, 256, 262-64
dreams, in Quaker journals, 14, 15; in Ferris, 26; in Woolman, 68-71; 74, 76; in Elizabeth White, 185; in Cole, 217
Dreiser, Theodore, 269

The Education of Henry Adams, 235, 252, 255, 256, 264-68
Edwards, Jonathan, 182ff; 222ff; *Personal Narrative*: 182-83, 187-208, 241, 250, 252, 254; texts of, 189-90; dating of, 190; public purpose, 191, 194; prose of, 200-203, 206; compared with *Educa-*

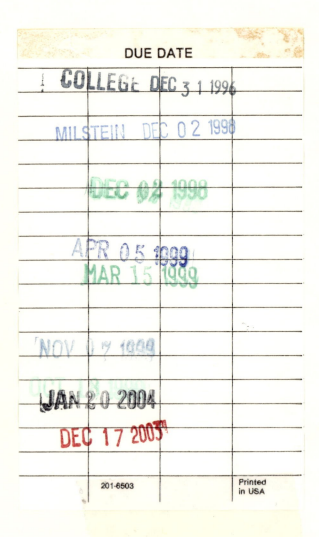